The Vegan Dairy

The Vegan Dairy

How to make non-dairy milks, butters, creams and cheeses – and then use them in your cooking

CATHERINE ATKINSON

LORENZ BOOKS

Contents

Introduction

It's never been easier to avoid dairy thanks to an ever-expanding choice of vegan products, from so-called milks, yogurts, creams and cheeses to butter and ice cream. As interest in vegan food has grown, the availability of these dairy alternatives has soared and they are now a standard feature on supermarket shelves; doubtless this trend will continue apace as consumer demand increases – from vegans, those who are intolerant to dairy, and those who simply enjoy the taste and nutritional benefits of products that tend to be high in healthy plant proteins and lower in cholesterol than their dairy counterparts.

In brief, vegans eat a wide range of foods but exclude all animal products, including eggs, dairy and any foods that contain ingredients from an animal source. It is increasingly common to live in a household where at least one person is a vegan and numbers have more than trebled in the last five years. If you are new to this way of eating, you are joining the millions of people around the world in a diet that goes back thousands of years.

For many, it is the exclusion of dairy that is their last hurdle to being vegan, but with a few tweaks to your diet, you can be dairy free and still enjoy a frothy latte, pizza, ice creams and treats such as fudge and chocolate. Rather than viewing a dairy-free diet as one that limits what you can eat and drink, think of it as a means of experiencing all kinds of different and exciting foods.

This book outlines many of the non-dairy ingredients that are available. Even better, lots of these dairy alternatives can be made at home – nut, seed and legume milks as well as dairy-free butters, spreads, creams, yogurts and 'cheeses'. You'll find them all here, with step-by-step techniques, as well as recipes that reveal how to use them in vegan cooking, from breakfasts, snacks and salads to main courses, desserts, drinks and sweet treats. We've zoned in on the dishes that are traditionally considered to be dairy classics, whether it's a macaroni cheese or cream-topped meringue, and transformed them into delicious vegan-friendly versions, just for you.

Going dairy free

The transition from traditional dairy products to vegan alternatives may seem daunting at first, but there are plenty of substitutes available to make the process easier. The supermarket is a good starting point, but there are also many that can easily be made at home. These include a wide range of milks made with all sorts of things, from nuts, seeds and coconut to oats, soya and tiger nuts, as well as butters, creams, yogurt and 'cheeses' of varying textures and flavours.

In order to successfully create vegan alternatives to dairy products and then to use them in recipes, it is worth considering what is available to buy and the relative merits of making your own. The following introductory section does just this, going through the major types of foods that are normally dairy, explaining what the options are, and how you can replace them. It includes lots of tips on making them the best they can be, and how to use them – blending different milks for economy and best flavour, or what type of vegan 'cheese' to use for different recipes, for example. Other tips include ideas for using the 'waste' products of, for instance, nut milks and cream, such as turning leftover damp nut or coconut pulp into a nutritious flour.

Key ingredients that form an important part of the vegan pantry are covered, from nutritional yeast to egg replacer, as well as advice on ways to replicate the various properties of eggs in dishes, whether for binding, volume or richness. Specialist equipment is also discussed, all of which is now readily available and will make the process easier.

Last, but not least, there is important advice on maintaining a healthy vegan diet. In addition to providing a guide to key nutrients that can be harder to obtain if you omit animal products – iron, certain vitamins and minerals – there are lots of ideas for how to obtain these from a plant-based diet, with quantities to help you consume an adequate amount.

In the chapters that follow are recipes for making your vegan dairy basics – milk; yogurts, creams, dressing and sauces; butters and spreads; and 'cheeses' – and then there is a selection of tempting 'dairy classic' dishes, all now made vegan-friendly, from breakfasts and drinks to main courses, desserts and baking. Whether you crave nachos slathered in cheese, or an ice cream, there's something here for everyone.

KEY VEGAN PRODUCTS

Milk: Finding the right milk alternative is important. The choice is mostly down to personal preference but you may also want to consider the nutritional benefits and price of different milks. You'll find lots of information on pages 10–13, as well as in the chapter of dairy-free milk recipes (see pages 24–46).

Cream: Soya cream, oat cream, sour cream and coconut cream can be used in the same way as dairy cream. You can make the latter two (see pages 58 and 64), but it's easier to buy oat and soya cream.

Butter and spreads: Plant-based vegan spread and 'butter' can be substituted for dairy versions weight for weight in recipes. A range of non-dairy spreads is available, many of which are suitable for spreading, baking and shallow-frying, unless stated otherwise on the packaging. These soft spreads are less successful for making pastry, though, so you should buy a block of hard vegan margarine or 'butter' for this. Coconut cooking butter can be used in place of dairy butter in most recipes. Then of course there are various nut and seed butters, which are easy to make yourself and have multiple uses (see pages 70–87).

Yogurt: Plain, flavoured and 'live' soya yogurt can be used in the same way as dairy yogurt, but make sure you buy or make an unsweetened one for savoury dishes. Recipes for almond, cashew nut and coconut yogurts are given on pages 52–55.

'Cheese': Dairy-free alternatives to many kinds of cheeses can be made from a range of plant-based foods such as nuts, soya and coconut oil; the latter is often used in cheeses where a melting quality is required. See pages 14–15 for more information on vegan 'cheese' and pages 88–113 for some recipes you can make yourself.

Opposite: You can make or buy plant versions of most dairy foods, from yogurt and butter to cheese and milk.

All about vegan milks

While store-bought cartons of nut milk are convenient, they may contain a higher proportion of sugar than nuts, as well as thickeners, preservatives and flavourings. Home-made milks, by contrast, are fresh, unprocessed and additive-free. Often more economical than commercially-made nut milks, they allow you to have complete control of the quality of ingredients included and the final taste, texture and thickness of the milk. They can be blended with additional ingredients too, for extra nutrition, flavour and colour.

NUT AND SEED MILKS

A range of nut- and seed-based 'milks' can be made simply by blending shelled raw unsalted nuts and seeds with water. These can be used neat as a drink or in cooking, or made into a selection of other dairy-free ingredients, such as cream, yogurt or 'cheese'.

Having said that, although it is possible to make milk by blending unsoaked raw nuts or seeds with water, for most types it is preferable to soak them first, even if only for a short time. This is because all nuts will absorb some water during soaking, which softens them so that they will yield more 'milk' than if they were processed without being soaked. Soaking also stimulates the germination process, causing beneficial enzymes to be activated and released into the milk.

In moderate conditions, nuts and seeds should be soaked at room temperature, but if the weather is hot, or you are soaking them for more than 12 hours, cover the bowl with clear film or plastic food wrap and put it in the fridge. Here are approximate soaking times for some different types of nuts and seeds:

• Brazil and pistachio nuts	1–4 hours
• cashew and macadamia nuts	3–6 hours
• walnuts and pecan nuts	4–6 hours
• hazelnuts and peanuts	6–8 hours
• sunflower and pumpkin seeds	8–14 hours
• almonds	8–24 hours

Different strengths and thicknesses

Making your own milk allows you to decide on the final thickness. For most uses, a medium-bodied milk works well, but you can also make richer, creamier ones or opt for more economical light-bodied milks by adapting the ratio of nuts or seeds to water. You can also leave the milks unstrained.

Full-bodied blends: These thick, creamy milks are ideal for making rich custards and ice creams, or for maximum flavour. Full-bodied blends can be used to replace single/light cream in many recipes. Use 225g/8oz/1½ cups nuts or seeds for every 750ml/1¼ pints/3 cups water.

Medium-bodied blends: These are what most store-bought milks are, and are ideal for drinking on their own, for serving with breakfast cereals, and to replace dairy milk in cooking. Use 175g/6oz/1 cup nuts or seeds for every 750ml/1¼ pints/3 cups water.

Light-bodied blends: The most economical to make since the ratio of nuts or seeds to water is less, these can be used on cereals and as a base in milkshakes and smoothies. Use 75g/3oz/½ cup nuts or seeds for every 750ml/1¼ pints/3 cups water.

It is normal for milks to separate slightly after you have stored them; you simply need to stir them before use or add up to 30ml/2 tbsp of lecithin and/or tocotrienols to every 800ml/1⅓ pints/3¼ cups nut milk after it has been strained.

Lecithin: This creamy-beige powder (also available as granules) is a derivative of the soy bean and acts as a thickener and emulsifier, helping to prevent the milk from separating. It will also lengthen the keeping time of the milk by 1–2 days.

As a bonus, lecithin is used by every living cell in the human body and is a source of inositol and choline, nutrients that play an important role in fat metabolism. Some claim it can help promote weight loss, although this benefit is still controversial.

Tocotrienols: Also known as 'rice solubles', these are excellent for thickening milk. Rich in vitamin E, they add a subtle sweetness.

Opposite: Many types of nuts and seeds can be used to make non-dairy milks, each with a different flavour.

How to make nut flour

Some nuts make better flour than others: cashew nuts, blanched almonds and macadamia nuts all make excellent flour that is virtually white in colour. The pulp from unskinned almonds and from hazelnuts can also be used for making flour, although it will be darker in colour (flour from unskinned almonds will be speckled).

1 Preheat the oven to 110°C/220°F/Gas ¼. Line a baking sheet with baking parchment (don't use foil). Spread the leftover pulp from making nut milk over the baking parchment in a thin, even layer, using a fork to break up the larger lumps.

2 Bake the pulp for 15 minutes, then remove it from the oven and stir it with a fork. Spread it out again into an even layer and bake it for a further 10–15 minutes or until it is completely dry. It can burn even at a very low temperature, so check it often towards the end of the cooking time.

3 Remove from the oven and leave until the dried pulp is completely cool. Tip it into a food processor and process for 3–4 minutes or until it is very finely ground. Store the nut flour in an airtight container at room temperature for a few weeks, in the fridge for up to 2 months, or in the freezer for up to 6 months.

Above: Cans of coconut milk yield both coconut cream and milk, and are extremely useful in the vegan kitchen.

COCONUT MILKS AND CREAM

Although you can make your own (see page 40), coconut milk is usually bought in cans and is a blend of thick and thin coconut milk. Every brand is slightly different and the fat content can vary between 7.5–15ml/1½ tsp–1 tbsp per 100ml/3½fl oz. Many contain additives such as thickeners, stabilizers and emulsifiers.

Coconut cream is the thick creamy part of coconut milk that rises to the top, in the same way that cream comes to the top of cow's milk. In the can, the coconut cream and the more watery milk tend to separate, so shake the can well before opening. You can also buy reduced-fat coconut milk, which contains 30 per cent less fat than its full-fat counterpart.

Coconut milk can also be bought in powdered form, which can be reconstituted to the desired thickness with water. This is particularly useful if you only require a small amount of coconut milk. It is typically mixed with double the amount of water to powder, but can be made with less water if you want to enrich a dish with coconut milk without diluting it.

Dairy evaporated milk and condensed milks can be replaced with evaporated coconut milk and condensed coconut milk. Again, they have a mild coconut taste, but this is hardly noticeable when they are combined with other ingredients.

SOYA AND OTHER NON-NUT MILKS

Delicious healthy milks can be made from beans such as soya, pulses such as yellow split peas, tubers such as tiger nuts, and grains like rice, oats and hemp. While some, such as tiger nuts and split yellow peas, benefit from generous soaking times, others like oats and hemp seeds need little or no soaking and can be ready to use in a very short amount of time.

Soya milk: Soya beans, also known as edamame beans when eaten fresh from the pod, are the basis of soya milk (and a number of other vegan products including tofu, miso and tempeh). A good source of protein, calcium and several vitamins, soya milk is made by soaking, blending, cooking and filtering the beans, so it is more time-consuming to make than nut milks. However, making it is more economical than buying it. NB: soya milk can be a problem for anyone with a thyroid condition as it can interfere with the absorption of medication, so always leave at least 4 hours after taking thyroid tablets before consuming soya milk or soya milk products.

Pea milk: Thick and rich, milk made from yellow split peas is high in protein (around eight times as much as store-bought almond milk) as well as being a good source of calcium and iron. It has a creamy-white colour and a mild, neutral flavour – nothing like peas – and is made in a very different way to nut-based milks. In commercial pea milk, the yellow peas are milled into flour and processed, separating the pea protein from the starch and fibre. The protein part is then blended with water and a little oil and often fortified with vitamin B12. It's particularly good from an environmental perspective as peas requires far less water for growing than do nuts such as almonds.

Oat milk: Oat milk can be a good option for those with allergies or intolerances as it is free of lactose, nuts, soya and gluten (if made from certified gluten-free oats). It also contains beta-glucan, a soluble fibre that can help reduce cholesterol. It is simple and inexpensive to make, but commercial varieties have the advantage of often being fortified with calcium and vitamins. If you buy it, rather than making your own, choose unsweetened varieties if possible.

Rice milk: This can be made from white or brown rice and has a neutral flavour. It contains less protein than nut and seed milk but it is cheap to make, and good blended with nut milks or used in dishes where a more delicately flavoured non-dairy milk would be wasted or a more strongly flavoured one would be overpowering.

BLENDING DAIRY-FREE MILKS

Combinations of nuts and seeds can be soaked together, following the timing of whichever type needs the longest soaking and calculating the amount of water needed depending on the proportions of nuts or seeds; it's better to use slightly less water, then dilute if necessary. There are several reasons you may choose to blend different nuts or seeds together:

- To create a milk with a wider range of vitamins and minerals, try blending walnuts, rich in vitamin E, with Brazil nuts, an excellent source of selenium.
- You may want to mix a more strongly flavoured milk, such as hemp milk, with a milder one, such as sunflower seed milk.
- Some types of milk work together well: Brazil nut and coconut milk, and macadamia nut milk and sunflower seed milk, are especially good combinations.
- To make nut or seed milk go further, blend it with some oat milk (almond and oat is a popular combination) or add inexpensive peanut milk.

SWEETENING MILKS

Most of the non-dairy milk recipes in this book are unsweetened, so can be used in savoury and sweet dishes, but when drinking, you may prefer a slightly sweeter taste. You can use a range of natural ingredients to do this, such as agave syrup, coconut palm sugar and syrup, dates, maple syrup or stevia, as well as caster/superfine or soft light or dark brown sugar, which dissolve quickly and easily in the milk. Bear in mind that dark-coloured sweeteners will alter the colour of the milk. Try to buy organic versions and use sparingly: 5–10ml/1–2 tsp is usually enough to sweeten 800ml/1⅓ pints/3¼ cups milk.

MILK STORAGE AND PASTEURIZATION

Home-made milk should be kept in the fridge in a glass jug or pitcher with a lid or covered with clear film. Avoid plastic or metal as these can taint the flavour. It will stay fresh for up to 3 days. After a day or two, the milk may separate, so give it a stir before using. If you are unable to use up all the milk in this time, it can be frozen.

It is also possible to pasteurize nut milk, so that it will keep for up to a week. Heat the milk to just below boiling point, then maintain the temperature for 3–4 minutes. Cool the milk quickly by putting the pan in a bowl of iced water. Pasteurization will affect the flavour of the milk and destroy some vitamins, so it is better to only make what you will drink in a few days.

Below: A glass jug or pitcher with a lid is the ideal vessel for storing home-made nut milks. This shape of jug is particuarly good since it should fit in the door of most fridges, saving space and meaning it stays upright.

Barista milks

Finding a plant-based milk to use in drinks such as coffee and tea can be challenging. It's worth experimenting and discovering one that is acceptable to your personal taste preferences. Many find that a light soya milk or cashew milk works well in hot drinks and those who take sugar may enjoy coconut milk or almond milk as even unsweetened versions of these have a slightly sweet flavour.

You can also buy 'barista blends', which are designed to be frothed to create latte and cappuccino-style coffees. There are several types available, including oat, almond, hemp seed and 'pea milk' – a blend of pea protein and oats.

Always allow hot drinks to cool for 2–3 minutes before adding plant-based milks to reduce the likelihood of curdling.

All about vegan 'cheeses'

Ranging from soft and spreadable to hard and sliceable, vegan cheese is often made by similar techniques to those used when making dairy cheese, including fermentation, but involve a range of ingredients to simulate the different flavours and textures.

Although some brands come close to producing 'cheeses' similar to dairy ones, if you were once a dairy-cheese lover and connoisseur, you will have to acknowledge that non-dairy cheese isn't quite the same. It is difficult to make plant-based ingredients taste and melt like dairy cheese rather than the vegetable oils, nuts, tofu, coconut and nutritional yeast they are made from; it is better to accept and enjoy vegan 'cheeses' for their own merits and find out by trial and error which types and brands suit your personal preferences, whether you are want a vegan cheese to eat with crackers or to use in cooking. The research into and production of vegan cheeses is constantly expanding and improving, so it is worth shopping around and looking for new products, and of course giving the recipes in the chapter on home-made vegan cheese a go.

Below: Home-made non-dairy 'cheeses' are attractive on a cheeseboard, to be eaten with bread or crackers.

VEGAN 'CHEESE' VARIETIES

In supermarket plant-based cheeses, the base is often made from a soya blend, coconut oil, brown rice protein or nuts, or a mixture. In the chilled aisle you will typically find blocks of plant-based cheeses, packets of wrapped slices ready for sandwiches or grilling, and bags of ready-grated cheese. Most of these are intended to be the equivalent of dairy cheeses such as Cheddar and mozzarella, with mild, neutral flavours. There are also now vegan alternatives for cream cheeses.

Vegan cheeses from smaller specialist makers tend to be sold online or in vegan stores. They offer a range of plant-based cheeses, mostly made from nuts, and often sell both 'fresh' and 'fermented' types. These easier-to-make cheeses are the ones that feature in the recipe section in this book, and vary from melting mozzarella-types to harder grating ones.

In specialist vegan 'cheese' stores, you can also buy cheeses akin to squidgy Brie as well as fermented blue-veined cheeses, and even ones flavoured by the addition of liquid smoke or truffle oil. These cheeses are harder to create at home, so it's generally worth buying them. They can be more expensive than standard supermarket types however, and are more intended for the cheeseboard rather than for use in cooking.

BENEFITS OF FERMENTING VEGAN 'CHEESE'

Fermentation is the only preservation method that increases the nutritional content of food as well as having numerous other health benefits. It works by preventing undesirable microbes from multiplying,and by increasing the number of beneficial microbes called probiotics, a word that literally means 'for life'. Other key benefits of fermenting include:

• Anti-nutrients are compounds that interfere with the absorption of nutrients and these are destroyed by fermentation. For example, phytic acid, which is found in all seeds, nuts, legumes and grains, reduces

Above: All sorts of vegan 'cheeses' can be made at home, using vegetables and coconut as well as nuts and seeds. The savoury sprinkles are a cheesy-style seasoning, a good alternative to grated Parmesan.

the absorption of vitamins and minerals such as niacin, calcium, iron and zinc. Fermenting food will neutralize much of the phytic acid, and allow the nutrients to be more absorbable.

• The fermentation process increases the availability of many vitamins and minerals, particularly the important B-group of vitamins, as well as vitamins A and K.

• A large proportion of the immune system is housed in the gut. Fermented foods help to repopulate your gut with friendly bacteria, which crowd out pathogenic bacteria and yeasts and provide health-supporting probiotics to make your immune system more robust.

Nutritional yeast flakes

These golden-coloured flakes can be used to give a cheesy Parmesan-like kick to all sorts of dishes and are invaluable for enhancing home-made vegan cheeses. Nutritional yeast differs from bread and beer yeasts as the yeast has been heat-treated to deactivate it. It can be dissolved in any liquid, so you can whisk a spoonful into a glass of vegetable juice or stir it into sauces, soups or stews before serving. High in protein (50g per 100g/2oz per 4oz), it's a good source of B-vitamins and is usually fortified with folic acid, zinc and vitamin B12 – an essential supplement to the vegan diet, so make sure you pick a brand with this addition. To preserve the B-vitamins, avoid adding to boiling/bubbling liquid where possible; let it cool for a minute or two first.

Egg substitutes

While eggs are not a dairy ingredient, they are usually grouped with them. They are frequently combined with dairy products – for instance, with milk in batters, quiches and custards, with butter in sauces such as hollandaise and béarnaise, and with cream in ice creams and other desserts – where they serve to thicken, aerate, bind or emulsify. Fortunately, there are numerous vegan alternatives to eggs. Just bear in mind that different recipes require different approaches and not all the substitutes are interchangeable.

FLAX AND CHIA SEEDS

High in protein and omega-3 fatty acids, the outer layer of flax and chia seeds is a mucilage; a sticky layer found in most plants to aid water storage. When combined with water, a gel emulsion is created, which binds ingredients together. To make the equivalent of 1 egg, mix 15ml/1 tbsp ground flax seed with 45ml/3 tbsp cold water and leave to soak for at least 5 minutes. The seeds will absorb the liquid, creating a thick, gloopy texture. You can buy ready-ground flax, or grind your own to a fine powder using a pestle and mortar, coffee grinder or spice grinder.

Chia seeds can be used in the same way (again mixing 15ml/1 tbsp seeds with 45ml/3 tbsp water). There's no need to grind them first, but you can if you prefer a finer texture and don't want tiny seeds in the finished dish. White chia seeds can be used rather than black ones for light-coloured bakes.

Only use flax and chia seeds as an egg replacer in recipes that need no more than 2 eggs.
Good for: pancakes, brownies, muffins and cookies.

Below, left to right: Flax seeds, smooth peanut butter, and aquafaba.

NUT BUTTER

Smooth peanut, cashew, almond and sunflower butters can be used as a replacement in recipes where eggs are purely used to hold the mixture together. They add both protein and a nutty flavour. Replace 1 egg with 45ml/3 tbsp nut butter but be aware that the nut butter won't 'set' mixtures in the same way as eggs, so the resulting bakes will have a softer texture.
Good for: cookies, cakes and traybakes.

AQUAFABA

Translating as 'water bean', this is a lovely name for the unpromising-looking liquid in a can of chickpeas. It can be used as an emulsifier or binder but is best known for its ability to be whisked to create a thick foamy mixture similar to whisked egg whites. Using juice from the can is the easiest way, though slowly cooking dried beans in a minimal volume of water for several hours will give the same result. Use 45ml/3 tbsp aquafaba for 1 egg, 30ml/2 tbsp for 1 egg white, or 15ml/1 tbsp to replace 1 egg yolk.
Good for: as an emulsifier in mayonnaise, and whisked to make pipeable meringues, macarons, Yorkshire puddings, and light and airy mousses or ice creams.

Above, left to right: Chickpea flour, silken tofu, and vegan egg replacer.

CHICKPEA FLOUR

Also known as garbanzo bean flour, besan, chana or gram flour, pale brown chickpea flour is high in protein and can be used to both bind and help aerate baked goods. To replace 1 egg, blend 45ml/3 tbsp chickpea flour with 45ml/3 tbsp plant-based milk until smooth and creamy.
Good for: baked custard-type mixtures, cakes, muffins and scones.

TOFU

Made from the curds of soya milk, tofu has little flavour of its own, but is highly versatile and absorbs other flavours well. Firm tofu, sold as a block, can be used to create a feta cheese substitute (see page 100). A softer, lighter set tofu called 'silken' tofu is a good substitute for milk or cream and egg mixtures. Use 65g/2½oz/¼ cup silken tofu per 1 egg, blending until smooth and creamy before use.
Good for: cheesecakes, creamy tarts, brownies, and cakes with a heavier and moist texture.

BICARBONATE OF SODA AND VINEGAR

Bicarbonate of soda/baking soda reacts with vinegar to produce lots of foamy bubbles that, when combined with plant milk, can produce surprisingly light eggless cakes and bakes. Use 5ml/1 tsp bicarbonate of soda mixed with 5ml/1 tsp vinegar to replace 1 egg and add an extra 45ml/3 tbsp plant milk to the mixture.
Good for: cakes and plain baked goods.

FRUIT AND VEGETABLE PURÉES

Puréeing or mashing fruit and vegetables is a flavourful way to replace eggs as it not only helps bind the mixture together but also provides moisture and sweetness as well. For the equivalent of 1 egg, use 1 mashed medium banana or 65g/2½oz/¼ cup puréed raw avocado or cooked and puréed apple, sweet potato, butternut squash or pumpkin.
Good for: reduced-sugar and reduced-fat bakes.

AGAR AGAR

This gelling agent extracted from red algae is often used instead of gelatine to set jellies, cold puddings, and some vegan cheeses. It can be used as a setting agent in cooking, although the recipe may have to be adapted if the recipe would usually be baked. Available as dried strips or a powder, agar agar has no colour, taste or aroma and needs to be activated by being boiled in liquid for 5 minutes.
Good for: custard-based fillings for tarts, crème caramel and panna cotta.

VEGAN EGG REPLACER

This is a commercial product made from a blend of potato starch, tapioca starch, raising/leavening agent and cellulose. A fine white powder, a 450g/1lb pack is the equivalent of about a hundred eggs. Reconstituted with water, it does a good job of mimicking the properties of whole eggs, yolks and egg whites in cooking and baking. It may not always work with your own recipes and it is better to follow those created for the product (often provided on the packet or website). As it is white, sponges and custards will not be yellow (although this may be an advantage if you want to add food colouring, to create pastel-tinted cakes for example). When used as a replacement for egg whites, the mixture will be softer and not suitable for defined piping.
Good for: cakes, bakes, quiches, batters and meringues.

Kitchen equipment

Making non-dairy milks, butters, 'cheeses' and yogurts requires little specialist equipment and, provided that you have a blender or food processor, they can be made simply and quickly. You will probably already own a few other pieces of equipment that will make the process easier, including a calibrated jug or cup, rubber spatula and a sieve or strainer. The following is an outline of the more useful items, all of which are readily available.

BLENDER

Nut and seed milks, butters and cheeses can be made in an ordinary blender or food processor, but the results may be slightly grainy. If you want to make ultra-smooth products, choose a machine with at least 600 watts of power and a blade that is suitable for crushing ice (and therefore capable of finely grinding nuts and seeds). While high-powered blenders such as Vitamix are more expensive, they are very powerful and will extract the maximum amount of 'milk', and produce creamier results. Bear in mind that when using such machines for butters and cheeses, you will need to make large enough quantities for the nuts or seeds to cover the blades of the machine and keep the mixture moving, at least 400g/14oz/3½ cups of nuts or 300g/11oz/2 cups of seeds. If you want to make less than this, a small high-powered food processor will be more suitable and do a better job.

NUT BAGS

While nut and seed milks don't have to be strained, a nut bag is a worthwhile investment if you prefer milks with a smooth, silky texture. These reusable bags have a very fine nylon mesh and are usually in a funnel shape for easy straining. Most have a drawstring so that you can hang the bag to drain. Nut bags are very strong but not unbreakable so, when using, squeeze them gently but do not twist the bag. The stitching on most nut bags is on the outside, which makes them easier to clean. After use, rinse the bag well and, if necessary, wash it in warm soapy water. Rinse thoroughly to remove all traces of detergent and then air dry it.

Alternatively, you can use a jelly bag. Jelly bags are made from calico or nylon and are usually used for straining juices from cooked fruit pulp for preserve-making. The weave is close, although not as fine as that of a nut bag. Some jelly bags come with a stand, which makes straining easier.

Muslin or cheesecloth can also be used instead of a nut or jelly bag: layer two or three squares in a sieve or strainer placed over a bowl or jug. Muslin is typically used for draining and thickening dairy-free yogurts and cheeses.

YOGURT MAKER OR VACUUM FLASK

A yogurt maker is useful if you intend to make a lot of yogurt, as it is designed solely for this purpose. If you make yogurt less often, you can use a sterilized vacuum flask instead.

Below: A nut bag, glass jars and a heavy, light-coloured baking tray are all useful bits of kit.

Above: You can use glass bottles in a range of sizes for storing your milks.

DEHYDRATOR

This can be used to quickly dry out and firm up some non-dairy 'cheeses', creating a harder rind or crust. If you don't have one, you can just wrap the cheese in baking parchment; it will just need to be left to mature for a little longer but will still work.

GLASS JUG

A glass jug or pitcher is preferable for storing non-dairy milk, as plastic can affect its flavour. Choose one with a closeable lid, so that the milk does not get contaminated by other food flavours during storage; one with a screw lid and with a pouring spout is best.

JARS AND CONTAINERS

When storing nut butters, dressings and sauces, glass jars are ideal as you can see the contents easily. Choose jars that are appropriately shaped and sized; wide-necked ones make filling and using much easier. Plastic containers are useful for storing cheeses, and nut butters can be frozen in sealed containers, too.

Sterilizing jars and bottles

It is a good idea to sterilize jars and bottles before using them, to destroy any micro-organisms that might affect dairy-free milks and butters. The simplest way is to put the jars, bottles and lids in a dishwasher and run it on the hottest setting, including drying. Alternatively, you can sterilize them in the oven or microwave:

Oven method: Stand the jars or bottles, spaced apart, on a baking sheet lined with kitchen paper. Rest any lids on top. Place in a cold oven, then heat to 110°C/225°F/Gas ¼ and bake for 30 minutes. Leave to cool completely before filling.

Microwave method: Half-fill the clean jars or bottles with water and heat on Full Power, until the water has boiled for at least 1 minute. Using oven gloves, remove from the microwave. Carefully swirl the water inside them, then pour it away. Drain the jars or bottles upside-down on a clean dish towel, then turn upright to dry.

CALIBRATED JUG OR CUP AND MEASURING SPOONS

For measuring the amount of liquid needed for a recipe, a calibrated jug is essential. You should also use accurate measuring spoons for other ingredients, such as oil and various sweeteners. If you make a note of the quantities used, you can then tweak them to suit your personal preferences the next time you make the food.

SPATULAS

A flexible rubber or plastic spatula can be used to scrape the last bits of food from the food processor or blender after you have mixed it. It also avoids damaging the jug or bowl of the machine.

BAKING SHEET AND NON-STICK FRYING PAN

A baking sheet is useful when oven-roasting nuts or seeds prior to making butters. Choose one with sides, and use a good-quality heavy one that won't buckle at high temperatures or develop hot spots that might cause burning. Avoid baking sheets that are very dark as they absorb more heat, which means nuts and seeds burn more easily. You can also toast them in a non-stick frying pan on the stove-top or hob.

A balanced vegan diet

As a vegan who has given up dairy foods, you will lose count of the times you are asked, 'but how will you get enough calcium?' and 'what about protein?' Many will be surprised to learn that an adequate intake of both of these isn't difficult, provided that you eat a balanced diet.

The foods we eat contain two main categories of nutrients: macronutrients and micronutrients. Macronutrients are needed in large amounts daily and include proteins, carbohydrates and fats. Vitamins and minerals are found in very small quantities in foods, and are micronutrients. They play a vital role in maintaining the body's normal functions. Most foods contain both macro- and micronutrients in varying proportions, so the key to a healthy diet is to eat a wide variety of different foods. Because the vegan diet avoids some foods that are common providers of certain vitamins and minerals, such as dairy, you need to be sure to obtain an adequate intake of these from your plant-based sources.

PLENTY OF PROTEIN

Protein is key for the maintenance and repair of every cell in the body and for producing hormones and antibodies. It is necessary to eat protein every day as it cannot be stored for future use.

Protein is made up of amino acids and nine of these are essential to obtain from foodstuffs because the body cannot make them itself. There are only a few vegan foods that contain all nine amino acids, such as quinoa, and soya beans and products made from them. Protein derived from most other plant sources such as nuts, legumes and rice do not contain all the nine amino acids, but so long as you eat a varied diet, it is easy to ensure that you do consume all the essential amino acids.

How much protein?

Try to eat a wide range of different protein foods from every group. Vegan dairy alternatives are a great way to increase this, from the non-dairy milk you pour over your cereal to the nut or tofu-based 'cheese' you have for lunch or as a snack. Protein can also be added in sauces and dressings, so consider those as well.

The recommended intake of protein is a minimum of 50g/2oz a day (depending on body weight), but remember that the individual vegetables and grains do not provide complete proteins, with the exception of quinoa and amaranth; a combination of foods is therefore important.

Soya products

- Soya milk, tofu (8g protein per 100g/3¾oz)
- Tempeh (20g protein per 100g/3¾oz)

Grains

- Amaranth (2g protein per 100g/3¾oz)
- Quinoa (3.5g protein per 75g/3oz)
- Buckwheat (5g protein per 100g/3¾oz)
- Rolled oats (6g protein per 50g/2oz)

Pulses

- Chickpeas (7g per 100g/3¾oz)
- Garden peas/petits pois (7g per 100g/3¾oz)
- Beans such as black beans, borlotti and cannellini (7–8g per 100g/3¾oz)
- Lentils including red, green and Puy (8–9g protein per 100g/3¾oz)

Nuts and seeds

- Chia seeds (2g per heaped tablespoon)
- Hemp seeds (5g per heaped tablespoon)
- Almonds (3g per 100g/3¾oz)
- Cashew nuts (3g per 100g/3¾oz)
- Brazil nuts (4g per 100g/3¾oz)

Vegetables

- Cauliflower (1.5g per 75g/3oz)
- Avocado (2g per medium fruit)
- Kale (2g per 75g/3oz)
- Broccoli (3g per 75g/3oz)

Top tips for healthy eating

• Include good sources of protein in most meals, such as lentils, pulses, tofu, nuts, non-dairy milks and yogurt.
• Choose some higher-fibre starchy carbohydrates such as wholemeal bread, wholewheat pasta, brown rice, sweet potatoes and oats most of the time; white bread and pasta are still healthy, but don't eat them too frequently.
• Eat a wide variety of fruit and vegetables daily, at least five portions. Remember that green vegetables such as broccoli and peas contain useful iron.
• Have plenty of calcium-rich foods, including calcium-fortified products.
• Eat nuts and seeds most days, especially those which are rich in omega-3, such as flax seeds, chia seeds and walnuts. Many dairy-replacement foods contain these, making it easy to get enough.
• Make sure you get enough vitamin D from the sun during spring and summer and take a supplement during autumn and winter.
• Ensure your diet contains vitamin B12; either from fortified foods or a supplement.
• Make sure you get iodine, selenium and zinc in your diet or take a supplement.
• Eat plenty of iron-rich foods and accompany them with foods high in vitamin C to ensure maximum absorption.

MUST-HAVE MINERALS

Important for muscles, bones and teeth, blood oxygenation and coagulation, there are five minerals that are typically sourced from animal products and for which vegans need to find alternative sources. These are: iron, calcium, zinc, iodine and selenium.

Iron

An essential mineral in all cells, iron is a component of haemoglobin that carries oxygen around the body in red blood cells and also sustains energy levels. Dietary iron from animal products is more easily absorbed than the iron found in plants. However, vitamin C (found in most fruit and vegetables) is known to increase the absorption of iron, so try to consume some at the same time as iron-rich foods. Other things can hinder the absorption of iron. Tea, for example, contains tannins that bind to iron, so it is best to leave at least an hour before and an hour after your meals before drinking it.

Other foods, including wholegrains, beans and pulses, contain compounds known as phytates, which can affect how well iron is absorbed. Again, vitamin C can help with this, as can vitamin A (found in orange and yellow fruits and vegetables), reducing the effects of phytates. You can also reduce phytates in grains, pulses and seeds by soaking them first – which is why fermenting nuts (used in some of our vegan cheeses) is so beneficial. One nutritional advantage of being vegan is that you avoid casein, found in dairy foods, as this also inhibits iron absorption.

Good vegan sources: beans, chickpeas, lentils, tofu, cashew nuts, peanuts, flax seeds, hemp seeds, pumpkin seeds, kale, dried fruits, quinoa and fortified breakfast cereals.

Calcium

A vital mineral for the formation and continuing strength of bones and teeth, our bodies contain about 1kg/2¼lb of this mineral. While dairy foods are often considered the best source, there are plenty of vegan foods that are rich in calcium (see box). Adults should aim to eat around 700mg a day, but teenage girls need around 800mg a day and teenage boys around 1,000mg a day as most of bone mass is laid down during these years of growth. If you are breastfeeding, you will need an extra 550mg a day. Vitamin D is essential for absorbing calcium.

Good vegan sources of calcium

Soya products

- Soya milk (240mg per 250ml/9fl oz/1 cup)
- Soya yogurt (200mg per 120ml/4fl oz/½ cup)
- Tofu (200mg per 115g/4oz)

Beans and pulses

- Baked beans (85mg per 200g/7oz)
- Red kidney beans (50mg per 75g/3oz)

Fruit and vegetables

- Kale (300mg per 200g/7oz cooked)
- Broccoli (50mg per 115g/4oz cooked)
- Canned tomatoes (50mg per 400g/14oz)
- Dried apricots (50mg for 8)
- Dried figs (100mg for 2)
- Oranges (50mg for 1 large)

Nuts and seeds

- Sesame seeds (100mg per 15ml/1 tbsp)
- Almonds (50mg for 10)

Fortified foods

- White pitta (100mg per 75g/3oz)
- Naan (80mg per 50g/2oz)
- White or wholewheat bread (50mg per thick slice)
- Pasta (50mg per 8oz/225g cooked)

Zinc

This mineral has a strong role in the immune system, is crucial during growth and reproduction, and is needed for the catalysis of around 200 enzymes that perform many functions in the body, including cell division and repair, and the breakdown of proteins, fats and carbohydrates. The richest sources are meat and fish, but there are vegan options.

Good vegan sources: pulses such as haricot and soya beans, nuts, especially Brazil nuts and seeds.

Iodine

Necessary for the body to make thyroid hormones, which control metabolic rate and help keep cells healthy, iodine is mainly found in fish, seafood and dairy produce, so it's important that vegans find an alternative source.

Good vegan sources: cranberries and cranberry juice,

strawberries, butter/lima beans, haricot/navy beans and seaweed. It is also possible to buy salt fortified with iodine, although you should try to reduce the amount of salt in your diet.

Selenium

This micromineral is an antioxidant that helps protect cells from the damaging effects of free radicals. Selenium is important for the immune system and the thyroid gland. It's also thought to have anti-cancer properties as it helps block the action of many of the enzymes that are involved in rapid cell division and growth. Fish, shellfish and poultry are the best sources but there are other options.
Good vegan sources: Brazil nuts; one nut a day will provide you with more than the daily requirement.

VITAL VITAMINS

For many of us, the first thing that comes to mind when the word 'vitamins' is mentioned are the pots of pills that can be purchased from a pharmacy or health food store. However, for the most part, vegans can get all the necessary vitamins from food and should only consider supplements for a very few.

Vitamins are a group of substances needed in minute quantities for normal cell function and growth. They are classified as fat-soluble or water-soluble, based on how they are absorbed by the body. Vitamins A, D, E and K are fat-soluble, while the water-soluble ones include vitamin C and the B-complex vitamins; the latter need to be consumed each day as the body cannot store them. There are two vitamins that vegans may need to consider taking a supplement for: vitamins B12 and D.

Vitamin B12

Necessary for producing oxygen-carrying red blood cells, for the correct and efficient functioning of the nervous system, the manufacturing of DNA and the processing of fats and carbohydrates, vitamin B12 is important for everyone, but is particularly important for growth and development in young children and teenagers. The vitamin is found naturally only in foods of animal origin. Some foods such as nutritional yeast (see page 15), breakfast cereals, some plant-based milks and a few vegan meal alternatives are fortified with this vitamin. If you do not include these daily in your diet, you should consider taking a supplement.

Vitamin D

This vitamin is vital to help your body to absorb calcium and phosphorus. It is found in two forms: vitamin D2, which is found in a small number of animal-based foods; and vitamin D3, which is easily obtained through sunlight exposure during the summer months. Make sure you buy a form of vitamin D3 that is derived from a plant rather than animal source; it should be clearly labelled as 'suitable for vegans'. Try to get periods of about 10 minutes of sun exposure to your bare skin once or twice a day in the summer months without sunscreen (in temperate climates, always take care not to burn). It is now recommended that vegans (and non-vegans) should take a supplement of vitamin D in the remaining months of the year.

Below, left to right: Cannellini beans, dried seaweed and nuts all contain vital vitamins and minerals.

Milks & water kefir

If you're new to dairy-free living, choosing a vegan milk will be on your priority list. Much will depend on personal preference, but you may find that it's worth keeping more than one type in the fridge: a creamy nut or seed milk for pouring over breakfast cereals and making protein-rich smoothies and shakes, an economical grain milk for everyday cooking, and one that is suitable for hot drinks, such as a barista-style milk for creating frothy coffees. As an alternative to milk, you can also have a go at making water kefir and coconut water kefir, both of which have beneficial properties and make a refreshing drink, without the dairy of classic kefir.

Cashew milk

Milk made from cashews has an almost neutral flavour, which means it is ideal if you want to blend it with other flavourings (see page 46) or use it in cooking without adding a distinctly nutty flavour. Because cashews are a relatively 'soft' nut, they require only a short soaking time, but if it is more convenient, you can leave them to soak overnight.

175g/6oz/1 cup raw unsalted cashew nuts
750ml/1¼ pints/3 cups filtered water, plus soaking water
pinch of sea salt (optional)

MAKES ABOUT 800ML/1½ PINTS/ 3¼ CUPS

Cook's tips

- Filtered water is best, as filtering removes impurities that may spoil the flavour of the milk, though you can use bottled or tap water.
- The damp nut pulp can be made into nut flour (see page 11) or nut pulp crackers (see page 214).
- The milk will keep in the fridge for up to 4 days.

1 Put the cashew nuts in a large glass, ceramic or stainless-steel bowl. Pour over enough water to cover by about 2.5cm/1in. Add a small pinch of sea salt as well if you like; this will help to soften the nuts, but isn't essential. Leave to soak at room temperature for 3–6 hours.

2 After soaking, strain the cashew nuts, then rinse them and tip them into a blender with a capacity of at least 1.5 litres/2½ pints. Add about a third of the filtered water (250ml/9fl oz/1 cup) to the blender. Pulse a few times to break up the nuts, then blend continuously for about 1 minute. Add a further 250ml/9fl oz/1 cup of water and blend for a further minute, until the mixture is well-blended and smooth. A high-powered blender such as a Vitamix is preferable to finely pulverize the nuts. If you are using a less powerful machine, you will need to blend the mixture for 1–2 minutes more.

3 Next, strain the liquid to give it a silkier texture and remove any fine pieces of nuts, pouring the mixture through a very fine-meshed sieve or strainer into a large bowl. For an even smoother end result, line the sieve first with a layer of muslin or cheesecloth, or use a nut bag, then pour in the mixture and leave it to filter for a few minutes, gently stirring the pulp to encourage the liquid to pass through.

4 To extract a little more nut milk, pour in the remaining water and leave to drain again. When the milk has filtered through, gather up the corners of the muslin or nut bag and squeeze out the last few drops.

5 Serve chilled, or pour into a glass bottle, cover and store in the fridge.

Almond milk

The most popular and widely consumed nut milk, almond milk has a silky-smooth texture and creamy taste as well as fantastic nutritional benefits. Its mild flavour makes it superb for drinking, pouring over cereals and for cooking, and because almonds have an affinity with many fruits, it is especially good when making fruity desserts. It also works well with chocolate and coffee.

175g/6oz/1 cup raw unsalted blanched almonds
750ml/1¼ pints/3 cups filtered water, plus soaking water

MAKES ABOUT 800ML/1½ PINTS/ 3¼ CUPS

Cook's tips
- Buy shelled almonds in their skins for the best flavour and for economy, then blanch them yourself (see Cook's tip opposite). This recipe makes a medium-thickness simple almond milk.
- The slightly damp nut pulp can be made into nut flour (see page 11) or crackers (see page 214).

1 Put the almonds in a large glass, ceramic or stainless-steel bowl. Pour over enough water to cover by about 2.5cm/1in. Leave to soak at room temperature for at least 8 hours or refrigerate and soak for up to 24 hours.

2 Drain and rinse the almonds, then tip them into a blender and add 250ml/9fl oz/1 cup of water. Pulse a few times to break up the nuts, then blend continuously for 1 minute. Add a further 250ml/9fl oz/1 cup of water and blend for 1–3 minutes or until the mixture is smooth.

3 Pour the mixture through a nut bag hung over a jug or deep bowl, or through a sieve lined with a layer of muslin or cheesecloth. Leave to drain for a few minutes. Slowly pour in the rest of the water, then leave to drain again.

4 When the milk has filtered through, gather up the nut bag or the corners of the muslin and gently squeeze with clean hands to extract the last few drops of nut milk. Store in glass bottles, or in a covered jug, in the refrigerator for up to 4 days.

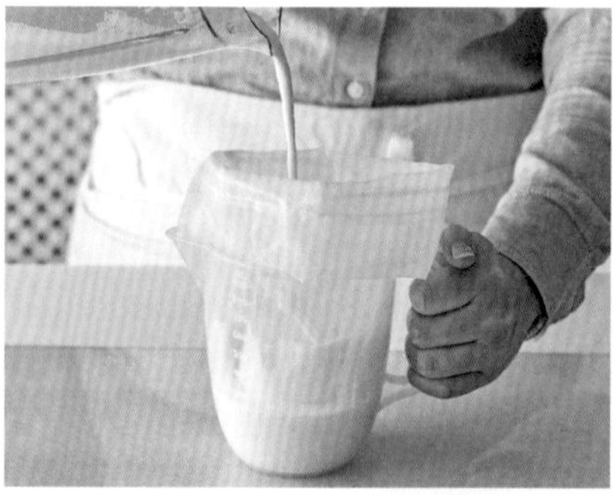

Light almond milk

In this recipe, fewer almonds are used than for simple unsweetened almond milk, and lecithin is added to give the milk a slightly thicker texture and to reduce separation. You may wish to add a few drops of vanilla extract and a little sweetener to the milk. This is an excellent economical nut milk for using as a base for milkshakes, serving with cereals, or making porridge.

1 Put the almonds in a large glass, ceramic or stainless-steel bowl. Pour over enough water to cover by about 2.5cm/1in. Leave to soak at room temperature for at least 8 hours or refrigerate and soak for up to 24 hours.

2 Drain the almonds and rinse, then tip them into a blender and add 250ml/9fl oz/1 cup of water. Pulse a few times to break up the nuts, then blend continuously for 1 minute. Add a further 250ml/9fl oz/1 cup of water and blend for 1–3 minutes or until the mixture is smooth.

3 Pour through a nut bag suspended over a jug or bowl, or through a sieve lined with a layer of muslin or cheesecloth, and leave to drain for a few minutes. Pour in the remaining water and leave to drain again. When the milk has filtered through, gather up the nut bag or muslin and squeeze with clean hands to extract the last drops.

4 Pour the almond milk back into a clean blender. Add the lecithin, vanilla extract and agave syrup or honey, if using, then blend again.

5 Store the milk, covered, in bottles in the fridge for up to 4 days.

75g/3oz/½ cup raw unsalted blanched almonds
750ml/1¼ pints/3 cups filtered water, plus soaking water
30ml/2 tbsp powdered lecithin
2.5ml/½ tsp vanilla extract (optional)
5ml/1 tsp agave syrup or clear honey (optional)

MAKES ABOUT 800ML/1½ PINTS/3¼ CUPS

Cook's tip
To blanch almonds, put them in a heatproof bowl and cover with boiling water. Leave for 1 minute, then drain, rinse in cold water, and slip off the skins.

Hazelnut milk

This is one of the few nut milks that benefits from being made with lightly roasted rather than raw nuts. You can buy ready-toasted hazelnuts, but you get a better flavour if you roast your own, as here. Some of the flavour will leach into the soaking water, so the nuts aren't drained after being soaked. The pulp can be made into nut flour (see page 11).

175g/6oz/1 cup raw unsalted skinned hazelnuts
750ml/1¼ pints/3 cups filtered water

MAKES ABOUT 800ML/1½ PINTS/ 3¼ CUPS

Cook's tip
To skin hazelnuts, place them on a baking sheet. Bake at 180°C/350°F/Gas 4 for 10–12 minutes or until the skins begin to split and the nuts are golden. Leave to cool for a few minutes, then place in a clean dish towel and rub to loosen and remove the skins. Continue from Step 2.

1 Spread the hazelnuts in a single layer on a baking sheet. Bake at 180°C/350°F/Gas 4 for 7–8 minutes; they should be very lightly browned and smell nutty. Watch carefully as over-roasting will make the nuts bitter. Leave the nuts to cool, then tip them into a bowl and pour over the filtered water. Soak at room temperature for 6–8 hours.

2 Tip the nuts and about half of their soaking water into a blender. Pulse a few times to break up the nuts, then blend continuously for about 1 minute. Add the remaining water and blend for 2–3 minutes or until the mixture is smooth.

3 Pour the mixture through a nut bag suspended over a jug or bowl and leave to drain. If you don't have a nut bag, pour the mixture through a sieve or strainer lined with muslin or cheesecloth.

4 Gather up the nut bag or the corners of the muslin and gently squeeze with clean hands to extract the last few drops of nut milk. Store the milk, covered, in the fridge for up to 4 days.

Pecan or walnut milk

Walnuts are less sweet than many other nuts and sometimes have a hint of bitterness. Soaking will eliminate this. Pecans are similar to walnuts but have a slightly sweeter taste. Both types taste wonderful in delicately flavoured foods such as porridge or custard, or are simply used for drinking or pouring. The pulp can be made into nut flour.

115g/4oz/¾ cup raw unsalted pecans or walnuts
700ml/1 pint 3fl oz/2¾ cups filtered water, plus soaking water

MAKES ABOUT 750ML/1¼ PINTS/ 3 CUPS

1 Put the nuts in a large glass, ceramic or stainless-steel bowl. Pour over enough water to cover by 2.5cm/1in. Leave to soak at room temperature for 4–6 hours. Drain and rinse.

2 Pulse the nuts and one-third of the filtered water a few times, then blend continuously for 1 minute. Add one-third more of the water. Blend for 2–3 minutes, until smooth.

3 Pour the mixture through a nut bag hung over a jug or bowl and leave to drain for a few minutes. If you don't have a nut bag, pour the mixture through a sieve or strainer lined with muslin or cheesecloth. Slowly pour in the rest of the water, then leave to drain again.

4 Gather up the nut bag or the corners of the muslin and gently squeeze with clean hands to extract the last few drops of nut milk. Store the milk, covered, in bottles or a jug in the fridge for up to 3 days.

Macadamia milk

High in fat, macadamias are soft enough to make a rich nut milk without the need for soaking, although the yield will be slightly higher if you soak the nuts first. To make it go further, you could blend it with some thinner, cheaper milk, such as oat or rice milk.

115g/4oz/¾ cup raw unsalted macadamia nuts
350ml/12fl oz/1½ cups filtered water, plus soaking water

MAKES ABOUT 400ML/14FL OZ/ 1⅔ CUPS

1 Put the nuts in a large glass, ceramic or stainless-steel bowl. Pour over enough water to cover by 2.5cm/1in. Leave to soak at room temperature for 3–6 hours.

2 Pulse the nuts and one-third of the filtered water in a blender a few times, then blend for 1 minute. Add one-third more of the water. Blend for 2–3 minutes, until smooth.

3 Pour the mixture through a nut bag hung over a jug or bowl and leave to drain for a few minutes. If you don't have a nut bag, pour the mixture through a sieve or strainer lined with muslin or cheesecloth. Slowly pour in the rest of the water, then leave to drain again.

4 Gather up the nut bag or corners of the muslin and gently squeeze to extract the last few drops of milk. Store the milk in the fridge, covered, for up to 3 days.

Pistachio milk

Since pistachios are expensive, this milk is best served in small quantities and used where it will play a starring role. Soaking is not essential but it will maximize the yield. The slightly damp nut pulp can be used to make excellent flour (see page 11) or nut pulp crackers (see page 214).

115g/4oz/¾ cup shelled raw unsalted pistachio nuts
350ml/12fl oz/1½ cups filtered water, plus soaking water

MAKES ABOUT 400ML/14FL OZ/ 1⅔ CUPS

1 Put the nuts in a glass, ceramic or stainless-steel bowl. Pour over enough water to cover by about 2.5cm/1in. Leave to soak at room temperature for 1–4 hours. Drain and rinse.

2 Use a small knife to remove any remaining skin that may still cling to the pistachios. Blend the nuts with 250ml/9fl oz/1 cup of the filtered water in a blender. Pulse a few times, then blend continuously for 1–2 minutes, until smooth.

3 Pour the mixture through a nut bag hung over a jug or bowl and leave to drain for a few minutes. If you don't have a nut bag, pour the mixture through a sieve or strainer lined with muslin or cheesecloth. Slowly pour in the rest of the water, then leave to drain again.

4 Gather up the nut bag or the corners of the muslin and gently squeeze with clean hands to extract the last few drops of nut milk. Store the milk, covered, in the fridge for up to 3 days.

Brazil nut milk

Selenium-rich Brazil nuts make a creamy, mild-flavoured, almost white milk. It is particularly good blended with tropical fruit such as bananas or goji berries. Do not drink this milk too often, however, since the daily allowance of selenium is quite low and it's easy to exceed it.

1 Put the nuts in a large glass, ceramic or stainless-steel bowl. Pour over enough water to cover by 2.5cm/1in. Leave to soak at room temperature for 1–4 hours. Drain and rinse.

2 Put the nuts in a blender with 250ml/9fl oz/1 cup of the filtered water. Pulse a few times, then add another 250ml/9fl oz/1 cup of water. Blend continuously for 1–2 minutes, until the mixture is smooth.

3 Pour the mixture through a nut bag hung over a jug and leave to drain for a few minutes; if you don't have a nut bag, pour the mixture through a sieve or strainer lined with muslin or cheesecloth.

4 Slowly pour in the rest of the water, then leave to drain again. Gently squeeze the nut bag or muslin with clean hands to extract all the milk.

5 Store the milk, covered, in the fridge for up to 3 days. The nut pulp can be made into a nutritious nut flour (see page 11).

75g/3oz/½ cup raw unsalted Brazil nuts

550ml/18fl oz/2½ cups filtered water, plus soaking water

MAKES ABOUT 600ML/1 PINT/ 2½ CUPS

Peanut milk

One of the least expensive nuts, peanut milk can be made with either raw or lightly roasted peanuts, but make sure they are unsalted and buy those without red papery skins if possible. They are slightly softer than nuts such as almonds, so take a little less time to soak.

1 If you want roasted peanut milk, spread the nuts in a single layer on a baking sheet. Bake at 180°C/350°C/Gas 4 for 5–6 minutes; they should be a slightly dark golden colour rather than brown.

2 Tip the nuts into a bowl (if you have roasted them, do this while they are still hot as this will speed up the soaking time). Pour over enough water to cover the nuts by 2.5cm/1in. Leave to soak at room temperature for 6–8 hours, or if preferred, overnight in the fridge (if you've roasted the nuts, let the water cool completely first).

3 Tip the nuts and about half of the filtered water into a blender. Pulse a few times to break up the nuts, then blend continuously for 2 minutes. Add most of the remaining water and blend for 2–3 minutes or until very smooth. Pour through a nut bag or a sieve or strainer lined with muslin and leave to drain. Pour in the rest of the water and leave to drain again.

4 Gently squeeze the nut bag or muslin with clean hands, to extract the last drops. Store in the fridge, covered, for up to 3 days.

175g/6oz/1 cup raw unsalted peanuts
750ml/1¼ pints/3 cups filtered water, plus soaking water

MAKES ABOUT 800ML/1½ PINTS/ 3¼ CUPS

Cook's tip
If you buy peanuts with the papery red-brown skins still on, you will need to lightly roast them first to remove the skins. Once roasted, the skins can quickly and easily be rubbed off in a clean dish cloth while the nuts are still warm.

Chestnut milk

Unlike other nuts, chestnuts are high in carbohydrates and low in fat. They make a thick, pale-brown milk with very little leftover pulp. The quickest, easiest method is to use ready-cooked and peeled vacuum-packed chestnuts, but you can use and prepare fresh ones if you prefer.

175g/6oz/1 cup cooked and peeled chestnuts
750ml/1¼ pints/3 cups filtered water

MAKES ABOUT 800ML/1½ PINTS/3¼ CUPS

Cook's tip
To prepare fresh chestnuts, slit the shells and place in a large pan. Cover with water, bring to a boil and cook for 15 minutes. Turn off the heat and leave for 5 minutes. Remove a few nuts at a time with a slotted spoon. When they are cool enough to handle, peel off the outer shell and the brown skin.

1 Halve the cooked, peeled chestnuts (or prepare 250g/9oz/1⅓ cups fresh ones, following the instructions in the Cook's tip).

2 Pulse the nuts in a blender with all of the filtered water a few times to break them up, then blend continuously for 2–3 minutes or until the mixture is smooth.

3 Pour the mixture through a nut bag suspended over a jug or bowl, and leave to drain. If you don't have a nut bag, pour the mixture through a muslin-lined sieve or strainer.

4 When the milk has filtered through, gather up the nut bag or the corners of the muslin and gently squeeze with clean hands to extract the last few drops of nut milk.

5 Discard the nut pulp (there won't be much). Store the chestnut milk in glass bottles or a covered jug or pitcher in the fridge. It will stay fresh for up to 3 days.

Tiger nut milk

Despite their name, tiger nuts, also known as chufa, are not actually nuts, but a starchy tuber that grows underground. About the size of a hazelnut, they are creamy-coloured with brown blotches or stripy patches. This milk, like chestnut milk, is ideal for anyone who can't have nuts.

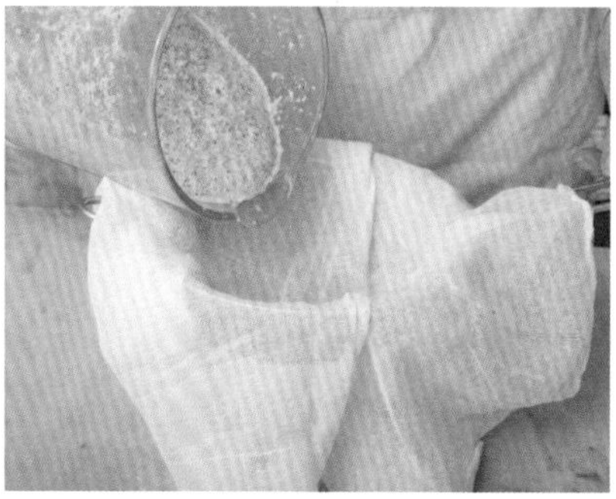

1 Put the tiger nuts in a large glass, ceramic or stainless-steel bowl. Pour over enough water to cover by 2.5cm/1in. Leave to soak in the fridge for 24–48 hours; the longer you soak them, the easier it will be to blend them to a smooth milk.

2 Drain and rinse the tiger nuts, then place in a blender and pour in 400ml/14fl oz/1⅔ cups of the filtered water. Add the salt and dates, if using. Pulse the blender a few times to finely chop the tiger nuts, then blend continuously for 2–3 minutes, until smooth and creamy.

3 Pour the mixture through a nut bag or a sieve or strainer lined with muslin or cheesecloth suspended over a bowl. Leave to drain. Return the pulp to the blender, add a further 400ml/14fl oz/1⅔ cups of the water and blend for a further 2–3 minutes or until very smooth. Strain again as before. Pour in the rest of the water and leave to drain again.

4 Gently squeeze the nut bag or muslin with clean hands to extract the last drops of milk. Discard the pulp. Stir in the vanilla and maple syrup, if using. Store the milk in the fridge, covered, for up to 3 days.

200g/7oz/1⅓ cups tiger nuts
1 litre/1¾ pints/4 cups filtered water, plus soaking water
1.5ml/¼ tsp salt
2 medjool dates or 15ml/1 tbsp maple syrup
5ml/1 tsp vanilla extract (optional)

MAKES ABOUT 1.2 LITRES/2 PINTS/ 5 CUPS

Cook's tip

Tiger nuts are quite fibrous, so you will have more leftover pulp than you do when making nut or seed milks.

Pumpkin or sunflower seed milk

Delicious and healthy milks can be made from seeds. Packed with protein, vitamins and minerals, sunflower and pumpkin seeds are high in fat, so make particularly rich and creamy milks. Seed milks tend to oxidize more quickly than nut milks, so for maximum nutritional benefit consume them within 2 days of making.

75g/3oz/½ cup pumpkin or sunflower seeds
350ml/12fl oz/1½ cups filtered water, plus soaking water

MAKES ABOUT 400ML/14FL OZ/ 1⅔ CUPS

Cook's tip
The seed pulp can also be made into a seed flour (as described on page 11).

1 Put the seeds in a bowl and pour in enough water to cover by about 2.5cm/1in. Leave to soak at room temperature for at least 8 hours, or place in the fridge and soak for up to 14 hours.

2 Drain and rinse the seeds, then tip them into a blender and add 300ml/½ pint/1¼ cups of the filtered water. Pulse a few times to break up the seeds, then blend continuously for 2–3 minutes or until smooth.

3 Pour the mixture through a nut bag or a sieve or strainer lined with muslin or cheesecloth suspended over a bowl. Leave to drain for a few minutes. When the milk has drained through, add the rest of the water and drain again.

4 When the milk has filtered through, gather up the corners of the nut bag or muslin and gently squeeze with clean hands to extract the last few drops of milk. Store the milk, covered, in the fridge. Ideally, sunflower seed milk should be used within 24 hours; pumpkin seed milk will keep for 2 days.

Hemp seed milk

While most seeds benefit from long soaking, others like hemp seeds need little or no soaking, so milks made from these can be ready to use in a very short amount of time. An excellent source of protein, hemp seeds provide all nine essential amino acids, so this milk is particularly beneficial for vegans. Don't add more seeds than suggested or the milk may have a bitter aftertaste.

50g/2oz/⅓ cup hemp seeds
475ml/16fl oz/2 cups filtered water

MAKES ABOUT 500ML/17FL OZ/ GENEROUS 2 CUPS

1 Put the seeds and filtered water in a blender. Pulse a few times to start breaking up the seeds, then blend continuously for 2–3 minutes or until the mixture is smooth.

2 Pour the mixture through a nut bag or a sieve or strainer lined with muslin or cheesecloth suspended over a bowl. Leave to drain for a few minutes.

3 When the milk has filtered through, gather up the corners of the nut bag or muslin and gently squeeze with clean hands to extract the last few drops of milk.

4 Discard any bits of hemp seed remaining in the nut bag or muslin (there should be very little).

5 Store the milk, covered, in the fridge and use it up within 3 days.

Coconut milk and coconut cream

Coconut milk is not the liquid from inside the coconut, but an extraction made from the coconut meat or flesh. It has a rich, creamy taste and a colour and appearance similar to that of cow's milk due to its naturally high fat content. It is made by soaking the coconut with hot water, then cooling and squeezing the resulting liquid through a fine cloth strainer to remove the solids.

1 mature coconut
150ml/¼ pint/⅔ cup near-boiling filtered water

MAKES ABOUT 250ML/9FL OZ/ 1 CUP COCONUT MILK AND CREAM

Cook's tip
You can buy two types of coconut milk: 'thick' coconut milk, which is made by directly squeezing grated coconut flesh through muslin or cheesecloth; and 'thin' coconut milk, where the already-squeezed flesh is then soaked in hot water for a second and third time before being strained.

1 Remove the flesh from a mature coconut and peel away the brown skin. Chop the white flesh into pieces and place in a food processor.

2 Pour over the near-boiling water. Blend until fairly smooth, then leave to cool for 5 minutes and blend again for just a few seconds.

3 Pour the mixture into a nut bag or sieve or strainer lined with muslin or cheesecloth suspended over a glass, china or plastic bowl (coconut reacts with metal) and leave it to drain for a few minutes.

4 Bring the corners of the nut bag or muslin together, then squeeze to extract the milk. Set aside the liquid for about 30 minutes. The coconut cream will float to the top of the milk and can be easily spooned off the surface into a bowl or container.

5 This process of soaking and squeezing can now be repeated to make more (slightly thinner) coconut milk. Use the coconut pulp to make coconut flour (see below).

Coconut flour

leftover pulp from making coconut milk and cream

1 Preheat the oven to 110°C/225°F/Gas ¼. Line a baking sheet with baking parchment (don't use foil as the metal may taint the flavour of the coconut).

2 Spread the leftover pulp from making coconut milk over the baking parchment in a thin, even layer, using a fork to break up any lumps.

3 Bake the pulp for 15 minutes, then remove it from the oven and stir with a fork. Spread it out again into an even layer and bake for 15–20 minutes more, or until it is completely dry. Coconut can burn even at a low temperature, so check it often towards the end of the cooking time and give it a stir.

4 Remove the coconut from the oven and leave it until it is completely cool. Tip it into a food processor and process for 4–5 minutes or until it is very finely ground. Store the flour in an airtight container and use within one year.

PYREX

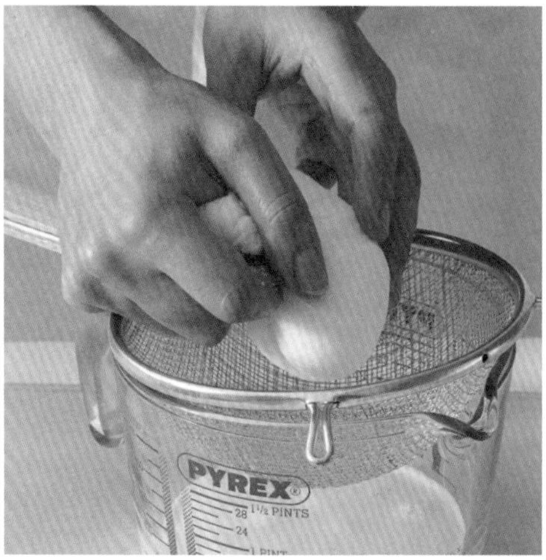
PYREX
1½ PINTS

Pea milk

Home-made pea milk differs slightly from the commercial variety as it is made from whole split yellow peas rather than isolated pea protein. It therefore contains a little more starch and fibre but has a similar rich and creamy taste and is good for pouring over breakfast cereals.

115g/4oz/½ cup yellow split peas
800ml/1½ pints/3¼ cups filtered water
3–4 medjool dates, stoned/pitted
30ml/2 tbsp sunflower oil
10–15ml/2–3 tsp vanilla extract
pinch of sea salt (optional)

MAKES ABOUT 850ML/1⅓ PINTS/3½ CUPS

Cook's tip
If you use an electric pressure cooker there is no need to soak the peas first. Select the beans/lentil setting and adjust the time to 30 minutes. When finished, allow the pressure to release naturally; this may take up to 15 minutes.

1 Rinse the split peas in a sieve or strainer under cold running water, then tip into a bowl. Pour over 250ml/9fl oz/1 cup of the filtered water, cover and leave to soak for 8 hours or overnight if possible.

2 Tip the peas and their soaking water into a medium-large pan and add a further 250ml/9fl oz/1 cup of the water. Bring to a rapid boil, skim off the foam, then lower the heat, cover and simmer for about 1 hour or until the peas are mushy. Turn off the heat, add the dates and leave to cool.

3 Transfer to a blender. Add the oil, vanilla and salt if using, and blend to a smooth purée. Add most of the remaining water and blend again.

4 Pour the mixture through a suspended nut bag or a sieve lined with muslin or cheesecloth. Leave to drain. Pour over the remaining water, leave to drain again, then gently squeeze to extract the last few drops.

5 If you'd like a thinner milk, return the pulp to the blender with an additional 250ml/9fl oz/1 cup water and repeat the draining process. Discard the pulp. Store, covered, in the fridge and use within 3 days.

Soya milk

Although soya milk is one of the most time-consuming non-dairy milks to make and needs to be simmered after straining, it isn't a difficult process and costs a fraction of store-bought versions. You can also adjust the thickness of the milk to suit your tastes and requirements.

1 Put the soya beans in a large glass, ceramic or stainless-steel bowl. Pour over enough boiling water to cover by 2.5cm/1in. Cover and leave to cool, then soak in the fridge for at least 12 hours and up to 24 hours.

2 Drain the beans and squeeze each one out of its skin; they will be loose after soaking and should pop out as you rub them. Discard the skins.

3 Put the beans in a blender and add 600ml/1 pint/2½ cups of the filtered water and the dates or maple syrup, if sweetening the milk. Blend until very smooth, then pour through a nut bag or a strainer lined with muslin or cheesecloth suspended over a pan. Leave to drain. Pour in a further 250ml/9floz/1 cup of water and leave to drain again.

4 Bring to the boil, reduce the heat, half-cover with a lid and simmer for 15 minutes, skimming off any foam. Turn off the heat and leave to cool.

5 Pour the milk into a jug or pitcher and leave as a full-bodied milk, or dilute with up to 150ml/¼ pint/⅔ cup filtered water. Bottle and store in the fridge for up to 4 days.

115g/4oz/⅔ cup dried soya beans, preferably organic
about 1 litre/1¾ pints/4 cups filtered water, plus soaking water
2 medjool dates or 15ml/1 tbsp maple syrup (optional)

MAKES ABOUT 1.2 LITRES/2 PINTS/ 5 CUPS

Cook's tip
Making your own soya milk has the additional benefit of giving you the chance to make it to the creaminess you want, which makes it more versatile for cooking.

Rice milk

Easy and inexpensive, rice milk can simply be made from freshly cooked leftover rice, or for a more intense flavour, you can lightly toast the raw grains first. It can be made from either white or brown rice; the latter has a nuttier taste and a darker colour.

75g/3oz/scant ½ cup long-grain white rice or 100g/3½oz/½ cup brown rice
1.2 litres/2 pints/5 cups filtered water
pinch of sea salt
45ml/3 tbsp maple syrup or agave syrup (optional)
2.5ml/½ tsp vanilla extract (optional)

MAKES ABOUT 1.2 LITRES/2 PINTS/ 5 CUPS

Cook's tip
A thick starchy-textured milk, this is best sweetened with a thin syrup rather than blitzing it with dates, which will make the milk too thick.

1 In a large deep stainless-steel frying pan or a saucepan, spread out the rice in a thin layer and toast over a low heat until it smells nutty and is just starting to colour. Stir towards the end to prevent it from burning. Carefully – as the rice will splutter – pour in 400ml/14fl oz/1⅔ cups of the filtered water. Cover with a tight-fitting lid and cook over a very low heat for about 10 minutes for white rice and 15 minutes for brown, until just tender; most of the water will be absorbed. Turn off the heat and leave to cool.

2 Tip the rice and a further 400ml/14fl oz/1⅔ cups of water into a blender. Add the salt, syrup and vanilla extract, if using, and blend until very smooth. White rice milk doesn't need to be strained; for brown rice milk, pour through a nut bag or a sieve or strainer lined with muslin or cheesecloth suspended over a bowl. Leave to drain; this will take a long time, so on a warm day, place it in the fridge.

3 Stir in about 400ml/14fl oz/1⅔ cups water, depending on how thick you like your milk; adding this amount will make a thickness and strength similar to store-bought rice milk. Pour into a jug or bottles, cover and store in the fridge for up to 3 days.

Oat milk

Home-made oat milk is simple and cheap to make, but has a somewhat bland flavour. It will also separate quickly unless you add an emulsifier such as lecithin. It is nevertheless a useful milk, especially for cooking and for blending with thicker, richer milks, to make them go further.

1 Put the oats in a bowl with enough cold water to cover by 2.5cm/1in. Leave to soak for 15 minutes, then drain and rinse under cold running water (this is essential or the milk will have a slimy texture). Drain.

2 Put the oats and filtered water in a blender and leave to soak for 5 minutes. Blend for 2 minutes, until smooth, then pour through a nut bag or a sieve or strainer lined with muslin or cheesecloth suspended over a bowl or jug. Gently stir the mixture to help it through.

3 If using a flavouring, sweeteners or emulsifier, return the milk to the rinsed-out blender, add these ingredients and blend for 1 minute.

4 Store, covered, in the fridge for up to 5 days. It will thicken, so stir it well before using.

90g/3½oz/¾ cup rolled oats
750ml/1¼ pints/3 cups filtered water, plus soaking water
pinch of sea salt (optional)
5ml/1 tsp agave syrup or clear honey (optional)
2.5ml/½ tsp vanilla extract (optional)
15ml/1 tbsp powdered lecithin (optional)

MAKES ABOUT 800ML/1½ PINTS/ 3¼ CUPS

Flavoured milks

All sorts of ingredients can be added to your plant milks to create flavoured blends, often in a gorgeous range of pastel colours. Some ingredients can be added and soaked at the same time as the nuts, seeds or grains, others need to be added to the made-up milk.

Superfood blends
Each of the following can be added to 250ml/9fl oz/1 cup nut or seed milk:

- Goji berries: Add 30ml/2 tbsp dried berries to the nut milk, leave to soak for 2–3 minutes, then blend until smooth. Also known as wolfberries, these berries are high in vitamin A and boost the immune system. They also promote a healthy heart and circulation.
- Açai berries: Add 5ml/1 tsp açai berry powder to the nut milk and blend for 1 minute. These are rich in antioxidants and may help to promote weight loss.
- Chia seeds: Sprinkle 5ml/1 tsp of the little black seeds over the milk and pulse in the blender a few times. Leave for 3–5 minutes, then blend for about 5 seconds. These tiny mucilaginous (moist and sticky) seeds contribute omega-3 and omega-6 to the diet in the optimum ratio needed for a healthy heart and brain.

Cook's tip
A pinch of salt can balance the flavourings in non-dairy milks. It can be added during soaking or when blending. Leave it out if you need to watch the sodium content of your diet.

Cacao or cocoa powder These complement all milks, but go especially well with hazelnut milk. Cacao and unsweetened cocoa powder are different names for the same thing, but cacao powder specifically refers to unsweetened powder made at a low temperature. Add 10–15ml/2 tsp–1 tbsp cacao or cocoa powder to every 250ml/9fl oz/1 cup nut or seed milk before or after blending, along with some vanilla extract, if liked. Sweeten to taste.

Carob powder This is made by grinding the roasted pods of the evergreen carob tree. The pods contain a very sweet pulp and hard brown seeds. Carob has a similar taste to chocolate but is free from caffeine and has around half the fat of cocoa. It should be used in the same quantity as cacao or cocoa powder, but because it is slightly sweeter, you should add less sugar or sweetener to the blend.

Fresh fruit juices These can be used instead of water when making nut milk. Try apple juice with almonds; pear or cranberry juice with walnuts; and orange or pomegranate juice with cashew or Brazil nuts.

Dried fruits Soak these with the nuts to extract maximum flavour. Apricots and peaches work well with almond milk, while dried tropical fruits, such as pineapple, are good with Brazil nut or coconut milk. Little or no additional sweetener will be required.

Spices Warm spices such as cinnamon and ginger add a lovely aroma and flavour to nut or seed milks, and turmeric is renowned for its anti-inflammatory properties. Add around 2.5ml/½ tsp ground spice to every 750ml/1¼ pints/3 cups milk. Alternatively, add chopped fresh stem ginger or some chopped preserved ginger from a jar along with a little of its syrup to the blender. Leave the milk to stand for a few minutes to let the spices infuse before straining. You will need to sweeten the milk to round out the flavour of the spices.

Vanilla This aromatic flavouring works well with all nut and seed milks. Add a few drops to enhance milks or, for a more pronounced taste, add 5–10ml/1–2 tsp vanilla extract or 1.5ml/¼ tsp pure ground vanilla bean paste to 750ml/1¼ pints/3 cups milk. This should be done after straining the milk, but if you don't want to see the little black specks of vanilla, blend the paste with the nuts and leave to stand for a few minutes before straining the milk.

Coconut water kefir

This makes an excellent dairy-free alternative to milk kefir. The crystal-like water kefir grains, which may be clear or golden, are cultured in coconut water with added sugar. The kefir grains feed on the sugar and most of it is converted to acetic acid, making a fairly low-sugar, low-calorie drink.

1 litre/1¾ pints/4 cups coconut water
45ml/3 tbsp water kefir grains (already cultured in a batch of plain water kefir, see below)

MAKES ABOUT 1 LITRE/1¾ PINTS/ 4 CUPS

Cook's tips
• Your new kefir water grains need to be cultured in a batch of plain water kefir before using them to make coconut water kefir.
• There are two different types of kefir grains, water and milk dairy; this uses the former.
• Some brands of coconut water have a small amount of sugar added, which is preferable for making kefir as the grains feed on sugar. If using unsweetened coconut water, stir in 5ml/1 tsp caster/superfine sugar.

1 Pour the coconut water into a sterilized 1-litre/1¾-pint glass jar or container. Add the water kefir grains and cover the top of the jar with muslin or cheesecloth, held in place with an elastic band. Alternatively, use a clip-top kilner-style jar and release the lid daily to allow some of the fermenting gases to escape.

2 Leave the jar away from direct sunlight for 24–36 hours, depending on the fermentation strength you like.

3 Strain the kefir liquid through a nylon sieve or strainer into a jug. Serve straight away with ice, and store any leftovers in the fridge.

4 Reserve the kefir grains in the strainer and use them to make a batch of plain water kefir (below); this will feed and rejuvenate the kefir grains. You can then make another batch of coconut water kefir with them.

5 If you don't want to make a new batch of kefir straight away, you can store the grains for a short time: mix together 300ml/½ pint/1¼ cups filtered water and 25g/1oz/1½ tbsp sugar in a jar until dissolved. Add the grains, cover and store in the fridge for up to 10 days.

Variation: As well as live fresh grains, you can buy dehydrated kefir grains. These are dormant and can be stored in a cool place for up to a year; note that they can take a while to become fully active. You can also buy ginger water kefir crystals.

Plain water kefir

900ml/1½ pints/3¾ cups filtered water
65g/2½ oz/⅓ cup caster/superfine sugar, preferably organic
25g/1oz/1½ tbsp organic raisins or other unsulphured dried fruit, such as apricots
5g/¼oz water kefir grains

MAKES 900ML/1½ PINTS/ 3¾ CUPS

1 Put the filtered water in a sterilized 1-litre/1¾-pint sterilized glass jar. Add the sugar and stir until dissolved, then add the fruit.

2 Add the water kefir grains and cover the top of the jar with muslin or cheesecloth, held in place with an elastic band. Leave at room temperature away from direct sunlight for 24–36 hours.

3 Strain the kefir through a nylon sieve into a jug, and discard the fruit. Serve straight away or store in the fridge. Reserve the kefir grains left in the strainer and use them to make coconut water kefir, another batch of plain water kefir, or store the grains in the fridge (see step 5 above).

Yogurts, creams & sauces

In this chapter you'll find all kinds of alternatives for traditional dairy classics, such as yogurt, sour cream, whipped cream, hollandaise sauce, ranch dressing and dulce de leche. You'll find the taste is almost identical or even better than their dairy counterparts. Soya and nut milk yogurts are easy to make at home and although you need to let them ferment and thicken for a few hours, they take very little hands-on time to prepare.

Soya or almond milk yogurt

This yogurt will not naturally thicken like dairy yogurt, so here nut milk is first thickened with cornflour. A little sugar, agave or maple syrup is essential as the probiotics 'feed' on it; the sweet taste will disappear by the end of the process so you may want to sweeten or flavour the yogurt again after making it. You can also strain the yogurt further to make it thicker.

10ml/2 tsp cornflour/cornstarch
7.5ml/1½ tsp caster/superfine sugar, agave or maple syrup
475ml/16fl oz/2 cups freshly made soya milk or almond milk (see pages 43 or 28)
2 vegan probiotic capsules (acidophilus 40mg) or 1 sachet non-dairy yogurt starter

MAKES ABOUT 475ML/16FL OZ/2 CUPS

Cook's tip
You can use unstrained almond milk to make this yogurt; the texture will be slightly less smooth but will be thicker than when using strained almond milk.

1 Blend the cornflour and sugar, agave or maple syrup in a pan with 30ml/2 tbsp of the milk until smooth, then stir in the rest of the milk. Bring to the boil and simmer for 1 minute, whisking until the mixture is slightly thickened.

2 Turn off the heat and leave to cool (you can speed up this process by placing the pan in a bowl of cold water), until the temperature falls to 90°F/32°C on a thermometer. Stir the mixture occasionally as it cools.

3 Open the probiotic capsules and sprinkle the powder over the warm milk (or add the sachet of yogurt starter, following the instructions on the packet) and whisk well.

4 Pour the mixture into a yogurt maker or a sterilized and cooled vacuum flask. Leave to stand for 8–10 hours; after 8 hours the yogurt will have a mild flavour, so if you prefer it tangy, leave it a little longer.

5 Transfer the yogurt from the yogurt maker or vacuum flask to a bowl and chill it, covered, in the fridge; it will thicken further as it chills. Use within 3 days of making.

Greek-style soya or nut milk yogurt

a batch of soya or nut milk yogurt

1 For thicker yogurt, strain it after chilling it. Line a sieve or strainer, large enough to hold all the yogurt, with a piece of muslin or cheesecloth, and suspend it over a bowl.

2 Tip the yogurt into the muslin and leave it to drain for 1–2 hours. The liquid will drain away, leaving a thicker yogurt behind in the muslin.

3 Discard the liquid and tip the yogurt into a container. Cover and chill until needed. It will keep for a few days in the fridge.

Coconut milk yogurt

This yogurt is deliciously creamy and decadent. Choose full-fat or whole coconut milk – diet or low-fat coconut milk will not work well – and make sure it is a brand that does not include any ingredients other than coconut, water and salt; no preservatives.

- 400ml/14fl oz can of full-fat coconut milk (or see page 40)
- 5ml/1 tsp coconut sugar
- 1 vegan probiotic capsule (contents only)

MAKES ABOUT 400ML/14FL OZ/ 1⅔ CUPS

Cook's tip
For a creamier yogurt, substitute 150ml/¼ pint/⅔ cup of the coconut milk with the same amount of canned coconut cream.

1 Refrigerate the can of coconut so that the liquid separates from the solids. Open the can and pour only the liquid into a glass – do not throw it away. Scoop the semi-solid cream into another glass or ceramic bowl.

2 Add the coconut liquid to the cream, stirring it in bit by bit until it is the consistency you like for your yogurt. Mix together well.

3 Add the sugar and the probiotic powder to the yogurt and mix well. Cover with cling film or plastic food wrap, or a wet cotton cloth. Make sure there is a gap at the top for the yogurt to expand.

4 Leave to ferment at room temperature or slightly warmer for 24 hours. Check after 24 hours and if you would like it more sour-tasting, ferment for another 12–24 hours. Once it is ready, eat it immediately or store it in the fridge. It will keep for at least a week.

Cashew yogurt

This can be enjoyed like dairy yogurt, perhaps with granola and some berries. It will continue to ferment very slowly when chilled, becoming a little thicker and tangier after a few days. The method for making soft fermented cashew nut cheese (page 104) is similar, but with less water .

250g/9oz/2½ cups raw unsalted cashew nuts, soaked for at least 2 hours and rinsed
10ml/2 tsp coconut sugar
pinch of salt
150–250ml/5¼–9fl oz/⅔–1 cup filtered water, as needed
1 vegan probiotic capsule (contents only)

MAKES ABOUT 300ML/½ PINT/ 1¼ CUPS

1 Put the cashew nuts, coconut sugar, salt and half the water in a blender and process until smooth and creamy. Add more water, a little at a time, and blend until it reaches the consistency you like. Add the probiotic powder and blend it in, or stir it in by hand.

2 Pour the mixture into a glass or ceramic bowl and cover with cling film or plastic food wrap, or a wet cotton cloth. Make sure there is a gap at the top so that the yogurt can expand.

3 Leave to ferment at room temperature or slightly warmer for 24 hours. Check, and if you would like it more sour-tasting, ferment for 12–24 hours more. When it's ready, enjoy it immediately or store it in sealed jars in the fridge. It will keep for about a week after opening.

Simple nut cream

The simplest nut creams can be made by blending nut butter with water or another liquid until smooth. For incorporating with other ingredients, a neutral-flavoured nut butter such as almond or cashew is ideal. This cream can even be turned into a quick- and-easy sauce for pasta with a little pasta cooking water; walnut butter or pine nut butter are both perfect for this.

115g/4oz/½ cup nut butter
up to 250ml/9fl oz/1 cup warm or hot water, vegan stock or nut milk

MAKES ABOUT 300ML/11FL OZ/ 1½ CUPS

1 Put the nut butter in a bowl. Stir in a few tablespoons of warm or hot water, stock if you are making a savoury recipe, or nut milk if you want a very rich mixture for a sweet recipe, then blend together until smooth.

2 Gradually work in more water, stock or milk; up to about 250ml/ 9fl oz/1 cup will make a thick cream. Add a little more liquid if you want a thinner cream. You can then either use it immediately, while the cream is still warm, or cool it before use. This nut cream will keep for a few days in the fridge.

Cashew cream

Cashews are ideal for making nut creams as the soft nuts blend to a rich product with a smooth consistency. The result can be as thick as you like and can be used in a wide range of recipes. It's great in any savoury or sweet dish where you need whipped cream, or if you prefer, thin it down with a little chilled cashew milk or water to make a pourable cream.

1 Put the raw unsalted cashew nuts in a large glass, ceramic or stainless-steel bowl. Pour over enough water to cover by about 2.5cm/1in and leave to soak for at least 8 hours, or overnight.

2 Drain and rinse the nuts, then tip them into a blender. Pulse a few times to break up the nuts. With the motor running, slowly pour in the filtered water, stopping to scrape down the sides. Blend until the mixture is as smooth and creamy as possible; this will depend on how powerful your blender is, but you should be able to make a fairly smooth cream with a standard kitchen blender.

3 Add more water or a splash of cashew milk if you want a thinner consistency. For a savoury dip, add a squeeze of lemon juice and season to taste with celery salt and ground black pepper; for a sweet cashew cream, stir in a little icing sugar, agave or maple syrup to taste.

250g/9oz/2½ cups raw unsalted cashew nuts
250ml/9fl oz/1 cup filtered water, plus soaking water

For a savoury use
lemon juice, celery salt and ground black pepper, to taste

For a sweet use
icing/confectioners' sugar, or agave or maple syrup, to taste

MAKES ABOUT 500ML/17FL OZ/ GENEROUS 2 CUPS

Sour cream

This is a versatile sour cream that can be used for both sweet and savoury dishes; simply vary the flavourings. Using silken tofu keeps the fat content lower, and it is also a good source of protein. The oil and lemon juice work together to help emulsify the sauce, making it thicker and richer.

175g/6oz/¾ cup silken tofu
10ml/2 tsp lemon juice
15–30ml/1–2 tbsp cold water

For a savoury use
10ml/2 tsp olive oil
1.5ml/¼ tsp Dijon mustard
salt and ground white pepper

For a sweet use
10ml/2 tsp sunflower oil
2.5–5ml/½–1 tsp caster/superfine sugar
2.5ml/½ tsp vanilla extract

MAKES ABOUT 200ML/7FL OZ/SCANT 1 CUP

1 Put the tofu in a blender with the lemon juice and 15ml/1 tbsp of the water. Blend for about 30 seconds until fairly smooth.

2 If making sour cream for a savoury dish, add the olive oil and mustard and season with a little salt and ground white pepper. If making sour cream for a sweet dish, add sunflower oil, sugar and vanilla extract.

3 Blend until completely smooth, adding the remaining 15ml/1 tbsp of water if you prefer a slightly thinner sour cream (it also depends on the brand of silken tofu used; some are softer and moister than others).

4 Pour and scrape the sour cream into a bowl, cover and chill until needed; it will thicken slightly as it chills. Use within 5 days of making.

Variation
You can use lime juice or apple cider vinegar instead of lemon juice if you prefer.

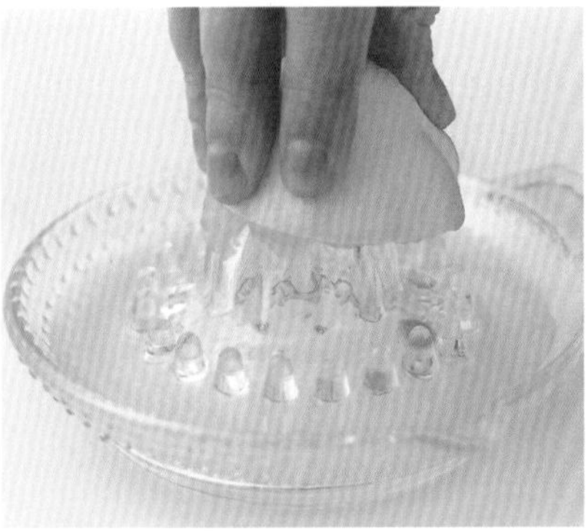

Hollandaise sauce

Hollandaise sauce is normally out-of-bounds for vegans as its main ingredients are egg yolks and butter. This creamy sauce is an excellent alternative and can be drizzled over asparagus and other lightly steamed vegetables or used as a dipping sauce – try it with 'mozzarella' sticks (page 144).

1 Put the cashew nuts in a bowl, pour over the filtered water and leave to soak for 30 minutes at room temperature or cover with clear film and soak in the fridge for up to 12 hours.

2 Tip the cashews and their soaking water into a blender. Add most of the lemon juice, turmeric and mustard and a little salt and ground white pepper. Pulse in the blender a few times to chop up the nuts, then blend for 2–3 minutes until very smooth.

3 If using, stir in the fresh herbs. Taste and adjust the seasoning and add a little more lemon juice if needed.

4 The sauce can be served cold or hot. For the latter, gently heat it in a small pan until just steaming.

75g/3oz/½ cup raw unsalted cashew nuts
120ml/4fl oz/½ cup water, preferably filtered
freshly squeezed juice of ½ lemon
small pinch of ground turmeric
2.5ml/½ tsp Dijon mustard
salt and ground white pepper, to taste
30ml/2 tbsp snipped fresh chives or chopped dill (optional)

MAKES ABOUT 200ML/7FL OZ/ SCANT 1 CUP

Avocado mayo

While you can make a simple avocado mayonnaise by blending a ripe avocado with store-bought vegan mayonnaise, this lighter version makes use of aquafaba instead of eggs for a reduced-fat, lower-calorie thick mayonnaise. You can adjust the flavourings depending on what you are planning to serve with it, and to your personal taste.

1 large ripe avocado
1 garlic clove, peeled and crushed (optional)
juice of ½ lemon
50–75ml/2–2½fl oz/¼–⅓ cup aquafaba (see page 16)
salt and ground black pepper, to taste

MAKES ABOUT 250ML/9FL OZ/ 1 CUP

1 Halve and peel the avocado, removing the stone/pit. Cut into chunks and put in a small food processor or blender with the garlic, if using, and most of the lemon juice. Season and blend until smooth.

2 With the motor running, slowly add the aquafaba to the food processor, stopping halfway through to scrape down the sides. Keep adding until the consistency is light and thick.

3 Taste and add a little more lemon juice or seasoning if needed. Spoon into a bowl and serve immediately if possible. It will keep in the fridge for 1–2 days, but it will start to discolour quite quickly.

Aioli

Traditional aioli is a rich garlicky mayonnaise sauce made with egg yolks that is perfect for dolloping, dipping and dunking. This vegan version is just as versatile and uses aquafaba as an egg substitute, emulsifying all the ingredients to make a rich creamy sauce. You can adjust the garlic and Dijon mustard to achieve the flavour and colour you like.

1 Put the aquafaba, mustard, garlic, salt, pepper, vinegar and lemon juice in a food processor or blender and blend for a few seconds until combined.

2 With the motor running, very slowly drizzle in the oil, making sure that it is fully combined before adding more. If the top starts to look slightly oily, stop adding oil for a few seconds and continue blending.

3 Continue to drizzle in the oil; the aioli will suddenly thicken. Once all the oil is added and thoroughly blended, add the lemon juice and garlic.

4 Spoon into a glass or stainless-steel (not plastic) container, bowl or sterilized jar, cover well (so the flavour doesn't transfer to other foods) and chill until ready to serve. It will keep for up to a week.

45ml/3 tbsp aquafaba (see page 16)
5–10ml/1–2 tsp Dijon mustard
2 garlic cloves, peeled and crushed
2.5ml/½ tsp salt
pinch of ground white pepper
15ml/1 tbsp apple cider vinegar or white wine vinegar
5ml/1 tsp lemon juice
200ml/7fl oz/scant 1 cup light olive or sunflower oil

MAKES ABOUT 250ML/9FL OZ/ 1 CUP

Ranch dressing

Ranch dressing has a smooth creamy texture, without being too heavy, and tastes mildly of garlic. It's traditionally made with dried herbs, but if you have fresh ones to hand, they are so much nicer. This vegan version has a base of cashew nuts, so the dressing is rich in protein, too.

75g/3oz/½ cup raw unsalted cashew nuts
120ml/4fl oz/½ cup cashew milk or almond milk (see pages 26 or 28)
10ml/2 tsp apple cider vinegar
2.5ml/½ tsp salt
2.5ml/½ tsp garlic powder
2.5ml/½ tsp American-style mustard or Dijon mustard
10ml/2 tsp maple syrup
45ml/3 tbsp sunflower oil
15ml/1 tbsp lemon juice
15ml/1 tbsp chopped fresh parsley or 5ml/1 tsp dried
15ml/1 tbsp snipped fresh chives or 5ml/1 tsp dried
freshly ground black pepper

MAKES 250ML/9FL OZ/1 CUP

1 Put the cashew nuts in a small bowl and pour over the nut milk. Cover and leave to soak in the fridge for 30 minutes, preferably longer.

2 Tip the nuts and milk into a blender, then add the vinegar, salt, garlic powder, mustard and maple syrup. Blend until very smooth.

3 Add the oil, a teaspoon at a time, briefly blending between each addition. Add the lemon juice, herbs and pepper and blend for just a few seconds to mix. Taste and adjust the seasoning.

4 Pour the sauce into a jug or glass bottle. Cover and chill in the fridge for at least 30 minutes to allow the dressing to thicken and for the flavours to develop. Whisk or shake well before use. The dressing will keep for 4–5 days in the fridge.

Variation

You can also make this dressing with water in place of nut milk, in which case it will keep for up to a week in the fridge. You also won't need to place it in the fridge for the soaking time.

Whipped coconut cream

This is a healthier and easy-to-make alternative to dairy whipped cream. It is very rich, so serve it in small helpings as a treat. This method does not work as well with coconut cream (page 40), so use the cream spooned from the top of a can of coconut milk, as outlined below. Here, it is flavoured with vanilla but you could use rose water or spices such as ground cinnamon or ginger.

400ml/14oz can of full-fat coconut milk
5ml/1 tsp vanilla extract

MAKES ABOUT 150ML/¼ PINT/⅔ CUP

Cook's tip
Whipped coconut cream is smoother than nut creams.

1 Chill the coconut milk in the fridge for several hours or overnight. Carefully open the can; the coconut cream will be at the top. Spoon out the coconut cream and place it in a glass bowl, preferably chilled, keeping the more watery coconut milk for other recipes.

2 Add the vanilla extract, then whisk for a few minutes with an electric beater, until the mixture is light and soft peaks form.

3 Serve the cream immediately or store it in the bowl, covered with clear film or plastic food wrap, in the fridge. It will keep for 2–3 days.

Vanilla custard

Desserts such as fruit pies and crumbles call for a generous serving of custard. Choose one of the creamier vegan milks to make this: cashew nut and soya milks are particularly good, as here, but the basic recipe can be varied to make the perfect partner to any pudding. For instance, hazelnut milk custard goes especially well with desserts containing apples and pears.

- 450ml/¾ pint/scant 2 cups soya milk or cashew milk (see pages 43 or 26)
- 30ml/2 tbsp caster/superfine sugar
- 45ml/3 tbsp cornflour/cornstarch
- 1.5ml/¼ tsp ground turmeric (optional)
- 10ml/2 tsp vanilla extract

MAKES ABOUT 475ML/16FL OZ

1 Spoon 60ml/4 tbsp of the milk into a heatproof bowl. Add the sugar, cornflour and ground turmeric, if using, and blend to a smooth paste.

2 Pour the remaining milk into a heavy pan and heat until steaming and beginning to bubble. Pour over the cornflour mixture, whisking.

3 Return it all to the pan. Simmer for 4–5 minutes, whisking constantly, until it bubbles and thickens. Cook for a few minutes more, whisking occasionally. Remove from the heat and stir in the vanilla. Serve hot.

Variation
For a chocolate custard, leave out the turmeric and reduce the vanilla to 2.5ml/½ tsp. Blend 30ml/2 tbsp cocoa powder with the cornflour, using an extra 30ml/2 tbsp milk to make a smooth paste, and mix in.

Cook's tip
The turmeric doesn't add flavour, just a subtle hint of yellow.

Warm chocolate sauce

Smooth and velvety chocolate sauce is divine for drizzling over ice creams and sponge puddings and as a dipping sauce for fresh fruit such as strawberries. This has a thick pouring consistency when warm but cools to a thick spoonable sauce and can be served chilled as well. For a much thicker, richer sauce with a mild coconut flavour, use coconut cream rather than soya cream.

150ml/¼ pint/⅔ cup soya cream
60ml/4 tbsp maple syrup
50g/2oz/¼ cup coconut sugar or light brown muscovado sugar
40g/1½oz unsweetened cocoa powder
15ml/1 tbsp tahini (see page 84)
75g/3oz/½ cup vegan dark chocolate chips or chopped vegan chocolate
5ml/1 tsp vanilla extract

MAKES ABOUT 250ML/9FL OZ/1 CUP

1 Pour slightly more than half of the cream into a heavy pan. Add the maple syrup, sugar and cocoa powder. Gently heat, stirring, until the sugar has dissolved and the mixture is smooth, then heat until it begins to boil. Stir continuously now as the mixture will start to thicken.

2 Remove from the heat and leave until the bubbles subside, then add the tahini, chocolate chips and vanilla. Stir until the chocolate has melted and the sauce is smooth. Stir in the rest of the cream.

3 Pour into a heatproof jug or bowl and serve warm. Alternatively, pour into a bowl and leave to cool, then chill. Use within 4 days of making.

Cook's tip
You won't be able to taste the tahini, but it gives a more rounded flavour to the sauce. Leave it out if you prefer or substitute smooth almond or cashew nut butter.

Butterscotch sauce

Super-sweet and buttery, this delicious sauce is almost clear rather than opaque, despite the addition of cream. It is thin when hot but thickens as it cools, making it ideal for spooning over ice cream or even drizzled over vegan yogurt. Serve in small helpings and try to reduce the amount of sugar in the dish it accompanies, or it will all be extremely sweet.

1 Put the vegan butter and the sugar in a heavy pan and gently heat until the butter has melted and the sugar has dissolved. Increase the heat a little, bring the mixture to the boil and let it bubble for 3 minutes, stirring occasionally.

2 Turn off the heat and carefully pour in the oat cream; the mixture may spit a little and will solidify in places.

3 Add the salt and return the pan to the heat. Slowly bring back to the boil and simmer for 2–3 minutes, stirring occasionally. Remove from the heat and leave to cool.

4 Pour the sauce into a jug or pitcher and serve at room temperature, or chill in the fridge. The sauce will thicken and have a pouring consistency. Use within 4 days of making.

75g/3oz/6 tbsp vegan margarine or 'buttery' spread (see page 72)
150g/5oz/⅔ cup coconut sugar or light muscovado sugar
150ml/¼ pint/⅔ cup oat cream or simple nut cream (see page 56)
1.5ml/¼ tsp salt

MAKES ABOUT 300ML/½ PINT/ 1¼ CUPS

Variation

If you prefer, swap in dark brown muscovado for the light muscovado or coconut sugar.

Coconut dulce de leche

This is quite calorific, so should be eaten in moderation as a special treat. It is fantastic combined with bananas in a banoffee pie or served as a dip with fruit, or even spread on toast. It can also be thinned by stirring in a little coconut, soya or oat cream if you want to make a delicious coconut caramel sauce to serve with puddings or ice cream.

400ml/14oz can of full-fat coconut milk (or see page 40)
75g/3oz/scant ½ cup coconut sugar
50g/2oz/¼ cup caster/superfine sugar
pinch of salt

MAKES 150ML/¼ PINT/⅔ CUP

1 Put the coconut milk, sugars and salt in a medium heavy pan. Gently heat, stirring occasionally, until the sugar has completely dissolved.

2 Bring to a boil, reduce the heat to low and simmer, stirring occasionally, for 20–25 minutes, until it darkens to a golden caramel and thickens.

3 Remove the pan from the heat and allow the mixture to cool, stirring occasionally; it will thicken further as it cools. Cover and store in the fridge for up to a week.

Coconut frosting

This is a dairy-free alternative to less-healthy buttercream and can be spread over cakes and cookies or piped. On a hot day, or if the coconut oil is very soft, chill it first for about an hour. For chocolate frosting, blend 20ml/4 tsp boiling water with 10ml/2 tsp unsweetened cocoa powder, leave to cool, then beat into the frosting.

1 Put the coconut oil in a bowl and beat for a few seconds with a wooden spoon. Sift over about one-third of the icing sugar, add the vanilla or coconut extract, and stir until mixed.

2 Gradually stir in the rest of the icing sugar along with 5ml/1 tsp coconut or soya milk. Beat well, then add more coconut or soya milk if needed, to make it thinner; this depends on whether you are planning to spread or pipe the frosting.

3 If liked, add 2–3 drops of food colouring. Beat until the frosting is light and completely blended. Spread or pipe as needed. Store any unused frosting in the fridge for 2–3 days.

50g/2oz/¼ cup virgin coconut oil
90g/3½oz/scant 1 cup icing/confectioners' sugar, sifted
5ml/1 tsp vanilla or coconut extract
10–15ml/2–3 tsp coconut milk or soya milk (see pages 40 or 43)
2–3 drops natural food colouring (optional)

MAKES ENOUGH TO FROST 12 CUPCAKES

Butters & spreads

Although you can buy dairy-free spreads, and nut and seed butters, it's rewarding to make your own and reassuring to know that they don't contain artificial additives or ingredients such as palm oil. You can blend them to the exact consistency you like, whether crunchy or smooth or somewhere in between, and you can also adjust the sweetness or saltiness to suit.

'Buttery' spread

Although you can buy vegan margarines, both soft ones for spreading and hard ones for baking, many contain ingredients such as palm oil and additives. It's often healthier to make your own. This versatile buttery spread is ideal for spreading on bread and can be used for frying and baking, too. Use refined coconut oil if you want a 'buttery' rather than a coconut flavour.

75ml/2½fl oz/⅓ cup soya milk or almond milk (see pages 43 or 28)
5ml/1 tsp apple cider vinegar
225g/8oz/1 cup refined coconut oil
30ml/2 tbsp sunflower or rapeseed oil
2.5ml/½ tsp nutritional yeast
1.5ml/¼ tsp ground turmeric
2.5ml/½ tsp salt

MAKES ABOUT 225G/8OZ/1 CUP

Cook's tips

• The spread will be hard when first removed from the fridge, but will quickly soften at room temperature. You should therefore take it out a few minutes before you need it, if you'll be spreading it on fresh bread, crackers etc.

• Ground turmeric gives the spread a buttery yellow colour, so reduce the quantity if you want a paler spread. You can use olive or avocado oil rather than sunflower oil if you prefer, in which case the spread will be slightly green rather than golden.

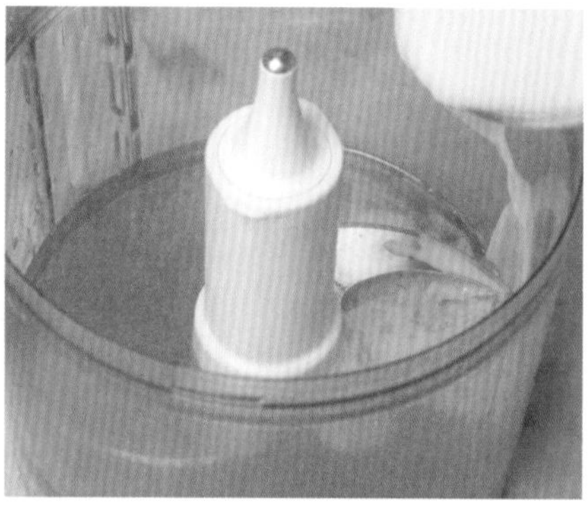

1 Pour the soya or almond milk into a small bowl. Add the apple cider vinegar and stir well; it will instantly thicken and may curdle slightly, which is fine. Leave the mixture at room temperature for a few minutes (if it is chilled, it will thicken the melted coconut oil before you pour it into a dish).

2 Put the coconut oil and sunflower or rapeseed oil in a small pan and gently heat, stirring occasionally, until the coconut oil has just melted; it should be barely warm.

3 Sprinkle the nutritional yeast, ground turmeric and salt over the liquid fat and stir until dissolved.

4 Pour the mixture into a blender or food processor. Add the milk and vinegar mixture and blend for about a minute until emulsified into a smooth and creamy spread.

5 Spoon and scrape the spread into a glass or ceramic dish, then chill in the fridge for about 2 hours or until the spread has set and hardened.

6 The spread keeps well for up to 10 days in the fridge. Ideally, store it in a less cold part of the fridge, such as the door or top shelf, so it doesn't become too hard. If you won't use it all in that time, divide it between smaller containers and freeze some for a later date. It will keep for up to 2 months in the freezer.

Smooth peanut butter

This is the simplest peanut butter, which is made with unroasted, unsalted nuts; ideal if you are following a 'raw' diet. Blended until smooth, it has a lighter colour and milder flavour than commercial peanut butter. If you wish to sweeten it, you can use brown sugar or, for a softer nut butter, add a liquid sweetener such as agave or maple syrup.

450g/1lb/2¾ cups raw unsalted peanuts
1.5ml/¼ tsp salt (optional)
5–10ml/1–2 tsp agave or maple syrup (optional)
5–10ml/1–2 tsp groundnut/peanut or sunflower oil (optional)

MAKES ABOUT 450G/1LB/2 CUPS

Cook's tips

• Be aware that the mixture is likely to heat up considerably while you are processing the nuts, so to avoid burns, leave the butter in the food processor to cool before tasting or decanting it. Pause frequently if you are using a low-powered machine to prevent it from overheating.

• For longer storage, decant the peanut butter into suitable freezerproof containers and freeze for up to 3 months.

1 Put the peanuts in a food processor or blender. Sprinkle with salt if you are using it. Pulse the blender a few times to start breaking up the nuts, then process for 1 minute or until the peanuts are finely ground.

2 Scrape the sides of the bowl with a rubber spatula, then add the sweetener, if using, and 5ml/1 tsp of the oil if you don't have a high-powered blender or food processor; this will help to soften the nuts so that they blend smoothly.

3 Process the mixture for 2–3 minutes, until the nuts come together in a clumpy paste. Stop and scrape down the sides of the bowl again. Take care not to overheat the machine; stop if necessary.

4 Continue processing the mixture for a further 2–3 minutes. At first, the peanut butter will get thicker, but gradually it will become smoother and creamier as it begins to flow freely through the blades. Add the remaining oil at this stage, if using.

5 Blend for an additional 1 minute, or until the desired consistency is reached; the motor of the food processor or blender will warm the mixture slightly, so bear in mind that it will be thicker once it has been removed from the blender and has cooled.

6 Use a rubber spatula to transfer the peanut butter into a clean container or sterilized jars. Store the peanut butter in the fridge (home-made nut butter doesn't contain preservatives, so it won't keep as long as commercial varieties). Use within 4 weeks of making.

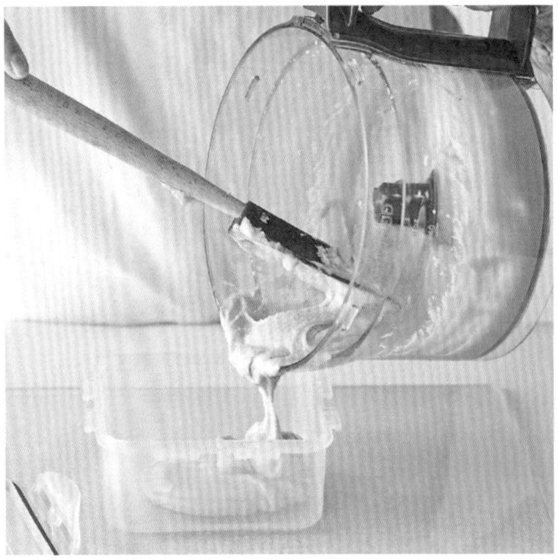

KENWOOD

Crunchy peanut butter

Here, the peanuts are roasted until golden before being turned into peanut butter. Roasting the nuts intensifies the flavour and will make a darker, richer peanut butter. It also warms and helps release the natural oils, so this nut butter is quicker and easier to make than one made with unroasted nuts. Watch carefully as nuts burn very quickly.

1 Heat the oven to 180°C/350°F/Gas 4. Spread out the raw peanuts in a single layer on a baking sheet. Bake for 5–6 minutes, until they are a light-golden colour and smell slightly nutty.

2 Remove from the oven, then leave the nuts on the baking sheet for 2–3 minutes. Set aside about 115g/4oz/¾ cup of the roasted nuts, then tip the rest into the food processor or blender. Sprinkle with salt, if you are using. Pulse the blender a few times to start breaking up the nuts, then process the peanuts for about 1 minute or until finely ground.

3 Scrape the sides with a spatula, then add the agave or maple syrup, if using, and 5ml/1 tsp of the oil if you do not have a high-powered blender or food processor. Blend for 1–2 minutes or until the nuts come together in a clumpy paste. Stop and scrape down the sides again.

4 Continue processing for 1–2 minutes more, until the peanut butter starts to become softer and creamier. Add the remaining oil, if using. Blend for 1 minute or until smooth.

5 Add the remaining nuts, then pulse until roughly chopped (if you want the pieces to be very even, chop the nuts by hand, then stir in).

6 Transfer the peanut butter to a clean container or sterilized jars. Store in a cool place, preferably in the fridge, and use within 4 weeks of making, or freeze for up to 3 months.

450g/1lb/2¾ cups raw unsalted peanuts
1.5ml/¼ tsp salt (optional)
5–10ml/1–2 tsp agave or maple syrup (optional)
5–10ml/1–2 tsp groundnut/peanut or sunflower oil (optional)

MAKES ABOUT 450G/1LB/2 CUPS

Cook's tip
Some nut butters will blend to a smooth consistency; others, such as almond butter, tend to be a bit more textured. If you want a crunchy nut butter, remove some of the nuts from the food processor once they are coarsely or finely chopped (depending on your preference). Blend the rest into a smooth nut butter, then add the reserved chopped nuts and pulse the machine until the chopped nuts and butter are just combined, or stir them in by hand.

How to skin peanuts
You can of course leave the skins on when making peanut butter (they will add fibre and red flecks to the nut butter), but if you want to remove them there are two easy ways:

1 Heat the oven to 180°C/350°F/Gas 4. Spread the nuts in a single layer on a baking sheet. Bake for 3–4 minutes or until the skins start to split away from the nuts (if you want to roast the nuts at the same time, cook them for a further 2–3 minutes; this will intensify the flavour). Put the nuts in a clean dish towel and rub to remove the skins. Pick out the skinned nuts.

2 Alternatively, put the nuts in the freezer for at least 4 hours. Take out a handful at a time and rub them vigorously in a clean dish towel. Most of the skins will be dislodged. Pick out the skinned nuts.

Almond butter

An increasingly popular nut butter, almonds are very hard, so will take slightly longer to process than some other nuts. If you are making the butter in an ordinary food processor, it's a good idea to warm the almonds in the oven for a few minutes first to soften them and start releasing the oils (you can leave this step out if you are using a high-powered blender).

400g/14oz/2⅔ cups raw unsalted blanched almonds
pinch of salt (optional)
5–10ml/1–2 tsp agave or maple syrup (optional)
5–10ml/1–2 tsp almond or sunflower oil (optional)

MAKES ABOUT 400G/14OZ/SCANT 2 CUPS

Variation
Pistachios and macadamias can be made into butters in exactly the same way. Both are soft nuts, so will blend into butters easily. Macadamia nuts are high in fat and the butter will be very soft, so don't add any additional oil.

1 Spread the almonds in a single layer on a baking sheet and place it in a cold oven. Turn on the oven to 150°C/300°F/Gas 2. Leave the baking sheet in the oven for 4–5 minutes or until the almonds are warm.

2 Remove the almonds from the oven and tip them into the food processor. Sprinkle over the salt, if using. Process for 1–2 minutes, until finely ground.

3 Scrape the sides with a rubber spatula, then add the sweetener and 5ml/1 tsp of the oil, if using. Blend for a few minutes or until the nuts come together in a clumpy paste. Stop and scrape down the sides again.

4 Add the remaining 5ml/1 tsp of oil, if using. Continue processing for 12–15 minutes, until smooth and creamy. The heat of the machine will help the nuts to soften and blend, but if using a low-powered one, take care not to burn out the engine; pause if necessary.

5 Transfer the butter to a clean container or sterilized jars. Store, chilled, for up to 4 weeks.

Cashew butter

You can make cashew nut butter with raw unroasted nuts, but the flavour is much more intense if they are roasted first. Cashew nuts are much softer than either peanuts or almonds so this nut butter will blend more quickly and tends to have a much finer, smoother consistency than some home-made nut spreads. Unroasted nuts make a pale creamy nut butter.

400g/14oz/$2^{2}/_{3}$ cups raw unsalted cashew nuts
pinch of salt (optional)
5–10ml/1–2 tsp agave or maple syrup (optional)
5–10ml/1–2 tsp almond or sunflower oil (optional)

MAKES ABOUT 400G/14OZ/SCANT 2 CUPS

1 Preheat the oven to 180°C/350°F/Gas 4. Spread the cashew nuts in a single layer on a baking sheet and roast for 5–6 minutes or until light golden. Take care not to let them burn.

2 Remove from the oven and leave the nuts to cool on the baking sheet for 2–3 minutes (very hot nuts could damage your machine), then tip them into the food processor. Sprinkle over the salt, if using. Process for 1–2 minutes or until finely ground.

3 Scrape the sides with a rubber spatula, then add the sweetener and 5ml/1 tsp of the oil, if using. Blend for a few minutes, until the nuts come together in a clumpy paste. Stop and scrape down the sides.

4 Add the remaining 5ml/1 tsp of oil, if using, and continue processing until smooth and creamy, scraping down the sides if necessary. Transfer the nut butter to a clean container or sterilized jars. Store in a cool place, preferably the fridge. Use within 4 weeks of making or freeze the butter in a suitable container for up to 3 months.

Hazelnut butter

Roasting brings out the distinctive flavour of hazelnuts and they make a delicious nut butter. You can roast them in the oven, but this will remove some of the moisture inside the nuts. In this recipe, the nuts are quickly toasted in a frying pan to lightly brown the outsides, without drying the nuts. Ready-roasted skinned hazelnuts can also be used instead.

400g/14oz/2⅔ cups raw unsalted hazelnuts, skinned or unskinned
pinch of salt (optional)
5–10ml/1–2 tsp light soft brown sugar, agave or maple syrup (optional)
10–15ml/2 tsp–1 tbsp hazelnut or sunflower oil

MAKES ABOUT 400G/14OZ/SCANT 2 CUPS

Cook's tip
Hazelnut butter is especially delicious in banana smoothies and on toast, where its flavour can shine through and a little will go a long way.

1 Put the hazelnuts in a single layer in a non-stick frying pan. Toast over a low heat for 4–5 minutes, stirring often. Remove from the heat as soon as they start to turn golden and smell nutty.

2 If the hazelnuts are still in their papery skins, tip them into a clean dish towel and rub them to remove most of the skins. Pick out the nuts and put them in a food processor or blender.

3 Sprinkle over the salt, if using. Process for 1–2 minutes or until finely ground. Scrape the sides with a rubber spatula, then add the sugar or sweetener and 5ml/1 tsp oil, if using.

4 Blend for a few minutes or until the nuts come together in a clumpy paste. Scrape down the sides of the bowl again with the spatula. Add the remaining oil, if using, and continue processing until the hazelnut butter becomes fairly smooth and creamy.

5 Transfer to a clean container or sterilized jars. Store in the fridge for up to 4 weeks or freeze in a suitable container for up to 3 months.

Chocolate hazelnut spread

Hazelnuts and chocolate have a natural affinity and it's not just children who adore this rich, nutty spread. This version contains a much higher proportion of nuts than commercial varieties and doesn't contain hydrogenated oils or thickeners. Use a good-quality vegan chocolate but one that is not too high in cocoa solids; it should have a slightly sweet flavour.

1 Break the chocolate into squares and melt it in a bowl set over a pan of near-boiling water, stirring occasionally. Do not let the bottom of the bowl touch the water. Remove the bowl from the pan and leave to cool.

2 Toast and skin the hazelnuts, as described opposite. Sprinkle over the salt. Process in a blender for 1–2 minutes, until the nuts are finely ground. Scrape the sides with a rubber spatula. Add the oil, then blend until the nuts come together in a fairly smooth nut butter.

3 Add the oil, sugar, cocoa powder and vanilla and continue processing until the mixture is smooth. Add the chocolate and blend well.

4 Transfer to a clean container or sterilized jars. The mixture will be thin initially, but will thicken as it cools. Store at room temperature or, if you prefer it very thick, keep it in the fridge. Use within 3 weeks.

350g/12oz vegan plain/semi-sweet chocolate
175g/6oz/1 cup raw unsalted hazelnuts
pinch of salt
30ml/2 tbsp hazelnut oil or sunflower oil
45ml/3 tbsp icing/confectioners' sugar
15ml/1 tbsp unsweetened cocoa powder
2.5ml/½ tsp vanilla extract

MAKES ABOUT 500G/1¼LB/GENEROUS 2 CUPS

Chestnut butter

Making a butter from chestnuts is different to making one from any other nuts as they have a high carbohydrate and low-fat content. If you buy whole unpeeled chestnuts, cook and peel them following the method on page 36. You will need 675g/1½lb unpeeled chestnuts.

250g/9oz/1½ cups cooked and peeled chestnuts
30ml/2 tbsp agave or maple syrup
pinch of salt
120–150ml/4–5fl oz/½–⅔ cup filtered water

MAKES ABOUT 400G/14OZ/SCANT 2 CUPS

1 Put the chestnuts in a food processor and pulse for 1–2 minutes to break them up. Add the agave or maple syrup and salt and blend for an additional few seconds to combine.

2 With the motor running, slowly add 120ml/4fl oz/½ cup of water. Blend for 1–2 minutes, then scrape down the sides. Blend until very smooth, adding a little more water if needed.

3 Spoon the chestnut butter into an airtight container or sterilized jar and seal. Keep the butter in the fridge and use it within 3 weeks of making it.

Coconut butter

Coconut butter is made by crushing and blending finely chopped coconut. It can be used as a spread and in baking, but should not be used for frying as it burns at a very low temperature. Sometimes the oil may separate and rise to the top, in which case give it a stir before using it.

1 Process the desiccated coconut in a food processor for 3–4 minutes, then scrape down the sides. Blend again, stopping after several minutes and scraping down the sides again.

2 Keep repeating this procedure and blend until the mixture has become oily and a fairly smooth, pale paste. This can take 20 minutes.

3 Transfer the butter to a sterilized jar and store it at room temperature. It will keep for at least a year. If it sets hard (in a cold room), warm it for a few seconds in the microwave.

250g/9oz/3 cups desiccated/ shredded unsweetened coconut

MAKES ABOUT 250G/9OZ/ 1¼ CUPS

Classic tahini

True tahini is a smooth, thick paste made from unroasted sesame seeds and usually contains olive oil. It is a key ingredient in Middle Eastern dishes such as hummus and baba ganoush. It is mild in flavour and pale in colour, and making it involves soaking the seeds before blitzing them to as a paste, as textured or as smooth as you prefer (or that your machine can manage).

150g/5oz/1 cup sesame seeds
cold filtered water, for soaking
pinch of salt
45–60ml/3–4 tbsp olive oil

MAKES ABOUT 200G/7OZ/¾ CUP

Cook's tip
Here, the seeds are soaked to soften them and give the butter a creamier consistency. It will thicken as it cools.

1 Put the seeds in a bowl and pour over enough cold filtered water to cover them by 2.5cm/1in (a lot will float on the top, but will sink as they absorb water). Leave to soak for 4–6 hours.

2 Drain, then tip into a food processor. Add the salt and process for 1–2 minutes, until finely ground. Scrape down the sides and process again.

3 With the motor running, add 30ml/2 tbsp of the oil. Blend until smooth, add 15ml/1 tbsp more oil and blend again, adding more oil until you achieve the desired consistency.

4 Transfer to a bowl or sterilized jar. Cover and store in the fridge for up to 4 weeks. Some of the oil may float to the top, so stir before using.

Toasted tahini

Toasted sesame seed butter is denser and deeper in taste and colour than classic tahini, as the seeds are roasted. They brown quickly, so watch carefully and stir continuously. This is the type of tahini that is most commonly sold in jars. It can be used to make hummus, as well as featuring in all sorts of dressings and even in some cakes and cookies.

150g/5oz/1 cup sesame seeds
approx 15–30ml/1–2 tbsp toasted sesame oil
pinch of salt

MAKES ABOUT 175G/6OZ/ GENEROUS ¾ CUP

1 Put the seeds in a non-stick frying pan. Toast over a low heat for 2–3 minutes, stirring constantly, until the seeds are just turning golden brown. Remove from the heat and continue to stir for 1 minute.

2 Leave the seeds to cool for 1 minute, then tip them into a food processor. Add the oil and salt. Pulse for 2–3 minutes, until finely ground. Scrape down the sides with a spatula.

3 Continue blending until the mixture is fairly smooth, scraping down the sides. Add a little more oil if necessary to keep the mixture moving over the food processor's blades.

4 Transfer to a bowl or sterilized jar. Cover and store in the fridge for up to 4 weeks. Some of the oil may float to the top, so stir before using.

Sunflower or pumpkin seed butter

Sunflower seeds make a dark cream-coloured butter, whereas pumpkin seeds blend to a speckled olive green. If you can't choose between the two types, use half of each to make a nutrient-rich spread. If you have a powerful blender you may not need to add all of the oil.

300g/11oz/2 cups sunflower or pumpkin seeds
pinch of salt
15–30ml/1–2 tbsp sunflower or pumpkin seed oil
10ml/2 tsp maple syrup (optional)

MAKES ABOUT 300G/11OZ/ 1½ CUPS

1 Put the seeds in a large non-stick frying pan. Toast over a low heat for 5–6 minutes, shaking the pan and stirring the seeds frequently. They are ready when some are just starting to colour, they smell nutty and you hear a sizzling sound. Remove from the heat and stir for 1 minute.

2 Leave to cool, then tip into a food processor or blender. Add the salt, then process for 1–2 minutes, until finely ground. Add 15ml/1 tbsp oil and the maple syrup if using, then process for 3–4 minutes.

3 Scrape down the sides with a spatula and continue processing until the butter becomes fairly smooth and creamy. Add a little more or all of the oil, if liked, to make a thinner butter.

4 Transfer to a clean container or sterilized jar. Store in the fridge. Use within 4 weeks or freeze for up to 3 months.

Pine nut pesto

Although this isn't a butter, it is included in this chapter as it is made in a very similar way. Normally pesto features grated Parmesan; in this vegan version, the tangy taste of cheese is replaced with some freshly squeezed lemon juice and a generous amount of seasoning.

1 Toast the pine nuts in a single layer in a non-stick frying pan over a low heat for 2–3 minutes, stirring, until just beginning to turn light golden. Tip the nuts on to a plate and leave until they are nearly cool.

2 Put the pine nuts, basil, garlic, olive oil, 10ml/2 tsp of the lemon juice, salt and pepper in a blender or food processor. Blend at high speed until the nuts and basil are finely chopped and the mixture is creamy.

3 Taste and adjust the seasoning as necessary, adding the remaining lemon juice if needed. Store in a screw-top jar in the fridge, spooning a little extra oil over the top. Use within 3 weeks.

50g/2oz/½ cup pine nuts
50g/2oz fresh basil leaves
1–2 garlic cloves, peeled
120ml/4fl oz/½ cup extra virgin olive oil
10–15ml/2 tsp–1 tbsp freshly squeezed lemon juice
salt and ground black pepper

MAKES ABOUT 225G/8OZ/1 CUP

'Cheeses'

Once you have mastered the simple recipes such as creamy almond soft cheese, easy-to-make seed and vegetable cheeses lightly set with agar agar, and savoury cheesy toppings ready for sprinkling, it's worth taking the time to also create some of the fermented vegan cheeses in this chapter. Fermenting not only adds to the final flavour of the cheese, but it also increases the nutritional content and provides healthy probiotics, too.

Simple almond milk 'cheese'

This mild, creamy nut cheese is made in the same way as almond milk, but here the pulp is used as a base for the cheese. Much less water is required when blending the almonds and some of the very creamy nut milk is left in the pulp. When freshly made, the cheese will have quite a sharp lemony flavour; this mellows and almost disappears after 24 hours.

175g/6oz/1 cup raw unsalted blanched almonds
175ml/6fl oz/¾ cup filtered water, plus water for soaking
45ml/3 tbsp freshly squeezed lemon juice
45ml/3 tbsp olive oil
salt and ground white pepper, to taste

MAKES ABOUT 350G/12OZ

Cook's tip
For the best flavour, buy the freshest unblanched almonds you can find (check use-by dates carefully) still in their brown skins and blanch them yourself (see page 29).

1 Put the almonds in a bowl and pour over enough water to cover by 2.5cm/1in. Leave to soak at room temperature for 2 hours, then drain and rinse. Return the nuts to the bowl, pour over the filtered water, cover and leave to soak again in the fridge for 24 hours.

2 Tip the nuts and soaking water into a food processor or blender (it's important that the mixture covers the blades or it will be impossible to blend it finely enough). Pulse a few times to break up the nuts, then blend continuously for 3–4 minutes, until very smooth.

3 Tip the mixture into a nut bag suspended over a bowl and leave to drain for 5 minutes; the pulp should still be fairly moist. Transfer the pulp to a separate bowl (keep the strained 'milk' to one side).

4 Whisk the lemon juice with the olive oil, salt and pepper, and stir it into the nut pulp. The mixture ought to be soft, but you should be able to shape it. If it is dry, stir in a little of the milk that has drained from the pulp. (The remaining milk can be diluted and used separately.)

5 Shape into a flattened round about 5cm/2in high and place on a baking sheet lined with baking parchment. Place in a cold oven and heat to 150°C/300°F/Gas 2. Bake for 25–30 minutes or until the outside of the 'cheese' is dry and slightly darker; this forms a sort of rind that will help keep the cheese fresh.

6 Leave to cool on the baking sheet, then transfer to a plate, cover and chill for 24 hours before serving. Eat within 5 days.

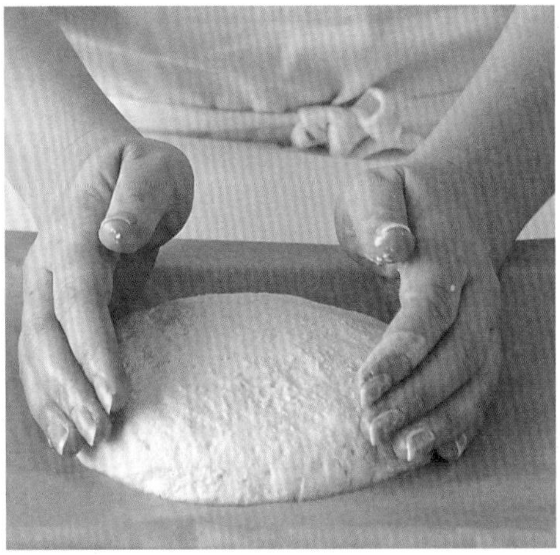

Firm sesame seed 'cheese'

Here, sesame seeds are ground to a fine flour-like texture, blended with rich sunflower seed milk, then set with agar agar to make a firm, sliceable cheese with a flavour not unlike tahini. You can also make this cheese successfully using other seeds such as hulled hemp, and other milks, such as cashew or unsweetened almond milk. Toasting the sesame seeds first gives additional flavour.

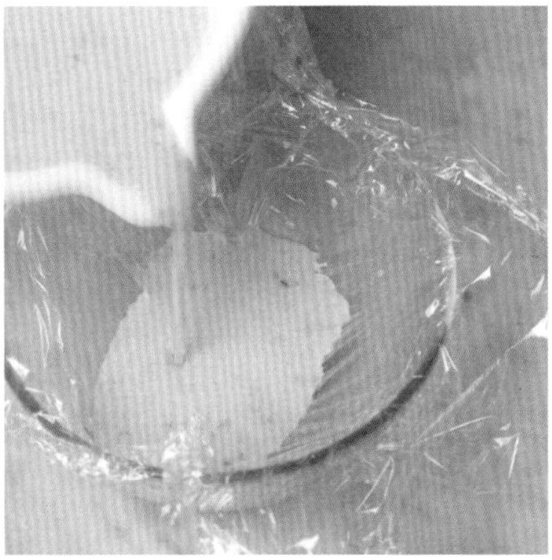

115g/4oz/¾ cup sesame seeds
45ml/3 tbsp nutritional yeast flakes
1.5ml/¼ tsp salt
10ml/2 tsp apple cider vinegar
250ml/9fl oz/1 cup sunflower seed milk
10ml/2 tsp powdered agar agar

Optional flavourings
5ml/1 tsp smoked paprika
2.5ml/½ tsp ground turmeric
30ml/2 tbsp chopped fresh herbs

MAKES ABOUT 350G/12OZ

1 If liked, lightly toast the sesame seeds first in a dry non-stick frying pan for 3–4 minutes, stirring frequently, until just beginning to turn golden. Take care not to burn the seeds. Leave to cool.

2 Tip the sesame seeds into a small blender. Add the yeast flakes and salt and blend to a fine flour-like texture. Towards the end, the oils from the seeds will make the mixture clump together. Add the vinegar and blend again.

3 Pour the sunflower seed milk into a pan, sprinkle over the agar agar and heat gently, whisking to dissolve. Bring to the boil, then lower the heat and simmer, uncovered, for 5 minutes.

4 Let the bubbles subside, then add the sesame seed mixture to the hot milk and whisk until smooth. Add flavouring of your choice, if using.

5 Pour the mixture into a wet dish or bowl, pre-lined with clear film if you want a smooth round cheese. Leave to cool, then cover and chill for at least an hour to firm up.

Firm smoked coconut 'cheese'

This has the taste and texture of those little sausage-shaped smoked cheeses you can buy – and it can be set in a cylindrical mould if you have one, to create a roll-shaped cheese. Although it does have a slight coconut taste, this is barely noticeable beneath the hickory smoke flavour, and the coconut milk does give a wonderful intense creaminess.

- 400g/14oz can of full-fat coconut milk (or see page 40)
- 15–30ml/1–2 tbsp hickory-flavoured liquid smoke
- 45–60ml/3–4 tbsp nutritional yeast flakes
- 2.5ml/½ tsp salt
- 2.5ml/½ tsp lemon juice
- 5ml/1 tsp tapioca flour/starch
- 15ml/1 tbsp powdered agar agar

MAKES ABOUT 350G/12OZ

Variation

If you prefer a softer set, use just 10ml/2 tsp agar agar.

1 Pour the coconut milk into a pan, add 15ml/1 tbsp of the hickory-flavoured liquid smoke, 45ml/3 tbsp of the nutritional yeast flakes, the salt and the lemon juice. Whisk everything together until the yeast flakes have dissolved. Taste the mixture and add more liquid smoke and another 15ml/1 tbsp yeast flakes if you prefer a stronger smoke/cheese flavour.

2 Sprinkle the tapioca flour and agar agar over the top. Whisk again to mix, then heat the mixture until it comes to the boil, whisking occasionally. Let the mixture boil, uncovered, for 5 minutes to allow the agar agar to activate and give a good set. This also allows some of the liquid to evaporate, making the 'cheese' richer and creamier.

3 Take the pan off the heat and allow the bubbles to subside. Pour the mixture into a glass dish or mould that has been rinsed out with cold water. Leave until completely cool, then cover and chill in the fridge for 2 hours until firm and set. Turn out to serve.

Courgette 'cheese' loaf

This attractive pale green cheese has a puréed courgette base complemented by hemp seeds and pumpkin seeds, both of which can be soaked beforehand for an hour or more if you want them to completely blend into the mixture. This makes a light yet still flavoursome 'cheese' that is firm enough to slice easily, but soft enough to spread as well.

75g/3oz/½ cup pumpkin seeds
2 large courgettes/zucchini, about 450g/1lb in total, trimmed and thickly sliced
2.5ml/½ tsp salt
2.5ml/½ tsp onion powder
175ml/6fl oz/¾ cup cup boiling water
10ml/2 tsp apple cider vinegar
50g/2oz/½ cup hulled/shelled hemp seeds (also sometimes called hemp hearts)
75ml/5 tbsp nutritional yeast flakes
pinch of ground white pepper
15ml/1 tbsp powdered agar agar

MAKES ABOUT 550G/1LB 6OZ

Cook's tips

• Keep the lid on the food processor to keep the courgette purée warm. If it is allowed to get cold, the agar agar will start to set before the mixture is poured into a dish.

• Some hemp seeds are harder and darker than others, which will affect how easily they break down during processing. Make sure you buy a type that has been treated so that they can be eaten whole if you do want to leave some seeds chunkier for a bit of texture.

• If you want a really smooth cheese, soak the hulled hemp seeds with the pumpkin seeds for 3–4 hours, and blitz the mixture well in step 3.

1 Put the pumpkin seeds in a small bowl and cover with cold water. Leave to soak for at least 1 hour, preferably longer if time allows.

2 Trim and thickly slice the courgettes. Put in a pan, sprinkle over the salt and onion powder and pour over the boiling water. Bring back to the boil, then reduce the heat, cover the pan with a lid and simmer for 7–8 minutes or until the courgettes are tender.

3 Lift the courgettes out of the water with a draining spoon (keep the cooking water) and put them in a food processor. Add the apple cider vinegar and blend to a fairly smooth purée. Drain the pumpkin seeds and add them to the purée with the hemp seeds, nutritional yeast and a little pepper. Blend again until very smooth, or leave some seeds slightly coarse (see Cook's tips).

4 Pour the courgette cooking water into a measuring jug; you will need 175ml/6fl oz/¾ cup, so discard some or add a little more water to make it up to this amount if necessary. Pour the courgette water back into the pan and sprinkle over the agar agar. Bring to the boil, stirring from time to time, and simmer for 5 minutes.

5 Remove the agar agar mixture from the heat and let the bubbles subside. Pour the mixture into the food processor and blend for a few seconds, until well mixed.

6 Pour and scrape the mixture into a wet dish, mould or loaf tin, and allow to cool. Chill for 2 hours in the fridge to set before turning out.

Mozzarella-style 'cheese' for melting

This is the go-to recipe when you're looking for a stretchy, melty 'cheese' to use as a mozzarella-type topping for foods like pizza or for toasted sandwiches. Although it is firm enough to set, it isn't a sliceable cheese, and is scooped into balls, which will spread out as they cook.

75g/3oz/½ cup raw unsalted cashew nuts
250ml/9fl oz/1 cup boiling water
75ml/2½fl oz/⅓ cup refined coconut oil, melted
45ml/3 tbsp nutritional yeast flakes
30ml/2 tbsp tapioca starch
15ml/1 tbsp agar agar
10ml/2 tsp lemon juice
5ml/1 tsp tahini
2.5ml/½ tsp salt
1.5ml/¼ tsp garlic powder (optional)

MAKES ABOUT 350G/12OZ

1 Put the nuts in a heatproof bowl and pour over the boiling water. Cover with a lid and leave for about 30 minutes to soak; the water should still be slightly tepid.

2 Tip the nuts and about half of the soaking water into a blender. Add the coconut oil, nutritional yeast, tapioca, agar agar, lemon juice, tahini, salt and garlic powder if using. Blend until the mixture is very smooth.

3 Pour into a pan and stir in the remaining soaking water. Bring to the boil, stirring continuously with a whisk. Simmer briskly for 5 minutes.

4 Remove from the heat and quickly pour the mixture into a heatproof glass or ceramic dish. Leave to cool, then cover and chill in the fridge until needed; the mixture will take about 1 hour to set firmly.

5 To use the cheese, scoop out pieces in the amount you require. For pizzas, roughly roll into small balls then pat into rounds slightly thicker than 1cm/½in. Use within 10 days of making.

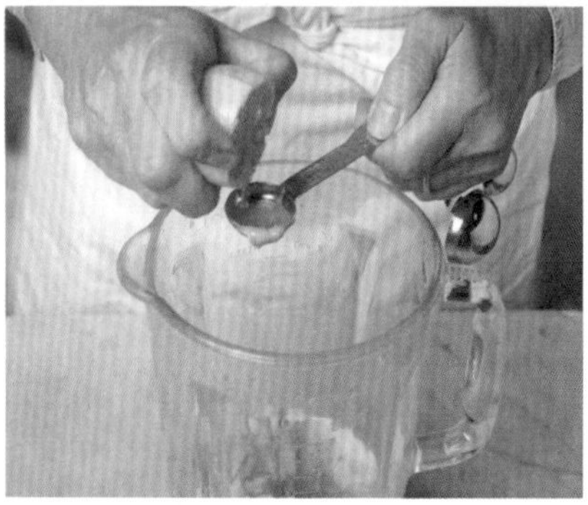

Mozzarella-style 'cheese' for grating

This is a nut-free alternative to dairy mozzarella, and has a mild cheesy flavour and smooth, creamy texture. It can be sliced, pulled into pieces, or coarsely grated, and can be eaten as is or cooked, where although not as stretchy as the cheese opposite, it will become meltingly soft.

50g/2oz/½ cup silken tofu, at room temperature
25g/1oz/¼ cup tapioca flour/starch
50ml/2fl oz/¼ cup coconut oil, preferably refined
15ml/1 tbsp white miso paste
30ml/2 tbsp nutritional yeast flakes
1.5–2.5ml/¼–½ tsp salt
250ml/9fl oz/1 cup cold water
15ml/1 tbsp powdered agar agar

MAKES ABOUT 250G/9OZ

1 Put the tofu and tapioca flour in a blender or small food processor. Gently heat the coconut oil in a pan until just melted. Remove from the heat, then stir in the miso paste, nutritional yeast and salt, and stir together. Add to the blender or food processor and blend until smooth.

2 Pour the measured cold water into the pan (there's no need to wash it out first), then sprinkle over the agar agar. Bring to the boil over a medium heat and contain whisking until it thickens and forms a thin gel. Cook for 2 minutes at full boil.

3 Add the agar agar gel to the blender or food processor and blend until combined. Working quickly (it will start to set almost immediately), pour the mixture into a glass dish.

4 Chill uncovered in the fridge for 1 hour or until set and firm. Loosen the sides of the 'cheese' and carefully turn out before using. It will keep in the fridge in a covered container for up to a week.

Tofu 'feta'

This slightly salty tangy vegan cheese tastes remarkably like the dairy version and is perfect for using in a Greek salad or any other dish that features feta. Tofu is spongy and porous, so after pressing it can be rehydrated with the marinade and will soak up all the flavour.

275g/10oz extra firm tofu
5ml/1 tsp white miso paste
10ml/2 tsp light olive oil
juice of ½ lemon
30ml/2 tbsp apple cider vinegar
30ml/2 tbsp nutritional yeast flakes
2.5ml/½ tsp dried oregano or dill
1.5–2.5ml/¼–½ tsp salt

MAKES ABOUT 275G/10OZ

1 Drain the excess liquid from the tofu and pat dry on kitchen paper. Place in a bowl, top with a piece of baking parchment, then place a small plate or saucer (that fits inside the bowl) on top. Place a couple of heavy weights or food cans on top and put in the fridge for 1–2 hours, so that the tofu is pressed and more liquid is squeezed out.

2 Remove the tofu from the bowl and pat dry again on kitchen paper. Tip away the liquid and wipe the bowl dry. Add the miso paste and blend with the olive oil. Gradually mix in the lemon juice, followed by the vinegar. Whisk in the nutritional yeast, oregano or dill, and salt.

3 Cut the tofu into 2cm/¾in cubes. Add to the marinade and gently toss in the mixture to coat all the pieces. Cover and allow to marinate in the fridge for at least 2 hours, stirring once, if possible. Store in the fridge until ready to use; the flavour will improve and mellow after 1–2 days and it will keep for up to 4 days.

'Labneh' balls

Labneh is a soft, tangy cheese made by draining the whey from yogurt, making it thicker and creamier. The longer you leave it, the firmer it will become. After 24 hours it will have the consistency of cream cheese and after 48 hours, you will be able to roll it into small soft balls of cheese.

500g/1¼lb unsweetened soya or almond yogurt or cashew yogurt (see pages 52 or 55)
5ml/1 tsp lemon juice
2.5ml/½ tsp salt

For the labneh balls
30ml/2 tbsp olive oil for rolling
30ml/2 tbsp chopped fresh coriander/cilantro or oregano

MAKES ABOUT 250G/9OZ OR ABOUT 12 BALLS

1 Line a large sieve or strainer with a double layer of clean muslin or cheesecloth and place over a large bowl.

2 Stir the lemon juice and salt into the yogurt. Pour the yogurt into the lined sieve or strainer, cover with a piece of clear film or plastic wrap and leave to drain in the fridge for 24 hours. You will now have a thick, spreadable labneh in the cloth.

3 Discard the whey that has collected in the bowl (or you can use it for cooking or smoothie-making, keeping in mind that it will be salty). Either spoon the labneh into a bowl and cover it with plastic wrap or clear film, or allow it to drain for a further 24 hours until really thick.

4 To make balls, oil your hands, scoop up heaped teaspoons of the 'cheese' and shape into small balls. Roll in the oil, then in the herbs to coat. Chill before serving and eat within 4 days.

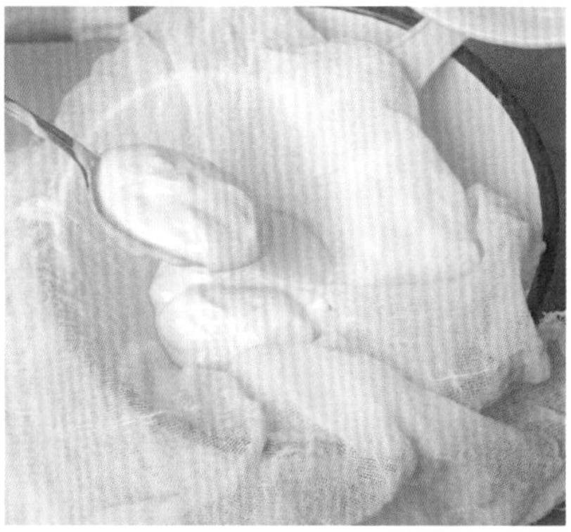

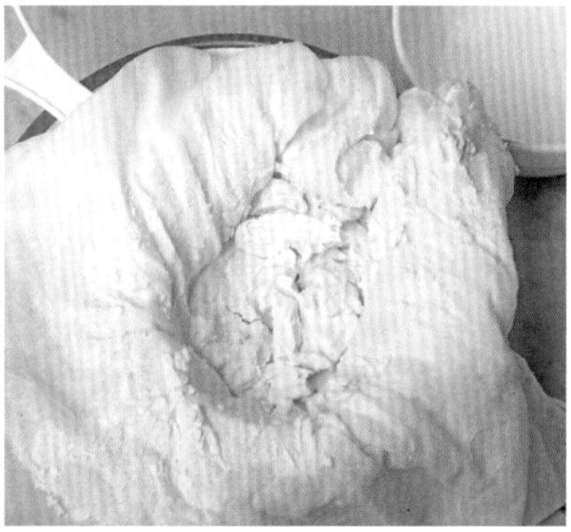

White bean 'cheese' sauce

This cheesy sauce is excellent for serving with pasta, layering in lasagne, or poured over vegetables. The beans give it texture and add a good amount of protein. The cheesy flavour in fact comes from nutritional yeast, but you can use grated vegan Cheddar-style 'cheese' if you prefer.

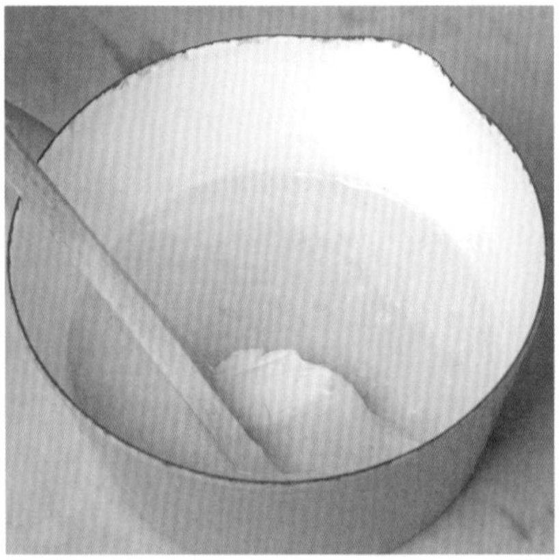

400g/14oz can of cooked white beans, such as cannellini
120ml/4fl oz/½ cup soya milk or almond milk (see pages 43 or 28)
10ml/2 tsp vegan 'buttery' spread
2.5ml/½ tsp apple cider vinegar or white wine vinegar
1.5ml/¼ tsp ground turmeric
1.5ml/¼ tsp salt
75ml/5 tbsp nutritional yeast flakes
freshly ground black pepper

MAKES ABOUT 400ML/14FL OZ/ 1⅔ CUPS

1 Drain and rinse the beans and tip them into a blender or food processor. Pour in about half the milk. Pulse a few times to finely chop the beans then blend to a smooth purée. Gradually add the rest of the milk, blending after each addition, until very smooth.

2 Transfer to a pan. Add the vegan spread, vinegar, turmeric and salt. Bring to the boil and let it bubble for a minute or two, stirring occasionally.

3 Remove the pan from the heat and stir in the nutritional yeast flakes and ground black pepper. Serve hot.

Variation
The vegan 'buttery' spread (see page 72) adds creaminess, but you can leave it out if you prefer a lower-fat sauce.

Carrot and potato 'cheese' sauce

As many vegan cheeses are nut- or seed-based, it's also good to have a vegetable-based option. This is a pourable cheesy sauce that works well over steamed vegetables (such as cauliflower cheese), on bakes, or even spooning onto toast and then grilling until browned and bubbling.

1 Peel the potato and carrot and cut into small chunks (cut the carrot in slightly smaller pieces than the potato). Put them in a pan and pour over just enough boiling water to cover.

2 Bring to the boil, cover with a lid and simmer for about 15 minutes or until the vegetables are just tender when pierced with a sharp knife. Drain the vegetables, reserving about 75ml/5 tbsp of the cooking water.

3 Tip the vegetables into a blender, add 45ml/3 tbsp of the reserved cooking water, the oil, nutritional yeast, celery salt and pepper, and blend until very smooth; add a little more of the cooking water until you achieve a thick, just-pourable consistency. Taste and adjust the seasoning if necessary.

4 Use the sauce straight away, or transfer to a jug or bowl and leave to cool. Cover and store in the fridge for up to 4 days.

1 large potato, about 200g/7oz
1 large carrot, about 115g/4oz
60ml/4 tbsp olive oil
60ml/4 tbsp nutritional yeast flakes
2.5ml/½ tsp celery salt
freshly ground black pepper

MAKES ABOUT 350ML/
12FL OZ/1½ CUPS

Variation

If you don't have any celery salt, add a pinch of powdered vegetable stock to the water when you cook the vegetables.

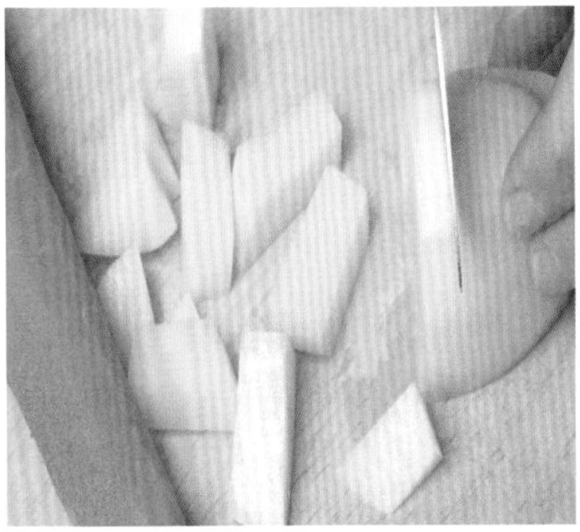

Soft fermented cashew nut 'cheese'

Cashews are good nuts to ferment as there is no skin on them, they have a neutral flavour, and they aren't too expensive compared to many other skinless nuts (although to be accurate, cashews are in fact a seed rather than a nut). You are also able to get a completely smooth consistency with cashews, like cream, which makes for a lovely texture. This is a soft, quite spreadable 'cheese' that forms the basis of other recipes that follow in this chapter.

250g/9oz/2½ cups raw unsalted cashew nuts
pinch of fine salt
2.5ml/½ tsp coconut sugar powder (optional)
75ml/5 tbsp filtered water, or as needed to assist in blending, plus soaking water
1–2 capsules of vegan probiotic powder (contents only)

MAKES ABOUT 350G/12OZ

Why ferment?
Nuts and seeds, commonly used to make vegan 'cheeses', are extremely nutritious, but can be hard for some people to digest. Sprouting or activating and then fermenting them before blending and turning them into cheeses will help them become more digestible as well as increasing the nutrient content tremendously. Nuts, unlike seeds and grains, cannot be sprouted, but they can be activated by soaking, while fermenting makes the digestion even easier.

1 Soak the cashew nuts for at least 3 hours. Discard the soaking water and rinse the nuts well.

2 Blend the nuts, salt and sugar, if using, in a blender or food processor until a smooth paste forms, adding just enough of the filtered water so that the blender will keep going but no more. You should be able to get this blend completely smooth but it might take you some time as you do need to stop quite often to scrape down the sides. If you have a high-speed blender, however, you will be able to do this in just a few minutes.

3 When the mixture has reached the desired consistency, scoop it into a glass or ceramic bowl. Sprinkle over the probiotic powder and mix in.

4 Leave the mixture to ferment for 12–24 hours at a temperature that's slightly warmer than your room; for example, in an airing cupboard, on the floor if you have underfloor heating, or on top of your dehydrator if it is on. Otherwise, just find the warmest place in your kitchen. It will work anyway, but might just take a bit longer. When it is ready it should smell slightly sour or bread-like, and if you stir it with a spoon it should be fluffy with air bubbles.

5 The fermented batch of cashew nut cheese can now be used. If you are not using it immediately, keep it covered in the fridge, where it will keep well for a few weeks. It also freezes very well.

Matured fermented cashew nut 'cheese'

You can age your nut cheese, just like normal cheese, for a more intense flavour. This is a very simple recipe but it is delicious. The nutritional yeast imparts a typical cheesy flavour. Onion powder works beautifully as well, and has a sweet taste; the result is not the same if you use fresh onion. Pink salt, fresh rosemary and bay leaves make attractive decorations.

batch of soft fermented cashew nut 'cheese' (see page 104)
7.5–15ml/½–1 tbsp nutritional yeast flakes
7.5ml/½ tbsp onion powder
5ml/1 tsp fine salt

MAKES ABOUT 450G/1LB

1 Blend all the ingredients in a food processor or mix thoroughly by hand, until smooth and evenly combined.

2 Turn the mixture out on to a board and shape the cheese how you want, using, for example, a ring or pastry cutter. If the dough is very runny it might not be mouldable – what you can do then is to keep it in the fridge for a while until it becomes a bit harder, or just flavour it and use it as a dip or soft cheese. If it is runny it could be because you added too much water in your original cashew nut cheese recipe; next time use less water.

3 Put the shaped cheeses into pieces of parchment paper, wrap them up and tie a string around. Alternatively, if you have a dehydrator you can put the cheeses (without the paper) here for a few hours at 42°C/107°F. This will give your 'cheeses' a rind that will keep them together.

4 Put the parchment-wrapped cheeses in your fridge for at least a few days to harden and mature. It is important not to seal up the cheeses, for example in a box with a lid. Since they are still very moist they need to evaporate and if they are covered completely at this point they will stay soggy and perhaps mould will even start to grow. If you keep them in a box, therefore, do not put a lid on; you could put a piece of kitchen paper over to protect them if needed.

5 The cheeses are ready to be eaten in a few days. The longer you leave them, the harder they will get and the more intense the flavour; 2–3 weeks is a good amount of time to give a fairly hard cheese that is easy to cut, though you can also leave them for a little while longer so long as you are careful not to dry them out. You can also freeze these cheeses well for several months. Sprinkle over herbs and pink salt for a decorative finish.

Variations

- The best nuts to use in nut 'cheese' making are cashews, almonds and macadamia nuts. These are good because they do not have skins, or it is easy to get rid of the skins. You can make this cheese from other nuts as well, but the skins can make it less appealing in colour and also taste slightly bitter. You can, however, swap any nut in these recipes for another of your choice.
- You can also make the recipes with seeds, although you should be aware that these have a more distinctive flavour and can turn bitter and darker in colour after fermentation; a good alternative can be to use about 50 per cent nuts and 50 per cent seeds.

Soft fermented macadamia or almond 'cheese'

There are two more nuts that you can use to make nut cheeses with. You can get a much harder consistency with these, if that is what you are after, as when it is ready you can press the nut paste to get more water out. Pressing works better with almonds and macadamia nuts than with cashews, though the latter will work if you take it slowly and are patient.

250g/9oz/2½ cups raw unsalted macadamias or raw unsalted blanched almonds
5ml/1 tsp agave syrup (optional)
pinch of sea salt
100ml/3½fl oz/scant ½ cup filtered water, or as needed
2 capsules of vegan probiotic powder (content only)

MAKES ABOUT 350G/12OZ

Hardening and pressing
If you want the 'cheese' to be harder you need to get rid of excess water. Put the nut paste in a cheesecloth or nut milk bag. Wring the cloth or bag so that the cheese sits tightly inside the cloth. If you squeeze it slightly you can see the water coming out – this should be clear. Place in a plastic colander set over a bowl, put a plate on the 'cheese' and then put something heavy on top of the plate to push the cheese down. Let it sit for 4–6 hours, allowing the weight to press the water through into the bowl underneath. The liquid should be clear; if it isn't, you are pressing too hard. Take the cheese out of the cloth or bag and store it in the fridge, to be flavoured, eaten or wrapped to mature further.

1 Soak the nuts for 10–12 hours. Discard the soaking water and rinse the nuts well.

2 If you are using almonds with skins, then you now have to soak them further in boiling water for 1–2 minutes. Discard the boiling water and rinse the almonds with cold water to stop them from going soft. Then you can simply squeeze the almonds out of their skins between your fingers.

3 Put the nuts, agave if using, salt and filtered water in a blender or food processor and process until a smooth consistency – you just need to add as much water as necessary for the blades to go round. It doesn't matter if you add a little too much water however as you can get excess water out at a later stage. This processing might take a little while depending on what blender or food processor you have at home. A top-of-the-range food processor will take only a few minutes. It is fine to use a normal processor but be aware it can take as long as 5–10 minutes, so be patient, stopping often to scrape the mixture down the sides.

4 When the desired consistency is reached, scoop the mixture into a glass or ceramic bowl and mix in the probiotic powder. Stir well to make sure it is fully dissolved in the mixture, then cover with a lid, cling film or a slightly damp cotton cloth.

5 Put the bowl in a warm place for 12–24 hours. This could be in an airing cupboard, on the floor if you have underfloor heating, or on top of your dehydrator if you have got one, or turn the light on in the oven and put it there, closing the door.

6 When it is ready it should have risen a little, smell slightly sour and if you stir with a wooden spoon it should be fluffy with air bubbles. Usually it takes 12 hours to ferment, but you might need to leave it for up to another 12 hours. Almonds and macadamias tend to take longer than cashews.

7 When ready, store it in the fridge. You can flavour it (see the following recipes), eat it straight away, or shape it, wrap in parchment paper and store in the fridge for several days to mature.

Matured fermented almond 'cheese'

When making a fermented nut cheese, almond is a good one to start with. It will develop a slighter harder rind-like crust while the centre remains a little softer and creamier. This is very similar to a dairy cheese in flavour and makes a nice addition to a cheeseboard.

batch of soft fermented almond 'cheese', pressed to remove extra water (see page 108, following the additional instructions for hardening and pressing)
7.5ml/1½ tsp miso paste
7.5ml/1½ tsp onion powder
5ml/1 tsp garlic powder
5ml/1 tsp lemon juice
5ml/1 tsp salt
5ml/1 tsp ground turmeric
2.5ml/½ tsp nutritional yeast flakes
2.5ml/½ tsp coconut sugar
2.5ml/½ tsp mustard powder (optional)

MAKES ABOUT 350G/12 OZ

1 Add the soft fermented cheese to the rest of the ingredients in a bowl and mix everything together well.

2 Turn the mixture on to a board and shape the nut cheese, using a ring mould, biscuit cutter or similar. Decorate if you like, perhaps with sprigs of thyme.

3 If you have a dehydrator you can dehydrate the cheese on 42°C/107°F for 12 hours to create a harder rind or crust.

4 Once dried, wrap in parchment paper and tie with string, and transfer to the fridge. If you don't have a dehydrator, wrap up in parchment paper and tie with string, and put into the fridge for a few days to harden and mature.

5 After a few days your 'cheese' is ready to be eaten, but the longer you leave it in the fridge the harder it will get, and the more intense the flavour. It will keep for at least a month if unopened.

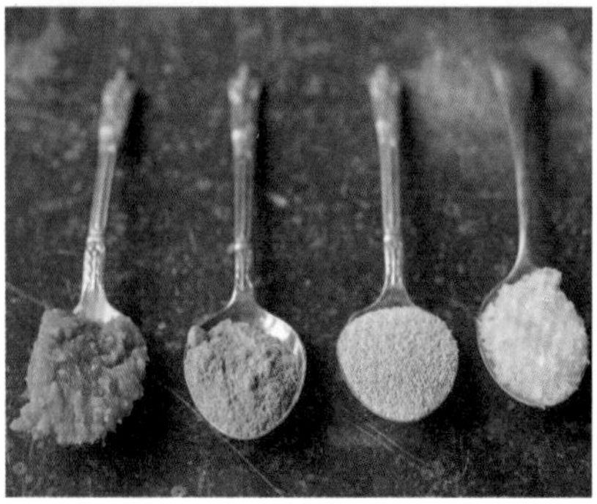

Garlic and herb fermented 'cheese' roll

This can be made with any of the three fermented nut cheeses. If you make it out of cashews, try to use as little water as possible when you blend the nuts. Shaping into a long rectangle or roll will allow you to cut it into fairly thin slices – perfect to top crackers.

1 Mix all the ingredients thoroughly in a food processor, or by hand.

2 Turn on to a board and mould the nut cheese into the size and shape you prefer. You can make one large or several small rolls, or other shapes using a ring mould, cookie cutter or similar. You can sprinkle some dried herbs on top for decoration.

3 If you have a dehydrator, dehydrate the cheese at 42°C/107°F for 4–6 hours to create a harder rind or crust. Once dried, wrap it in parchment paper and tie with string. If you don't have a dehydrator, wrap up the cheese in parchment paper and tie with string, then put it into the fridge for a few days to harden and mature.

4 After a few days your cheese is ready to be eaten, but you can leave it for several weeks if you want before eating it. Untouched, the cheese will last for 1–2 months. You can also freeze it.

batch of soft fermented cashew nut 'cheese' (see page 104) or soft fermented macadamia or almond 'cheese' (see page 108)
30ml/2 tbsp nutritional yeast flakes
15ml/1 tbsp mixed dried herbs (thyme, rosemary and oregano for example), plus extra for decoration if liked
5ml/1 tsp garlic powder
5ml/1 tsp salt, or to taste

MAKES ABOUT 350G/12 OZ (1 LONG ROLL OR 3 ROUNDS)

Paprika and tomato fermented 'cheese' balls

This is a tasty nut cheese, which you can make using a batch of soft fermented cashew, macadamia or almond 'cheese'. The flavourings can be varied; including a little harissa adds heat. It looks good if you decorate the balls by dipping them in paprika or dried herbs.

batch of soft fermented macadamia or almond 'cheese' (see page 108)
4–5 sun-dried tomatoes, finely chopped
15ml/1 tbsp nutritional yeast flakes
10ml/2 tsp smoked paprika
5ml/1 tsp sweet paprika, plus extra for dusting, if liked
5ml/1 tsp salt, or to taste
5ml/1 tsp harissa paste
2.5ml/½ tsp dried mixed Italian herbs, plus extra for dusting if liked

MAKES ABOUT 12 BALLS

1 Make your batch of macadamia or almond 'cheese' as described in the recipe on page 108, including the additional hardening and pressing stages to get all the excess water out.

2 Put the nut cheese and all the listed ingredients into a food processor and pulse until blended together well. The cheese will have a slight pink tint to it now.

3 That's it! The 'cheese' is now ready to mould into whatever shapes you want – little balls, rolls or rounds. You can decorate them further, for example by dipping the balls into paprika powder or dried herbs.

4 If you like, you can also mature this cheese to deepen the flavour and make it even firmer in texture by putting it in an airtight box and storing it in the fridge for a few days.

Savoury 'cheesy' sprinkles

As an alternative to grated Parmesan, it's handy to have savoury cheese-like toppings for sprinkling over dishes such as lentil bolognaise, vegetable soups, or on top of mac 'n' cheese, where they add both umami flavour and texture. These will keep for several weeks, ready for use.

1 For the seedy seasoning, put the sunflower seeds in a non-stick frying pan and gently toast over a low heat for 3–4 minutes, stirring frequently, until golden. Take care not to burn them. Leave to cool.

2 Put the seeds in blender or small food processor with the nutritional yeast flakes, paprika, salt and onion powder. Pulse the mixture in the blender until the seeds are coarsely chopped. Store in the fridge in an airtight container.

3 For the nutty seasoning, put the cashew nuts in a blender or small food processor and pulse a few times until roughly chopped.

4 Add the nutritional yeast flakes, salt and garlic powder. Continue to pulse until the nuts are finely chopped. Store the seasoning in an airtight container in the fridge.

For the seedy seasoning
130g/4½oz/¾ cup sunflower seeds
45ml/3 tbsp nutritional yeast flakes
5ml/1 tsp smoked paprika
2.5ml/½ tsp salt
1.5ml/¼ tsp onion powder

For the nutty seasoning
175g/6oz/1 cup raw unsalted cashew nuts
60ml/4 tbsp nutritional yeast flakes
2.5ml/½ tsp salt
1.5ml/¼ tsp garlic powder

EACH MAKES ABOUT 175G/6OZ

Breakfasts & drinks

It's easy to start the day with a bowl of cereal and non-dairy milk or a slice of toast topped with vegan spread or nut butter. However, when you have a little more time, there are plenty of other dairy-free breakfast options, such as the recipes for pancakes, muffins and granola bars included in this chapter, along with healthy vegan 'milky' drinks that can be enjoyed at any time of the day.

Coconut milk and quinoa porridge

Prepared with a mixture of high-protein quinoa flakes and rolled oats, this coconut-milk porridge is quick and easy to prepare, and fresh or frozen berries add a boost of vitamin C. It's also good made with almond milk or hazelnut milk. For a treat, serve this topped with some extra-thick almond milk or soya yogurt (see page 52).

600ml/1 pint/2½ cups coconut milk (see page 40), plus extra to serve (optional)
115g/4oz/1 cup quinoa flakes
50g/2oz/½ cup rolled oats
115g/4oz/1 cup frozen mixed berries or fresh berries
coconut sugar, to serve

SERVES 4–6

1 Put the milk and quinoa flakes in a pan, bring to the boil and simmer on a low heat for 5 minutes. Add the oats and simmer for 2 minutes, stirring often.

2 Gently stir in the berries and simmer for a further 1–2 minutes, until the berries are warmed through and just beginning to release their juices and the porridge has thickened.

3 Spoon into bowls and serve immediately, sprinkled with coconut sugar and some extra coconut milk, if liked.

Multigrain banana berry porridge

40g/1½oz/⅓ cup multi-grain mix, see box
about 250ml/9fl oz/1 cup soya milk (see page 43) or any nut milk

For the topping
a small banana, dried cranberries, blueberries, pecan halves and pumpkin seeds

SERVES 4–6

1 Add the multi-grain mix and milk to a small pan and bring the milk just to the boil, then reduce the heat and simmer for about 5 minutes, stirring from time to time until the grains are soft and have absorbed most of the liquid. Add a little extra milk or some water, if needed.

2 Mash half the banana and stir into the porridge then spoon the mixture into a serving bowl.

3 Arrange the remaining banana slices down the centre of the bowl, then add a thin line of cranberries down each side, the blueberries, then the nuts and seeds. Serve immediately.

Multi-grain mix
Make up a jar of this multi-grain mix to keep handy, and have sliced bananas and blueberries in the freezer ready and waiting so that you can rustle up this warming and super-satisfying breakfast in no time.

Add 50g/2oz/½ cup each of rolled oats, barley flakes, rye flakes and quinoa flakes to a bowl and stir together, then spoon into a screw-topped jar and store until required.

MAKES 200G/7OZ OR 5 PORTIONS

Overnight oats with non-dairy yogurt

These delicious Bircher-style dairy-free yogurt, porridge and fruit pots are easy to make and will fill you up until lunchtime. Make the pots the day before, or even 2 days in advance, add a well-fitting lid and keep in the fridge ready and waiting for a colourful fruit topping to be added.

50g/2oz/⅓ cup mixed unblanched hazelnuts, almonds and Brazil nuts, roughly chopped
20ml/4 tsp ground flax seeds
115g/4oz/1 cup rolled oats
1.5ml/¼ tsp ground cinnamon
1 dessert apple, cored and coarsely grated (no need to peel)
250ml/9fl oz/1 cup non-dairy yogurt (see pages 52–55)
60ml/4 tbsp fresh orange juice

MAKES 6 POTS

1 Put the nuts, seeds, oats and cinnamon in a bowl and stir together. Add the grated apple, yogurt and orange juice, then stir together.

2 Divide the mixture between 6 small glass pots with lids and smooth the tops level. Cover and chill in the fridge until ready to top and serve.

Toppings, each enough for 2 pots

Mixed berry: Purée 100g/3½oz hulled strawberries in a blender until smooth. Spoon over the pots and add a few blueberries and a couple of blackberries.

Mango and chia: Purée 100g/3¼oz prepared mango flesh with 30ml/2 tbsp lime or orange juice or water in a blender until smooth. Stir in 2.5ml/½ tsp chia seeds, then spoon over the top of the pots and decorate with a few pomegranate seeds.

Banana, cacao and coconut: Mix 60ml/4 tbsp non-dairy yogurt with 15ml/1 tbsp cacao powder and 10ml/2 tsp date syrup, and spoon over the pots. Top each pot with a few slices of banana, a few roughly chopped goji berries and a sprinkling of coconut flakes.

Kiwi and grape: Peel and dice a kiwi fruit and mix with a few halved green seedless grapes. Spoon over the top of the pots.

Strawberry and raspberry: Purée 100g/3½oz hulled strawberries in a blender until smooth. Spoon over the pots and top each with 4 raspberries and a couple of hulled and halved strawberries.

Cook's tips

- If you find these Bircher-style pots are a little too thick for your taste, just add a little extra non-dairy milk to the mix.
- You could use a mixture of buckwheat and quinoa flakes in place of the rolled oats.
- Use walnuts in place of the other nuts for an omega 3 boost.

Fruity rice milk and buckwheat bowl

Satisfying slow-simmered buckwheat in rice milk provides a great energizing start to the day and makes a change from oats. You can of course use any other non-dairy milk, too. Sweetened with dried apricots and spiced with ginger, the hot cereal is finished with fresh peaches and nuts, although you can simply serve it with an extra drizzle of non-dairy milk if you prefer.

115g/4oz/½ cup buckwheat groats (see Cook's tip), rinsed several times with cold water and drained well
550ml/18fl oz/2¼ cups rice milk (see page 44) or other non-dairy milk, plus extra if necessary
75g/3oz/½ cup dried apricots, diced
5ml/1 tsp grated fresh root ginger (optional)
2 fresh peaches, stoned/pitted and sliced

For the topping
2 medjool dates, stoned/pitted and sliced
pomegranate seeds
chopped pistachio nuts

SERVES 2–3

Cook's tip
Buckwheat comes from the seeds of a plant related to rhubarb and is not from the wheat family. Nor, technically, is it a grain. Gluten free, it is a great source of protein, containing all the essential amino acids. Make sure you buy hulled buckwheat 'groats' that have been roasted or toasted (it should state this in the list of ingredients on the packet).

1 Put the buckwheat in a heavy pan and pour over the rice milk. Slowly bring to the boil, then reduce the heat and simmer gently for 5 minutes, stirring frequently.

2 Add the apricots and cook for a further 5–7 minutes, stirring until the buckwheat is tender and most of the milk has been absorbed. Cover the pan with a lid and leave to stand for a few minutes.

3 Transfer the buckwheat porridge to a blender and add the ginger, if using, and half of the peach slices. Screw on the lid and blend until smooth. Add extra milk if needed to get the consistency that you like.

4 Spoon into bowls and top with the remaining peach slices and the medjool date slices, then sprinkle with the pomegranate seeds and pistachio nuts and serve while hot.

Variations
- 50g/2oz/½ cup buckwheat flakes can also be used in place of the whole seeds; these cook quicker – in just 4–5 minutes – and get very thick, so stir the mixture constantly as it cooks or it will stick to the pan.
- You can of course use other fruit combinations for this dish, if you like. Prunes or dates work well, with slices of apple or banana for the topping.

Drop scones

These egg-free American-style pancakes (also known as Scotch pancakes) are wonderfully light and fluffy. They can be left plain if preferred, but adding raisins and lemon zest gives them a new twist. Serve with a drizzle of maple or date syrup and some non-dairy yogurt if liked.

200g/7oz/scant 2 cups self-raising/self-rising flour
7.5ml/1½ tsp baking powder
pinch of salt
30ml/2 tbsp soft light brown or coconut sugar
250ml/9fl oz/1 cup almond milk or soya milk (see pages 28 or 43)
finely grated rind of 1 lemon (optional)
25g/1oz/¼ cup raisins (optional)
sunflower or coconut oil, for frying
vegan 'buttery' spread and maple syrup or date syrup, to serve

MAKES 16

1 Sift the flour, baking powder and salt into a bowl and stir in the sugar. Make a hollow in the middle. Pour in the non-dairy milk and lemon rind if using, and stir it all together to make a smooth, thick batter.

2 Put a little of the oil into a frying pan. Place the pan over a medium heat and, when hot, spoon in enough batter to form two or three pancakes, spreading out each with the back of the spoon until they're about 6–7cm/2½–3in in diameter.

3 Sprinkle a few raisins on each pancake, if including. Keep the pan at a steady heat and when bubbles rise to the surface and burst, after 2–3 minutes, turn them over with a palette knife. Cook for a further 2–3 minutes, until golden brown on the other side.

4 Remove the pancakes to a warm plate in a single layer and keep them warm by covering with a clean dish towel while you cook the remaining batter. Serve with spread, if you like, and maple or date syrup.

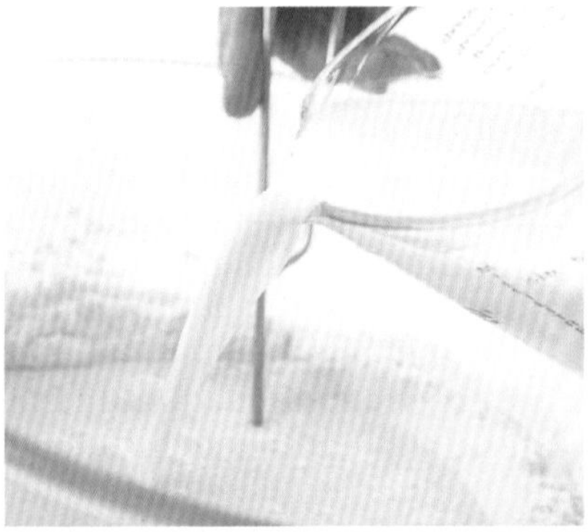

Date double-deckers

Naturally moist and sticky, dates are a great source of iron and potassium and help sweeten these tasty breakfast bars. Peanut butter gives them a protein boost, making them ideal for days when you need to eat on the go. Pack one to enjoy at coffee break or for a quick afternoon snack.

1 Preheat the oven to 180°C/350°F/Gas 4. Line a shallow square 20cm/8in cake tin or pan with a larger piece of baking parchment, snip into the corners of the paper and press down to line the base and sides.

2 Put the dates in a food processor with the water and vanilla. Pulse briefly until roughly chopped, then blend to a coarse purée.

3 Melt the margarine in a medium pan then stir in the peanut butter and sugar. Mash the banana with a fork then add to the pan with the quinoa flakes, oats and seeds. Stir the mixture together then spoon two-thirds into the prepared tin and spread into an even thickness.

4 Spoon the date purée over the top and spread into an even layer, then sprinkle with the remaining oat mixture and lightly press into the date layer. Bake for about 25 minutes until, the top is golden brown.

5 Mark into 12 pieces then leave to cool in the tin. Remove from the tin, peel off the paper and store in an airtight container. Eat within 2 days.

200g/7oz/1 cup ready-to-eat pitted dates
90ml/6 tbsp water
5ml/1 tsp vanilla extract
100g/3¾oz/½ cup non-dairy margarine or 'buttery' spread (see page 72)
30ml/2 tbsp smooth unsweetened peanut butter (see page 74)
50g/2oz/⅓ cup light muscovado/brown sugar
1 medium banana
100g/3¾oz/1 cup quinoa flakes
150g/5oz/1½ cups rolled oats
40g/1½oz/¼ cup sunflower seeds

MAKES 12

Cranberry and apple muesli bars

Flapjack-style cereal bars tend to be loaded with butter, but here a combination of fresh apple purée, flax seeds and chia seeds are used instead of butter and eggs to moisten and bind the ingredients together and make a healthier low-fat, dairy-free alternative.

250g/9oz or 2 small dessert apples, cored and diced (no need to peel)
75ml/5 tbsp water
30ml/2 tbsp coconut oil
15ml/1 tbsp ground flax seeds
150g/5oz/1½ cups sugar-free muesli (see below)
10ml/2 tsp chia seeds
30ml/2 tbsp dried cranberries
50g/2oz/scant ½ cup light muscovado/brown sugar

MAKES 12

Sugar-free muesli

100g/3¾oz/1 cup jumbo rolled oats
75g/3oz/¾ cup barley flakes
75g/3oz/¾ cup rye flakes
50g/2oz/½ cup quinoa flakes
60ml/4 tbsp sunflower seeds
60ml/4 tbsp pumpkin seeds

MAKES 350G/12OZ/3½ CUPS

1 Put all the ingredients in a bowl and mix together.

2 Spoon into a jar, screw or clip on the lid and store in a cool place for up to 4 weeks, using as required.

1 Preheat the oven to 180°C/350°F/Gas 4. Line the base and sides of a shallow 20cm/8in square cake tin or pan with baking parchment.

2 Put the apples, 30ml/2 tbsp of the water and coconut oil in a medium pan, cover and simmer for about 5 minutes, until the apples are soft.

3 While the apples are cooking, blend the flax seeds with the remaining 45ml/3 tbsp water in a small bowl and leave to soak.

4 Mash the apples in the pan, then stir in the flax seed mixture. Stir in the muesli, chia seeds and cranberries, then mix in the sugar. Tip into the lined tin and press into an even layer with the back of a spoon.

5 Bake for 30–35 minutes, until golden brown. Mark into bars and leave to cool in the tin.

6 When cold, lift the paper and muesli bars out of the tin, peel off the paper and cut into bars. Store in an airtight container in the fridge for up to 2 days.

Variation

You can use all sorts of dried fruits instead of cranberries in these tasty bars – raisins, sultanas or golden raisins, dried cherries, or larger fruits such as dried apricots, figs, dates or prunes which you should snip into smaller pieces.

Mushroom muffins

These craggy-topped savoury muffins use non-dairy milk, oil and margarine instead of dairy ingredients, and use vinegar to bind instead of eggs. They make a delicious breakfast or a great savoury snack at any time of the day. They are best served warm from the oven.

15ml/1 tbsp white wine vinegar
5ml/1 tsp bicarbonate of soda/ baking soda
250g/9oz/2½ cups plain/all-purpose flour
15ml/1 tbsp baking powder
pinch of salt
60ml/4 tbsp sunflower oil
150g/5oz mushrooms, sliced
pinch of cayenne pepper (optional)
large pinch of mace (optional)
75g/3oz/¾ cup pine nuts
120ml/4fl oz/½ cup non-dairy milk
75g/3oz/6 tbsp non-dairy margarine or 'buttery' spread (see page 72), melted, plus extra for greasing

MAKES 6 LARGE MUFFINS

1 Preheat the oven to 180°C/350°F/Gas 4. Lightly grease the cups of a muffin tin or pan.

2 In a small bowl, mix together the vinegar and bicarbonate of soda with 15ml/1 tbsp of water, and set aside while it bubbles. Sift the flour, baking powder and salt into a large bowl, then set aside.

3 In a frying pan, heat 30ml/2 tbsp of the oil. When just bubbling, add the mushrooms. Season with cayenne and mace, if using. Fry gently, stirring, until softened. Scrape into a bowl and set aside to cool. Fry the pine nuts in the remaining oil for 30 seconds. Add to the mushrooms.

4 In a bowl, beat together the milk, melted margarine and vinegar mixture. Stir into the dry ingredients along with the cooked mushrooms and pine nuts.

5 Spoon the batter into the tins and bake for 25 minutes until the tops are golden. Remove to a wire rack to cool slightly, but serve warm.

Apricot bran muffins

Dried apricots are naturally sweet and are a good source of iron and vitamin A. They pair beautifully with creamy and mildly nutty almond milk. The slight acidity of non-dairy yogurt combined with bicarbonate of soda helps the muffins rise, giving them a lovely light texture.

1 Grease the cups of a muffin tin or pan or line them with paper cases.

2 Soak the dried apricots in a small bowl of warm water for 15 minutes. Remove and roughly chop into small bitesize pieces. Preheat the oven to 220°C/425°F/Gas 7.

3 In a large bowl, mix together the flour, oat bran, bicarbonate of soda, sugar and chopped apricots.

4 Add the melted margarine, yogurt and almond milk to the bowl of dry ingredients. Mix lightly until just combined.

5 Two-thirds fill the cups of the prepared tin with batter. Bake for 15–20 minutes until a skewer inserted into the centre of one comes out clean.

6 Leave to set for 5 minutes, then turn out on to a wire rack to cool. Serve warm or eat within 2 days.

115g/4oz/½ cup dried apricots
225g/8oz/2 cups self-raising/self-rising flour
50g/2oz/½ cup oat bran
2.5ml/½ tsp bicarbonate of soda/baking soda
30ml/2 tbsp soft light brown sugar
30ml/2 tbsp non-dairy margarine or 'buttery' spread (see page 72), melted, plus extra for greasing
150ml/¼ pint/⅔ cup non-dairy yogurt (see pages 52–55)
200ml/7fl oz/¾ cup light almond milk (see page 29)

MAKES 12 STANDARD MUFFINS

Pecan milk and pear milkshake

A fruity, creamy, vegan milkshake. Although fresh fruit cannot be beaten for flavour, canned varieties are a good alternative and it's certainly worth stocking up on a few cans for those occasions when your fruit bowl is empty. Go for ones in natural juices rather than syrup.

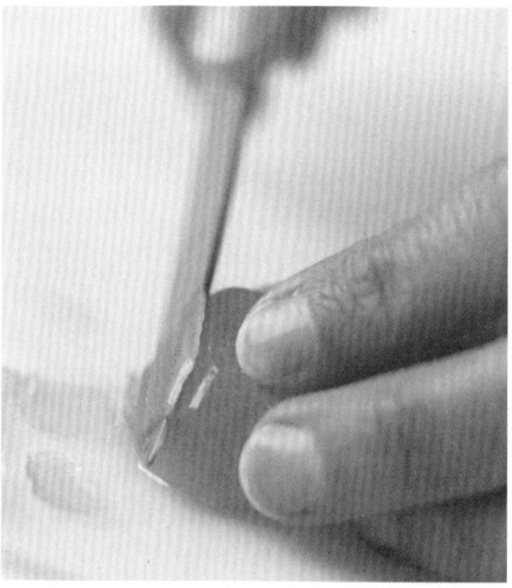

3 pieces preserved stem ginger, plus 15ml/1 tbsp ginger syrup from the jar
400g/14oz can of pears in natural fruit juice
450ml/¾ pint/scant 2 cups cold pecan milk (see page 31)
ice cubes

SERVES 2

1 Shave off some wafer-thin slices from one of the pieces of ginger and set aside. Roughly chop the remaining ginger. Drain the pears, reserving about 150ml/¼ pint/⅔ cup of the juice.

2 Put the pears, measured juice and chopped ginger in a blender or food processor and blend until smooth, scraping the mixture down from the sides if necessary.

3 Strain through a sieve or strainer into a jug or pitcher. Whisk in the milk and ginger syrup and pour into two glasses. Serve with ice and top with the reserved ginger shavings.

Creamy coconut and hazelnut smoothie

This nutty, creamy coconut drink should be sipped slowly. Sustaining and nourishing, it makes a good start to the day, or can be served as a nutritious snack-in-a-glass. It uses both coconut milk and cream. For a 'thinner' and less calorific version, swap the coconut milk for coconut water.

90g/3½oz/scant 1 cup whole blanched hazelnuts
10ml/2 tsp coconut sugar
2.5ml/½ tsp almond extract
120ml/4fl oz/½ cup coconut cream (see page 40)
250ml/9fl oz/1 cup coconut milk (see page 40)
ice cubes or crushed ice

SERVES 2

1 Roughly chop the hazelnuts and lightly toast them in a small frying pan, turning frequently, until aromatic and golden. Leave to cool, then tip the nuts into a blender or food processor with the sugar and blend well until finely ground.

2 Add the almond extract and coconut cream. Blend thoroughly until smooth, scraping down the sides if needed. Strain the mixture through a sieve or strainer into a jug, pressing the pulp down with the back of a spoon to extract as much liquid as possible. Stir in the coconut milk.

3 Put a couple of ice cubes or some crushed ice in two glasses and pour over the coconut smoothie. Serve the drinks immediately, or chill in the fridge until ready to serve.

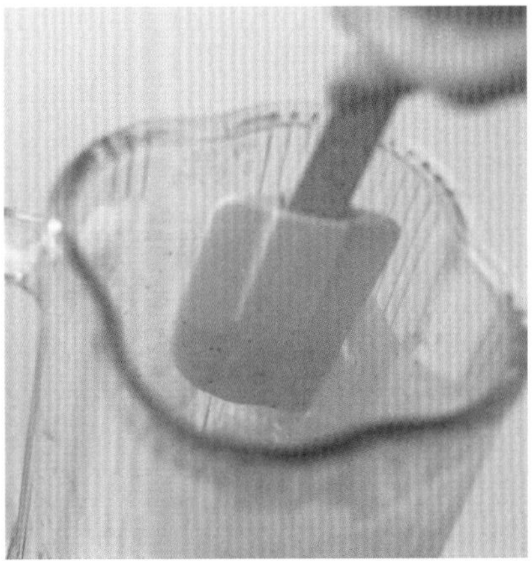

Brown rice and almond drink

This version of the refreshing Mexican drink *horchata* is made with brown rice and almonds and flavoured with cinnamon and a hint of vanilla. It is often loaded with sugar, but here dates are used as a healthier sweetener. Serve well chilled or pour it over ice.

50g/2oz/¼ cup brown basmati rice
½ cinnamon stick
600ml/1 pint/2½ cups very hot (not boiling) filtered water
115g/4oz/¾ cup whole skin-on almonds
3 medjool dates, stoned/pitted
2.5ml/½ tsp vanilla extract
pinch of salt (optional)
150ml/¼ pint/⅔ cup cold filtered water
ground cinnamon, to serve (optional)

SERVES 4

Cook's tips

- This rice-based *horchata* (pronounced 'or-cha-ta') is popular all over Latin America. In Spain, *horchata* (also known as *orxata*) is made from tiger nuts.
- *Horchata* can be served hot if you prefer. Heat until steaming hot (but do not boil) and serve in warmed mugs with a sprinkling of ground cinnamon or some cacao powder.

1 Rinse the rice in a sieve or strainer under cold running water. Tip into a large glass, ceramic or stainless-steel bowl and add the cinnamon stick. Pour over the measured hot water. Leave until the water is cool.

2 Cover the bowl and leave it in the fridge to soak for at least 8 hours; the rice should be soft enough that you can snap a piece in half with your fingernail without effort.

3 Remove and discard the cinnamon stick and put the rice, with its soaking liquid, in a blender with the nuts, dates, vanilla and a pinch of salt, if using. Pulse for a few seconds to break up the rice and nuts, then blend until very smooth.

4 Pour the mixture through a nut bag suspended over a jug, or through a sieve or strainer lined with muslin or cheesecloth. Leave to drain. Pour in the cold filtered water and leave to drain again.

5 Squeeze the nut bag or muslin with clean hands to extract the last drops. The drink can be stored, covered, in the fridge for up to 3 days. Serve in glasses with a sprinkling of ground cinnamon if you like.

Hot chocolate

Proper hot chocolate, made with good-quality vegan chocolate, rich non-dairy milk and, if you like, a hint of cardamom, is a sophisticated treat. It can be made with any non-dairy milk you like – tiger nut milk or oat milk makes a great option for those who can't have a nut-based one.

900ml/1½ pints/3¾ cups almond milk (see page 28)
2 cardamom pods, bruised (optional)
200g/7oz dark vegan chocolate, broken into pieces
whipped coconut cream, to serve (see page 64, optional)

SERVES 4

1 Put the nut milk in a pan with the cardamom pods, if using, and bring to the boil.

2 Add the chocolate and whisk until melted. Using a slotted spoon, remove the cardamom pods and discard, if necessary.

3 Pour the hot chocolate into heatproof glasses, mugs or cups and serve – topped with whipped coconut cream, if you like.

Turmeric almond milk latte chai

Turmeric gives this fragrant almond milk tea a beautiful golden colour. It's delicious served steaming hot on chilly days. Coconut milk or tiger nut milk make good alternatives to almond milk, and you can top it with some hot frothed 'barista' type milk if you like.

½ cinnamon stick
2.5cm/½in piece of fresh root ginger, thinly sliced
4 green cardamom pods, lightly crushed
4 whole cloves
5ml/1 tsp fennel seeds (optional)
1.5ml/¼ tsp ground turmeric
1.2 litres/2 pints/5 cups filtered water
5 bags Darjeeling or other black tea
350ml/12fl oz/1½ cups light almond milk (see page 29)
45ml/3 tbsp date syrup, or to taste

SERVES 4

1 Put the cinnamon, ginger, cardamom, cloves, fennel seeds if using, and turmeric into a pan. Pour over the filtered water and slowly bring to the boil. Lower the heat and simmer very gently for 10 minutes.

2 Turn off the heat, add the tea bags and cover with a lid. Leave to steep for 5 minutes. Remove and discard the tea bags and larger pieces of spice, then strain the chai through a fine tea strainer or sieve into a warmed jug or pitcher.

3 While the chai is brewing, gently heat the milk and date syrup, stirring to mix them together. When warm, add to the tea. Serve immediately.

Variation
You can use 1.5ml/¼ tsp ground cinnamon and 1.5ml/¼ tsp ground ginger instead of the cinnamon stick and fresh root ginger, if you prefer. Alternatively, you can omit them for a plainer drink.

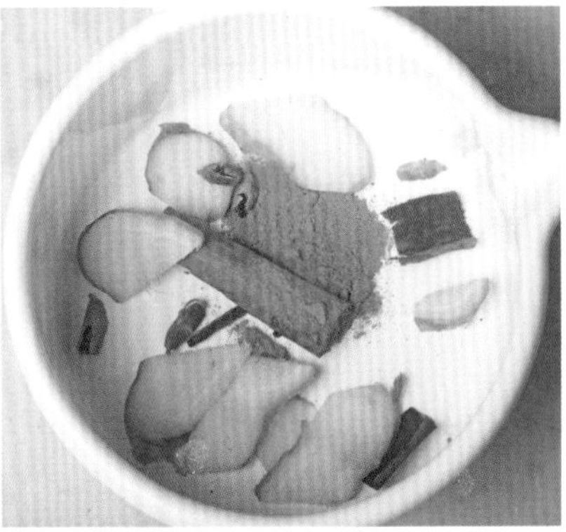

Soups, snacks & salads

Ready-made vegan soups and snacks are available, but many on dairy-free diets do miss their favourites such as fried mozzarella sticks, cheesy nachos and crispy quesadillas. You'll find these all here, carefully reworked with vegan substitutes, that are as delicious and satisfying as the original versions. Rich and creamy dressed salads also feature, for those days when you fancy a salad but are looking for something more substantial.

Coconut milk golden soup

Roasting cauliflower, yellow bell pepper and garlic brings out all their natural sweetness and adds a delicious slightly smoky flavour to this creamy yellow soup. Use either home-made or canned coconut milk – not coconut milk drink from a carton – when making the soup.

30ml/2 tbsp light olive or sunflower oil
finely grated zest and juice of 1 lime
15ml/1 tbsp water
1 small cauliflower, broken into little florets
1 large yellow bell pepper, quartered and seeds removed
2 garlic cloves, unpeeled
2 slices of canned or fresh pineapple, peel cut away and cored, and diced
150g/5oz/½ cup canned or frozen corn, defrosted
400ml/14fl oz/1⅔ cups coconut milk (canned or see page 40)
400ml/14fl oz/1⅔ cups vegetable stock
salt and ground black pepper, to taste

For the topping
20ml/4 tsp chia seeds
40g/1½oz roughly chopped pistachio nuts
torn nasturtium or English marigold petals
few small rocket/arugula leaves

SERVES 4

Cook's tips

• If this soup is left to stand the chia seeds will swell and it will take on a jelly-like texture, so serve it as soon as it is made.
• You could replace the chia seeds with hemp seeds if preferred.

1 Preheat the oven to 190°C/375°F/Gas 5. Lightly grease a non-stick baking tray with 10ml/2 tsp of the oil, then whisk the rest with 15ml/1 tbsp of the lime juice and the water in a small bowl.

2 Put the cauliflower florets on one side of the baking tray and drizzle with the oil mixture, turning to coat the pieces. Arrange the yellow pepper quarters on the other side, skin-side up. Add the unpeeled garlic cloves to the tray.

3 Roast the vegetables for 20 minutes or until the cauliflower is tender and very lightly browned. Remove the cauliflower and garlic from the tray and return the peppers to the oven for a further 5–10 minutes or until the skins are blistered and wrinkly.

4 Put the yellow peppers in a plastic bag and leave to steam until cool enough to handle. Peel off the skins and put the flesh in a blender with the pulp squeezed from the garlic. Reserve a few pieces of cauliflower to garnish, then add the rest to the blender with the pineapple, corn, coconut milk and about a third of the stock. Blend to a smooth purée.

5 Pour into a pan and stir in the remaining stock (use a little less if you prefer a thicker consistency). Gently reheat until piping hot, then season with salt and pepper to taste.

6 Ladle the soup into warmed bowls and top with the reserved pieces of cauliflower, lime zest, and a sprinkling of chia seeds, nasturtium petals and rocket, if liked. Serve immediately.

Mushroom and hemp milk soup

The earthy flavour of brown cap or chestnut mushrooms is subtly enhanced with hemp seed milk in this warming soup, and there is an additional hint of aniseed from the tarragon. Serve in small bowls with rolls as an appetizer or in larger portions with crusty bread for a hearty lunch.

4 shallots
15ml/1 tbsp sunflower or coconut oil
450g/1lb/6 cups brown cap/ chestnut mushrooms, chopped
300ml/½ pint/1¼ cups vegetable stock
300ml/½ pint/1¼ cups hemp seed milk (see page 39)
15–30ml/1–2 tbsp chopped fresh tarragon, plus sprigs to garnish
salt and ground black pepper, to taste

SERVES 4

1 Finely chop the shallots. Heat the oil in a large pan, add the shallots and cook for 5 minutes, stirring occasionally.

2 Add the mushrooms and cook gently for 3 minutes, stirring, then add the stock and milk. Bring to the boil, then cover and simmer for about 20 minutes, until the vegetables are soft.

3 Stir in the chopped fresh tarragon and season to taste with salt and ground black pepper.

4 Allow the soup to cool slightly, then purée it in a blender or food processor, in batches if necessary, until smooth. Return to the rinsed-out pan and reheat gently, until steaming hot.

5 Ladle the soup into warmed bowls and serve immediately, garnished with sprigs of fresh tarragon.

Curried cauliflower and cashew milk soup

This lightly spiced soup is both simple and satisfying, and can be made with most non-dairy milks as well as cashew – chestnut and hazelnut are also good with the cauliflower. Garnish with sprigs of fresh coriander, and serve with warm, crusty bread or with naan.

1 Put the cashew milk, cauliflower, garam masala and seasoning in a pan and place over a medium heat. Bring to the boil, then reduce the heat, partially cover the pan and simmer for 20 minutes, until the cauliflower is tender.

2 Leave the mixture to cool for a few minutes, then transfer to a blender or use a stick blender, and process until smooth. Return to the pan if necessary, and heat through without boiling.

3 Ladle the soup into warmed bowls. Sprinkle with a few fresh coriander leaves and serve immediately.

750ml/1¼ pints/3 cups cashew milk (see page 26)
1 large cauliflower, broken or cut into florets
15ml/1 tbsp garam masala
salt and ground black pepper, to taste
fresh coriander/cilantro leaves, to garnish

SERVES 4

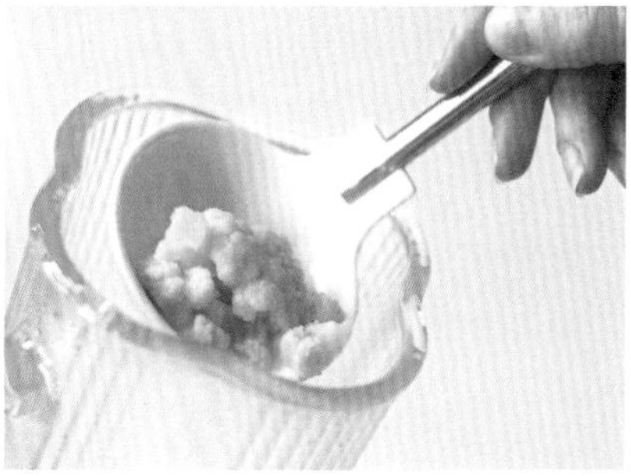

Aubergine dip with tahini-almond yogurt

This smoky aubergine and tahini dip is also known as baba ganoush. Some cooks add chopped flat leaf parsley and others sharpen it with lemon juice, or make it creamy with some thick yogurt. This recipe contains all of these for maximum flavour and a thick texture.

2 large aubergines/eggplants
30–45ml/2–3 tbsp tahini (see page 84 or 85)
juice of 1–2 lemons
45ml/3 tbsp Greek-style almond milk yogurt (see page 52)
2 garlic cloves, crushed
1 small bunch of flat leaf parsley, chopped
salt and ground black pepper, to taste
olive oil, for drizzling
griddled flat breads, to serve (optional)

SERVES 4

1 Place the aubergines on a hot griddle, or directly over a gas flame or charcoal grill, turning them from time to time, until they are soft to the touch and the skin is charred and flaky.

2 Place the charred aubergines in a plastic bag and leave for a few minutes to sweat. When they are cool enough to handle, hold them by the stems under cold running water and peel off and discard the skin. Squeeze out the excess water, then chop the flesh to a pulp.

3 In a bowl, beat the tahini with the lemon juice – the mixture stiffens at first, then loosens to a creamy paste. Beat in the yogurt and then, using a fork, beat in the aubergine pulp until everything is well combined. Add the garlic and parsley (reserving a little to garnish), season with salt and pepper and beat the mixture thoroughly.

4 Transfer the dip to a serving dish, drizzle over a little olive oil and sprinkle with the reserved parsley. Serve with flat breads, if liked.

Mini baked potatoes with 'blue cheese'

Brushing new potatoes with a mixture of olive oil and salt before baking gives them lovely crisp skins and soft fluffy centres. These are filled with a vegan version of 'blue cheese', made with silken tofu and crumbled firm tofu for texture; it has no 'blue' as such but plenty of umami tang.

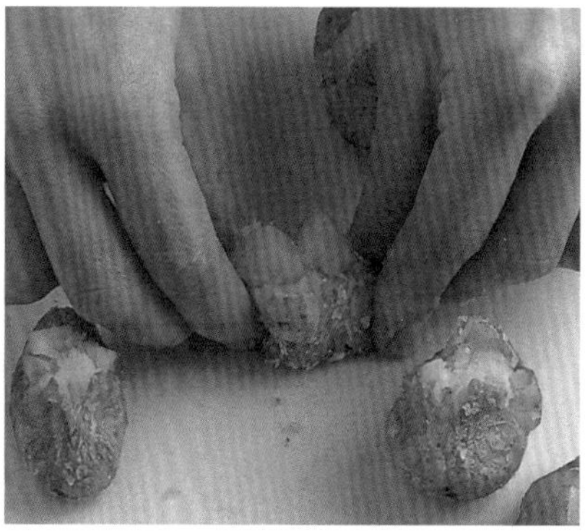

1 Preheat the oven to 180°C/350°F/Gas 4. Wash and dry the potatoes. Pour the oil into a bowl. Add the potatoes and toss to coat well with oil.

2 Dip the potatoes in the coarse salt to coat lightly. Spread out the potatoes on a baking sheet in a single layer. Bake for 45–50 minutes, until tender.

3 Meanwhile, make the blue 'cheese' topping. Put the silken tofu in a blender with the nutritional yeast, vinegar, miso paste, onion powder and a little salt and pepper. Blend together until smooth, scraping down the sides as required. Stir in the dill and crumbled firm tofu.

4 Cut a cross in the top of each cooked potato. Press gently with your fingers to open the potatoes. Spoon a little of the blue 'cheese' topping over each and sprinkle with chives.

5 Arrange on a serving dish and serve hot or at room temperature.

20 small even-sized new or salad potatoes
45ml/3 tbsp vegetable oil
coarse salt
30ml/2 tbsp snipped fresh chives

For the 'blue cheese' topping
150g/5oz silken/soft tofu
15ml/1 tbsp nutritional yeast
10ml/2 tsp apple cider vinegar
10ml/2 tsp white miso paste
1.5ml/¼ tsp onion powder
1.5ml/¼ tsp dried dill
50g/2oz firm tofu, finely crumbled
salt and ground black pepper

MAKES 20

Courgette and 'feta' fritters

Here, juicy courgettes and vegan feta are added to a thick batter made with non-dairy milk and flavoured with spring onions and fresh mint, and then pan-fried in big spoonfuls to make tasty fritters. Enjoy as a light lunch, snack or vegetable accompaniment.

- 450g/1lb courgettes/zucchini
- 30ml/2 tbsp olive oil, plus extra for frying
- 6 spring onions/scallions, trimmed and thinly sliced
- 25g/1oz/¼ cup chickpea/garbanzo flour
- 30ml/2 tbsp cornflour/cornstarch
- 45ml/3 tbsp pea milk (see page 42) or any other non-dairy milk
- 1 small bunch of fresh mint, leaves finely chopped
- 150g/5oz tofu 'feta' (see page 100), finely chopped or crumbled
- freshly ground black pepper
- green salad, to serve (optional)

SERVES 4

1 Lay a clean dish towel on the work surface and grate the courgettes on to it. Gather up the corners of the towel, then use your hands to squeeze the excess liquid out.

2 Heat the oil in a heavy non-stick frying pan or skillet and gently fry the spring onions for 3–4 minutes, until soft. Transfer to a large bowl.

3 In a separate bowl, blend the chickpea flour, cornflour and pea or other non-dairy milk together. Season with ground black pepper and add to the spring onions with the grated courgette and mint.

4 Stir everything together (the batter will seem quite thick at first, but moisture from the courgettes will loosen it), then stir in the crumbled feta. Let the batter stand for 3-4 minutes, then stir again.

5 Add a little more olive oil to the frying pan and place over a medium heat. When hot, drop large spoonfuls of the fritter batter into the pan – make three or four fritters at a time – and cook for 3–4 minutes, or until set and lightly browned, then turn over and cook the other side for 3–4 minutes, or until browned.

6 Drain the fritters on kitchen paper and keep them warm while you cook the remaining mixture in the same way. Serve warm, with a green salad if you wish.

Variation

Instead of mint, flavour the fritters with chopped fresh coriander/cilantro and a red chilli, seeded and finely chopped.

Fried 'mozzarella' sticks

These little cheesy sticks coated in crisp breadcrumbs are delicious with a tomato-based salsa or a sweet chilli dipping sauce, or try them with the aubergine dip with tahini-almond yogurt (see page 140). Prepare ahead for a snack or party food, then bake to heat up before serving.

250g/9oz mozzarella-style 'cheese' (see page 99)
30ml/2 tbsp chickpea/garbanzo flour
pinch of salt
2.5ml/½ tsp onion powder (optional)
2.5ml/½ tsp dried mixed herbs (optional)
120ml/4fl oz/½ cup almond milk (see page 28)
50g/2oz/½ cup plain/all-purpose flour
90g/3½oz/1 cup fresh white breadcrumbs
sunflower oil, for shallow frying
tomato salsa (see page 147), dipping sauce or quick tomato relish (see Cook's tip), to serve

MAKES 20

Cook's tip
For a quick tomato relish, mix 90ml/6 tbsp tomato ketchup, 10ml/2 tsp malt vinegar and 8 red or yellow cherry tomatoes, finely chopped, together. Stir in 15ml/1 tbsp chopped fresh herbs such as parsley or basil, if you like.

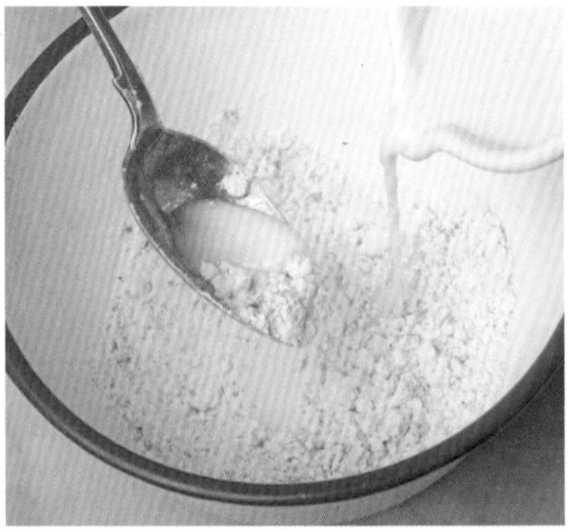

1 Cut the 'mozzarella' in half lengthways and then into 1cm/½in strips. Keep these in the fridge, covered, while preparing the other ingredients.

2 Put the chickpea flour in a bowl with a pinch of salt, and the onion powder and herbs if using. Blend to a paste with a little of the milk, then stir in the rest. Put the plain flour in a second bowl and the breadcrumbs in a third bowl.

3 Using a pair of forks, dip a stick of 'mozzarella' into the batter. Shake off the excess, then dip into the flour and turn to coat. Shake off the excess, dip into the batter again, then into the breadcrumbs, turning to coat all over. Place on a baking tray lined with baking parchment.

4 Repeat with the remaining sticks of mozzarella, then chill in the fridge. About 20 minutes before cooking, put the tray of sticks into the freezer to ensure they are really firm.

5 Heat about 2cm/¾in of oil in a large frying pan until hot (check by dropping in a small cube of stale bread; it should brown within 30 seconds). Add the 'mozzarella' sticks a few at a time (don't overcrowd the pan or the temperature of the oil will drop) and cook for about 30 seconds or until the breadcrumbs are dark golden and crisp, carefully turning them over halfway through cooking.

6 Lift the mozzarella sticks on to a plate lined with kitchen paper and keep warm while cooking the rest in the same way. Serve immediately with a dipping sauce, tomato salsa or quick tomato sauce.

'Cheesy' nachos bake with guacamole

Whether you are watching the match or a family movie on TV, a Mexican-style traybake of cheesy nachos is perfect for sharing, and it's easy to prepare the elements ahead. You could also serve the beans, salsa and guacamole separately as dips for the cheesy-baked tortilla chips.

200g/7oz corn tortilla chips
1 jalapeño chilli, seeded and cut into thin strips
115g/4oz mozzarella-style 'cheese' (see page 99), coarsely grated
30ml/2 tbsp savoury sour cream or cashew cream (see page 58 or 57)

For the bean mash
400g/14oz can of black beans, drained (not rinsed)
1 garlic clove, crushed
2.5ml/½ tsp mild chilli powder
1.5ml/¼ tsp ground cumin
salt and ground black pepper, to taste

For the tomato salsa
15ml/1 tbsp olive oil
15ml/1 tbsp lime juice
¼ red onion, finely chopped
6 ripe tomatoes, skinned and seeded, diced
30ml/2 tbsp chopped fresh coriander/cilantro, plus a few small leaves for garnishing

For the guacamole
2 medium ripe avocados, halved, stoned and roughly chopped
15ml/1 tbsp lime juice
2 spring onions/scallions, trimmed and finely chopped
2–3 drops Tabasco sauce (optional)

SERVES 4–6

1 Preheat the oven to 190°C/375°F/Gas 5. Tip the tortilla chips into a large baking tray and spread out evenly.

2 For the spiced bean mash, tip the black beans into a bowl, and add the garlic, chilli powder and cumin. Season with a little salt (don't use too much as the tortilla chips are already salty) and pepper, then roughly mash with a fork. Mix in about 30ml/2 tbsp cold water or enough to make a creamy-textured mash. Set aside.

3 For the tomato salsa, whisk the olive oil and lime juice together in a bowl, then stir in the chopped onion, tomatoes and chopped fresh coriander. Set aside.

4 For the guacamole, put the chopped avocados in a bowl, sprinkle over the lime juice and roughly mash with a fork, keeping some texture. Stir in the chopped spring onions and Tabasco sauce, if using. Spoon into a serving bowl and set aside.

5 Spoon the bean mash in little mounds all over the tortilla chips, then, using a draining spoon so that the juices are left behind, spoon over the tomato salsa. Scatter over the chilli strips and grated 'mozzarella'.

6 Bake for 4–5 minutes until everything is hot, but take care not to over-brown the tortilla chips. Remove from the oven.

7 Spoon over the sour cream and scatter with the reserved fresh coriander leaves. Serve on small plates with a scoop of the guacamole.

'Cheese' and tomato quesadillas

This easy-to-prepare snack is a great vegan alternative to cheese toasties. There are many variations, but here, non-dairy cheese is combined with chopped tomatoes, chilli and fresh coriander. Vary the filling depending on the ingredients in your fridge.

225g/8oz mozzarella-style 'cheese' (see page 99), grated, or store-bought grated vegan Cheddar-style 'cheese'
8 flour tortillas
4 tomatoes, chopped
1 fresh chilli, seeded and chopped
½ bunch of fresh coriander/cilantro leaves, roughly chopped
salt and ground black pepper
sunflower or light olive oil, for brushing

SERVES 4

1 Sprinkle the 'cheese' over four of the tortillas, dividing equally. Mix together the tomato, chilli, fresh coriander and a little salt and pepper.

2 Scatter the tomato mixture over the 'cheese', then top with the remaining tortillas, firmly pressing the pairs together.

3 Lightly brush a ridged griddle pan or frying pan or skillet with a little sunflower or light olive oil. Cook the tortillas one at a time in the pan, carefully turning, for 1½–2 minutes on each side, until the 'cheese' has begun to melt and the tortillas are crisp. Brush the pan with a little more oil before cooking the next one.

4 Serve the tortillas immediately, while they are still hot, cutting each into four wedges.

Chicory avocado salad with tofu cream

A rich dressing can transform a salad, and this dairy-free version offers a piquant creamy blend of tofu and dill, with a hint of French mustard. In this fresh, crunchy salad the bitterness of chicory is perfectly complemented by rocket leaves, crunchy walnuts and smooth avocado.

1 Toss the chicory and rocket leaves together in a bowl and then heap on to four individual serving plates. Peel, stone and slice the avocados, then toss the slices in the lemon juice to prevent them from going brown.

2 Divide the avocado slices evenly among the plates, arranging them among the chicory and rocket leaves. Sprinkle over the walnuts and season lightly with salt and pepper.

3 Make the tofu cream dressing by blending all the ingredients except the oil in a food processor or blender. With the machine running, gradually add the oil. Taste and adjust the seasoning.

4 Drizzle the dressing over the salad and serve immediately.

Variations

• The dressing could be made with other fresh herbs, such as fresh coriander/cilantro, basil or parsley.
• You could top this salad with savoury 'cheesy' sprinkles (see page 113) for a flavoursome crunchy alternative to walnuts.

3 chicory/Belgian endive heads, leaves separated
50g/2oz rocket/arugula
2 large ripe avocados
juice of ½ lemon
90g/3½oz/scant 1 cup walnut halves
salt and ground black pepper

For the tofu dressing
350g/12oz silken tofu
15g/½oz/½ cup dill fronds
5ml/1 tsp light soy sauce
5ml/1 tsp French mustard
1 small garlic clove, crushed
juice of 1 lemon
pinch of salt
50ml/2fl oz/¼ cup olive oil

SERVES 4

Creamy slaw salad with vegan mayo

A cross between potato salad and coleslaw, this makes a great alternative to both and is lower in carbohydrates and calories. The dairy-free dressing is a combination of vegan mayonnaise and soya yogurt, flavoured with mustard, lemon juice and chives.

1 sweet potato, about 200g/7oz
1 celeriac, about 350g/12oz
1 medium turnip, about 175g/6oz

For the mayo dressing
5ml/1 tsp wholegrain mustard
5ml/1 tsp lemon juice or rice vinegar
30ml/2 tbsp aioli (see page 61) or vegan mayonnaise
30ml/2 tbsp soya yogurt or cashew yogurt (see pages 52 and 55)
30ml/2 tbsp snipped chives
salt and ground black pepper, to taste

SERVES 4

Variations
• Other flavourings can be added to the dressing to complement the food.
• This salad works well with most types of root vegetable; try swede/rutabaga or beetroot for a change.

1 Bring a pan of lightly salted water to the boil over a high heat. Cut or grate the sweet potato, celeriac and turnip lengthways into long thin strips. Or if you have a spiraliser, you can create lovely curling strips of the root vegetables using a medium (3mm/⅛in) noodle blade, and then cut these into slightly shorter lengths.

2 When the water is boiling rapidly, add the sweet potato and cook for 2 minutes, then add the celeriac, followed by the turnip. Bring back to the boil and simmer for 2 minutes. The sweet potato should be just cooked through and the other vegetables tender, but still slightly crisp. Tip the vegetables into a colander to drain, then leave to cool slightly for 5 minutes.

3 Meanwhile, for the dressing, blend the mustard with the lemon juice or rice vinegar, then stir in the aioli or mayonnaise, yogurt and chives. Season to taste with salt and pepper.

4 Add the vegetables to the dressing and gently toss together to coat. Leave to cool completely for the flavours to mingle. Serve at room temperature or chilled, if preferred.

Cook's tip
Take care not to overcook the vegetables, and drain them thoroughly, or the salad will be soggy. When cooling the vegetables in the colander, stir occasionally to let the steam escape.

Main dishes

For cheese-lovers, it's good to know that quiches, pizza, macaroni cheese, lasagne and carbonara can be made without dairy cheese. All of these favourite dishes usually contain dairy milk or cream as well, so this chapter makes good use of the wide range of plant-based foods that you can make yourself or buy. The aim is not just to recreate the traditional dairy main-course dishes, but to make vegan versions that taste fantastic – and in many cases healthier, too.

Margherita pizza

A home-made pizza is vastly superior in flavour to store-bought versions and you know exactly what's in it! This simple Margherita pizza is spread with a rich tomato sauce and covered with stretchy mozzarella-style 'cheese', but you could add other toppings as well.

1 Sift the flour and salt into a mixing bowl and stir in the yeast. Make a well in the middle and pour in the water and olive oil. Mix to a soft dough, adding a little extra water if needed.

2 Knead the dough on a lightly floured work surface for 10 minutes, until smooth and elastic. Put the dough in a lightly oiled bowl, cover and leave in a warm place for 1 hour or until doubled in size.

3 Meanwhile, make the topping. Heat the olive oil in a pan and gently cook the onion and garlic for 3–4 minutes until soft. Add the tomatoes, sugar and a pinch of salt and pepper and bring to the boil. Turn down the heat and simmer uncovered for about 15 minutes or until well-reduced and thick. Turn off the heat and leave to cool.

4 Turn out the dough on a lightly floured surface, lightly knead for a minute or two, then roll out to a circle about 30cm/12in in diameter. Transfer to a lightly oiled baking sheet. Spread the tomato sauce over the dough to within 1cm/½in of the edges.

5 Preheat the oven to 200°C/400°F/Gas 6. Scoop up walnut-sized pieces of the mozzarella-style 'cheese', then flatten each slightly and arrange on the top of the pizza. Leave in a warm place for about 10 minutes to allow the pizza base to rise a little.

6 Bake for 15–20 minutes or until the crust is risen and golden-brown and the cheese is melted and bubbling. Scatter the top with basil leaves and a grinding of black pepper, cut into wedges and serve hot.

350g/12oz/3 cups white bread flour, plus extra for dusting
2.5ml/½ tsp salt
7g/¼oz sachet of easy-blend/rapid-rise dried yeast
200ml/7fl oz/scant 1 cup tepid water
30ml/2 tbsp olive oil, plus extra for greasing

For the topping
30ml/2 tbsp olive oil
1 small red onion, finely chopped
1 garlic clove, crushed
400g/14oz can of chopped tomatoes
1.5ml/¼ tsp caster/superfine sugar (optional)
150g/5oz mozzarella-style 'cheese' for melting (see page 98)
small handful of fresh basil leaves, to garnish
pinch of salt and ground black pepper

SERVES 4

Variation

Adapt this recipe to create your favourite pizza. You can add finely chopped red fresh chilli or smoked paprika to the tomato sauce and top with vegetables such as red and yellow bell peppers, courgettes/zucchini or mushrooms (lightly sauté them first or the juices will make the pizza base soggy). Or try sliced canned artichokes and a scattering of pitted olives.

Grilled 'cheese' polenta with mushrooms

Polenta makes a great dairy-free (and gluten-free) base. Here, it is made with half stock and half rice milk for both flavour and creaminess. This is also a quick and easy way to use up leftover polenta. You can make and serve one large 'pizza' rather than single squares if you prefer, and vary the flavour of the topping by using fried onions instead of mushrooms.

300g/11oz/3 cups instant polenta
600ml/1 pint/2½ cups boiling vegetable stock
600ml/1 pint/2½ cups hot unsweetened rice milk (see page 44)
45ml/3 tbsp olive oil, plus extra for greasing
400g/14oz mushrooms, sliced
2 garlic cloves, thinly sliced
250g/9oz mozzarella-style 'cheese' (see page 99), sliced
45ml/3 tbsp finely chopped fresh flat leaf parsley, to garnish
sea salt and ground black pepper

SERVES 4

1 Cook the polenta in the stock and rice milk in a large pan for about 4–5 minutes, or according to the packet instructions, until thick.

2 Remove the pan from the heat, and season to taste with a little salt. Spoon the polenta on to a lightly oiled board and spread out. Cut the polenta into 8 squares.

3 Put the olive oil in a frying pan over a medium heat and stir-fry the mushrooms and garlic for 10 minutes, until the mushrooms are cooked. Season and keep warm.

4 Heat the grill or broiler, and lightly oil the polenta squares. Grill the polenta on both sides for a minute or two, until golden and crisp. You might want to place them on a sheet of foil before grilling.

5 Cover each square of grilled polenta with a slice of the mozzarella 'cheese', and grill for another 3–5 minutes until the cheese is hot and bubbling.

6 Place two polenta squares on each serving plate and spoon the cooked mushrooms evenly over the top, then sprinkle each portion with chopped flat leaf parsley and serve immediately.

Cook's tip

Unsweetened rice milk is a good choice for the polenta base as it has a neutral flavour, but you can use any unsweetened non-dairy milk; soya or oat milk both work well here (see pages 43 or 45).

Leek and 'feta' tart

For this tart, a crisp hazelnut pastry case is filled with tender leeks and tofu feta baked in a lightly set silken tofu and hazelnut milk savoury custard, instead of a traditional egg-based quiche filling. You can use this pastry for all sorts of other vegan tarts, too.

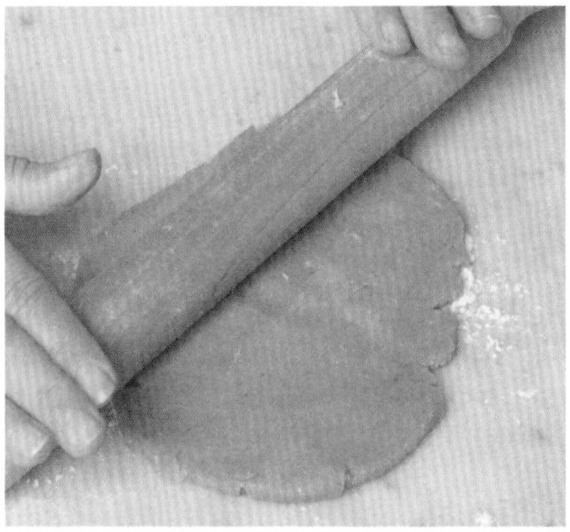

350g/12oz leeks, thinly sliced
15ml/1 tbsp olive oil
300g/11oz/1½ cups silken tofu
15ml/1 tbsp white miso paste
10ml/2 tsp chickpea/garbanzo flour
45ml/3 tbsp hazelnut milk (see page 30) or other non-dairy milk
15ml/1 tbsp wholegrain mustard
115g/4oz tofu 'feta' (see page 100), crumbled
salt and ground black pepper, to taste

For the pastry
115g/4oz/½ cup vegan hard/ baking margarine, at room temperature
25ml/1½ tbsp smooth hazelnut butter (see page 80)
175g/6oz/1½ cups plain/ all-purpose flour
30ml/2 tbsp cold water

SERVES 4

1 For the pastry, put the margarine and hazelnut butter in a bowl and blend together. Transfer the paste to a piece of baking parchment and chill for 30 minutes (or freeze for 10 minutes), until hardened.

2 Sift the flour into a bowl, add the margarine-nut paste, and rub it in until the mixture resembles breadcrumbs. Sprinkle over the cold water, mix until the crumbs begin to stick together, then gather into a ball.

3 Roll out the pastry and line a 25cm/10in flan tin or pan. Chill for 10–25 minutes. Meanwhile, put a baking sheet in the oven and preheat it to 200°C/400°F/Gas 6.

4 In a pan, sweat the leeks in the oil for 10 minutes, until soft, and set aside. Prick the base of the pastry case and line with baking parchment and dried beans. Put on the hot baking sheet and bake for 10 minutes. Remove the paper and beans and return to the oven for 4 minutes.

5 Put the silken tofu and miso paste in a blender with a little salt and pepper to taste. Blend until smooth. Spoon and scrape into a bowl.

6 Blend the chickpea flour with a little of the hazelnut milk, then stir in the rest of the milk. Add to the tofu paste along with the mustard and mix well. Add the leeks and tofu 'feta', and gently stir all together.

7 Spoon into the pastry case and level the top. Put into the hot oven and bake for about 30 minutes, until set and golden. Leave to stand for about 5 minutes before slicing and serving.

Cook's tips

• Make sure you use a smooth hazelnut butter rather than a crunchy one as it will help to bind the pastry together.
• Walnut butter (made in the same way as hazelnut butter, just with walnuts) and walnut milk (see page 31) are good alternatives, if you prefer.

Macaroni 'cheese'

This tasty pasta dish topped with a crisp layer of herby breadcrumbs should be in every vegan's repertoire. Quick and easy to make from store-cupboard ingredients, it makes a satisfying lunch or supper dish when served with a simple side salad.

1 litre/1¾ pints/4 cups cashew milk (see page 26)
1 small onion, peeled and quartered
1 bay leaf
350g/12oz/3¾ cups dried macaroni
75g/3oz/6 tbsp vegan 'buttery' spread (see page 72) or margarine
75g/3oz/⅔ cup plain/all-purpose flour
2.5ml/½ tsp English mustard powder
30ml/2 tbsp nutritional yeast flakes
1.5ml/¼ tsp ground turmeric
50g/2oz Cheddar-style vegan 'cheese', grated (or mozzarella-style 'cheese' see page 99)
½ bunch fresh thyme
40g/1½oz/¼ cup fresh breadcrumbs
15ml/1 tbsp olive oil
salt and ground black pepper, to taste

SERVES 4

Variations

• Ground turmeric adds just a hint of flavour to the dish, but its main purpose here is to give the sauce a pale golden cheesy colour. You can leave it out, if you prefer.
• Instead of the breadcrumb topping, you could sprinkle over a few spoonfuls of savoury 'cheesy' sprinkles (see page 113) after you've baked the macaroni.

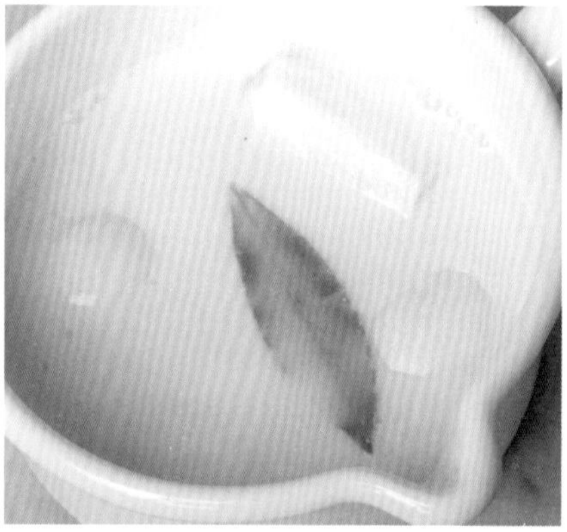

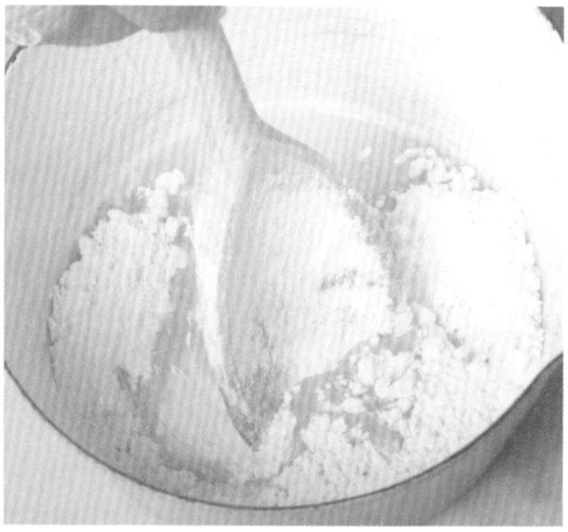

1 Pour the milk into a heavy pan. Add the onion and bay leaf and heat until steaming. Turn off the heat, cover with a lid and leave to infuse for 15–20 minutes. Strain the milk into a jug or pitcher, discarding the onion and bay leaf.

2 Preheat the oven to 180°C/350°F/Gas 4. Cook the macaroni in a pan of lightly salted boiling water according to the packet instructions, until just tender.

3 Meanwhile, melt the spread or margarine in the pan, then add the flour, stirring continuously. Cook over a low heat for a few seconds, then turn off the heat and gradually add the warm milk, whisking continuously. Bring to a boil and simmer for 3–4 minutes, until thick and smooth. Remove the pan from the heat and stir in the mustard, nutritional yeast, ground turmeric and grated 'cheese'.

4 Drain the macaroni well, then add to the sauce, mixing well. Tip the mixture into an ovenproof baking dish, about 30 x 20cm/12 x 8in.

5 Pick the thyme leaves off the stalks and put the leaves in a food processor with the breadcrumbs. Season with black pepper. Drizzle over the olive oil, then blitz for a few seconds. Sprinkle the crumb topping over the macaroni mixture.

6 Bake in the oven for 15–20 minutes or until the topping is lightly browned and the macaroni is bubbling. Serve warm.

Vegetable moussaka with tofu topping

This vegan adaptation of the famous Greek dish has all the savoury succulence of the traditional version. A flavoursome almond and tofu topping is used instead of the usual egg-enriched dairy-heavy béchamel. Aubergines in a mushroomy sauce create a substantial and tasty filling.

1 Preheat the grill or broiler to high. Place the aubergine slices in one layer on the rack. Lightly brush with oil and grill for 2–3 minutes on each side until golden. Alternatively, sear them in batches in a very hot heavy frying pan or skillet.

2 Make the sauce. Heat the oil in a large pan and fry the onions, garlic and carrots for 5–7 minutes. Add the remaining sauce ingredients to the pan and season. Bring to the boil, then simmer for 20 minutes.

3 Meanwhile, make the topping. Toast the ground almonds in a heavy frying pan or skillet, without any oil, for 1–2 minutes until golden, tossing occasionally.

4 Put the toasted almonds in a food processor or blender and add the rest of the topping ingredients. Process the mixture until smooth and well combined. Taste and adjust the seasoning as required.

5 Preheat the oven to 180°C/350°F/Gas 4. Spread half the sauce in a 35 x 23cm/14 x 9in ovenproof dish. Add a layer of aubergine slices and spread over the remaining sauce. Finish with a layer of aubergine slices.

6 Spoon the topping over the aubergine slices, ensuring it is spread evenly. Bake for about 20–25 minutes until the topping is set and has turned golden brown. Garnish with a sprinkling of paprika and some fresh basil leaves. Serve immediately.

600g/1lb 8oz aubergines/eggplants, cut into 2.5cm/1in slices
30ml/2 tbsp olive oil
ground paprika and fresh basil leaves, to garnish
salt and ground black pepper, to taste

For the sauce
30ml/2 tbsp olive oil
2 large onions, coarsely chopped
2 garlic cloves, crushed
2 large carrots, finely chopped
4 courgettes/zucchini, sliced
200g/7oz mushrooms, sliced
2 x 400g/14oz cans of chopped tomatoes
30ml/2 tbsp balsamic vinegar
20ml/4 tsp yeast extract
5ml/1 tsp ground nutmeg

For the topping
75g/3oz/¾ cup ground almonds
350g/12oz silken tofu
30ml/2 tbsp tomato ketchup
15ml/1 tbsp soy sauce
15ml/1 tbsp lemon juice
2.5ml/½ tsp English/hot mustard powder
salt and ground black pepper, to taste

SERVES 8

Vegetable and almond milk lasagne

A hearty vegan dish packed with flavour, this is ideal for a family meal or casual entertaining, as it can be made several hours in advance. Lightly browned vegetables are layered with sheets of lasagne and tomato sauce and covered with a creamy almond milk sauce before baking.

8 lasagne sheets

For the tomato sauce
15g/½oz dried porcini mushrooms
120ml/4fl oz/½ cup hot water
30ml/2 tbsp olive oil
1 onion, chopped
1 carrot, chopped
1 celery stick, chopped
2 x 400g/14oz cans of chopped tomatoes
15ml/1 tbsp tomato purée/paste
5ml/1 tsp dried basil

For the vegetable mixture
45ml/3 tbsp olive oil
450g/1lb courgettes/zucchini, thinly sliced
1 onion, finely chopped
450g/1lb chestnut mushrooms, thinly sliced
2 garlic cloves, crushed
salt and ground black pepper, to taste

For the white sauce
40g/1½oz/3 tbsp sunflower margarine or 'buttery' spread (see page 72)
40g/1½oz/⅓ cup plain/all-purpose flour
900ml/1½ pints/3¾ cups almond milk (see page 28)
salt and ground black pepper, to taste

SERVES 6

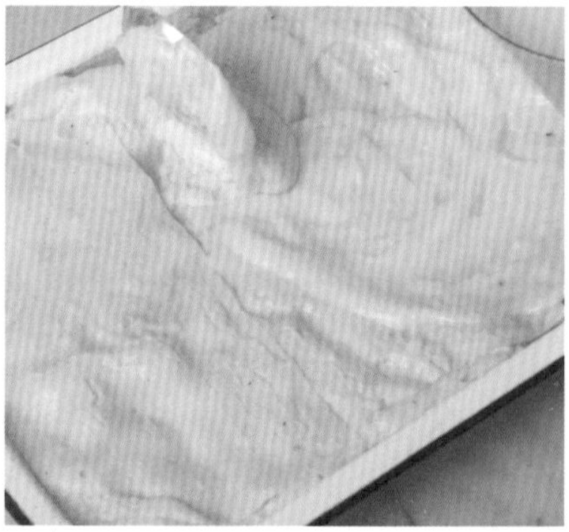

1 To make the tomato sauce, put the mushrooms in a bowl. Pour over the hot water and soak for 15 minutes. Tip the porcini and liquid into a sieve or strainer set over a bowl and squeeze the mushrooms with your hands to release as much liquid as possible. Chop the mushrooms finely and set aside. Pour the liquid through a fine sieve or strainer and reserve.

2 Heat the oil in a pan, add the onion, carrot and celery and fry for about 10 minutes, until softened. Place in a food processor with the tomatoes, tomato purée, basil, porcini and soaking liquid, and blend to a purée.

3 For the vegetable mixture, heat 30ml/2 tbsp of the oil in a large pan and cook the courgette slices over a medium heat for 5–8 minutes, until lightly coloured all over (cook in two batches if it's easier). Season to taste and remove the cooked courgettes to a bowl.

4 Heat the remaining 15ml/1 tbsp oil in the pan and cook the onion for 3 minutes. Add the mushrooms and garlic and cook for 5 minutes. Add to the courgettes. Preheat the oven to 190°C/375°F/Gas 5.

5 For the white sauce, melt the margarine or spread in a pan, then add the flour and cook, stirring, for 1 minute. Gradually whisk in the milk, then bring to the boil and cook, stirring, until smooth and thick. Season to taste.

6 Spread half the tomato sauce in a shallow ovenproof dish. Spread over half the vegetable mixture, then one-third of white sauce, then half the lasagne sheets. Repeat these layers, topping with the remaining white sauce. Bake for 30–45 minutes, until golden and the lasagne is tender.

Courgetti with dairy-free pesto

This Italian-inspired dish uses vegan pesto sauce: a blend of pine nuts, olive oil, fresh basil and garlic. Instead of spaghetti, here it is served with thin strips of just-cooked vegetables for a lighter take on the carb-heavy classic. It makes a good vegetable side dish as well.

- batch of pine nut pesto (see page 87)
- 3 large courgettes/zucchini, about 800g/1¾lb
- 1 large carrot
- 1 medium waxy potato, peeled and cut into 1cm/¾in cubes
- sprigs of fresh basil, to garnish

SERVES 4

1 First, make the pine nut pesto as described on page 87. Then, spiralise the courgettes and carrot using the 3mm/⅛in (medium) noodle blade. If you do not have a spiraliser, cut the vegetables into long, fine strips.

2 Simmer the potato cubes in a pan of water for 7 minutes. Add the carrot and, when the water comes back to the boil, add the courgette.

3 Cook for a further 3 minutes or until all the veg are tender. Tip into a colander and drain, shaking gently to allow the steam to evaporate.

4 Tip the vegetables back into the pan and heat gently for a few seconds to evaporate any juices. Spoon over the pesto sauce, stir to coat, then serve straight away on warm plates. Garnish with basil sprigs.

Pasta with a creamy nut-mushroom sauce

A satisfyingly simple supper. Here, cashews are blended into oat milk and combined with mushrooms to make a protein-rich and irresistibly creamy sauce that is ready in as little time as it takes to cook the pasta. Tagliatelle is used but the sauce would be delicious on any pasta.

1 Cook the tagliatelle in lightly salted boiling water for 10 minutes, or according to the packet instructions, until tender.

2 Meanwhile, in a food processor blend together the cashew nuts, garlic, mustard and oat milk to make a sauce.

3 Put the sauce in a separate pan, then add the sliced mushrooms. Simmer the sauce for about 10 minutes, stirring occasionally.

4 Dry-roast the pine nuts in a small, heavy pan until they turn golden brown and give off a nutty aroma. Remove from the heat.

5 Drain the pasta, stir in the watercress, then stir in the sauce. Serve while still hot, topped with toasted pine nuts and watercress garnish.

4 nests dried egg-free tagliatelle
150g/5oz/1½ cups unsalted cashew nuts
4 garlic cloves
5ml/1 tsp Dijon mustard
250ml/9fl oz/1 cup oat milk (see page 45)
150g/5oz chestnut mushrooms, cleaned and sliced
50g/2oz/½ cup pine nuts
a pack of watercress, chopped, plus leaves for garnishing

SERVES 4

Creamy carbonara with smoked carrot 'bacon'

Classic carbonara sauce is made with egg yolks, dairy cream and Parmesan cheese. This vegan version combines silken tofu and soya milk to make a deliciously rich sauce without the dairy. The final flourish is a scattering of carrot 'bacon' with a lovely smoky flavour and crispy texture.

350g/12oz spaghetti

For the carrot bacon

2 large carrots, trimmed and peeled
15ml/1 tbsp tahini (see page 84 or 85)
15ml/1 tbsp sunflower oil
10ml/2 tsp maple syrup
5ml/1 tsp dark soy sauce
5ml/1 tsp liquid smoke

For the carbonara sauce

250g/9oz/2½ cups silken tofu
120ml/4fl oz/½ cup unsweetened almond milk or soya milk (see pages 28 or 43)
75ml/5 tbsp nutritional yeast flakes
15ml/1 tbsp lemon juice
15ml/1 tbsp tahini (see page 84)
5ml/1 tsp white miso paste
2.5ml/½ tsp ground turmeric
salt and ground black pepper, to taste

SERVES 4

Cook's tip

Plate and serve the carbonara quickly once it is mixed together as the pasta will soak up the sauce if left to stand too long.

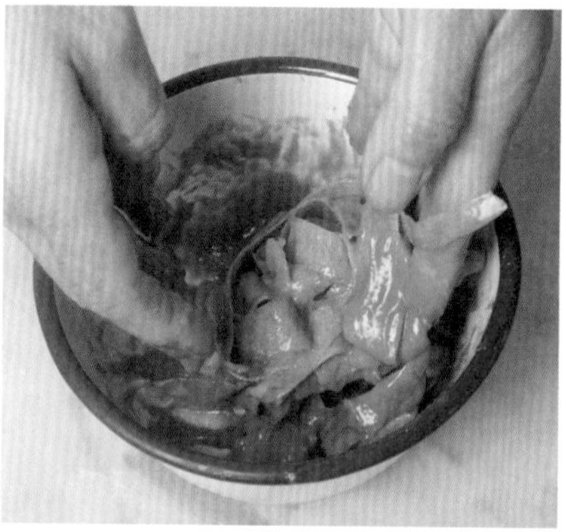

1 To make the carrot bacon, slice the carrots lengthways using a vegetable peeler to get thin even slices. Mix the tahini, oil, maple syrup, soy sauce and liquid smoke together in a bowl. Add the carrot slices and mix with your hands to coat all over. Cover the bowl and marinate the carrot strips at room temperature for about 15 minutes.

2 Preheat the oven to 180°C/350°F/Gas 4. Line a baking sheet with baking parchment. Arrange the carrot slices on the baking parchment and bake for 10–12 minutes or until dark golden and crisp, turning over halfway through the cooking time. Leave to cool.

3 For the pasta, bring a large pan of lightly salted water to the boil, add the spaghetti and when the water comes back to the boil, cook at a constant simmer, covered, for 10 minutes or until al dente (just cooked).

4 Meanwhile, blend the tofu, almond or soya milk, nutritional yeast, lemon juice, tahini, miso paste and turmeric together in a blender until very smooth. Season to taste.

5 Drain the spaghetti in a colander, reserving 60ml/4 tbsp of the cooking liquid. Cover the colander with the pan lid to keep it hot. Return the reserved cooking liquid to the pan and heat until steaming. Pour the carbonara sauce into the pan and bring to the boil, stirring. Turn off the heat, add the pasta and gently stir to coat in the sauce.

6 Divide the spaghetti between warmed bowls, adding a few pieces of carrot bacon to each. Serve immediately with a grinding of black pepper.

Courgettes stuffed with tofu 'feta'

Stuffed vegetables are a classic supper dish, usually topped with melting dairy cheese. This vegan recipe brings stuffed veg up to date with a filling of spiced rice, toasted pine nuts, tofu feta and pomegranate. You can prepare them ahead and keep in the fridge, ready to cook when you are.

115g/4oz/1 cup pine nuts
8 courgettes/zucchini
30ml/2 tbsp olive oil, plus extra for drizzling
1 onion, finely chopped
2 garlic cloves, crushed
2.5ml/½ tsp ground allspice
2.5ml/½ tsp ground cinnamon
185g/6½oz/scant 1 cup long grain rice
seeds of 1 pomegranate
60ml/4 tbsp chopped fresh parsley
115g/4oz tofu 'feta' (see page 100)
salt and ground black pepper, to taste

SERVES 4

1 Put the pine nuts in a dry pan and toast over medium-high heat, tossing regularly, for 1–2 minutes, or until golden brown. Set aside.

2 Halve the courgettes lengthways. Using a small sharp knife, carefully hollow them out, removing all the seed pulp from the middle.

3 To make the stuffing, heat the olive oil in a large sauté pan and add the onion, garlic, allspice and cinnamon. Sauté for a few seconds, then add the rice and cook for a further 2 minutes, making sure that the rice grains are well coated with the spice and oil mixture.

4 Add 150ml/¼ pint/⅔ cup water and season to taste, then cook until the rice is al dente: tender with a bite in the middle.

5 Remove from the heat, add the pine nuts, pomegranate seeds and parsley, then leave to cool. Preheat the oven to 180°C/350°F/Gas 4.

6 Fill the courgette halves with the stuffing and put into an ovenproof dish. Drizzle with a little olive oil and add about 100ml/3½fl oz/scant ½ cup water to the dish.

7 Bake, uncovered, for about 30 minutes, or until tender, basting occasionally with the pan juices. Crumble the tofu 'feta' over the top and serve warm.

Variation

This filling is also delicious used as a stuffing for green bell peppers, topped with mozzarella-style 'cheese' for melting (see page 98), rather than the tofu 'feta', before being baked in the oven.

Cook's tip

It's important to remove as much of the soft pulp in the middle of the courgettes as possible, since not only does creating a larger hollow allow them to be filled more easily, but removing the seeds and pulp prevents the finished dish from being too watery, too.

Creamy 'paneer' curry

This Indian-style dish is traditionally made with cubes of paneer and cow's milk, but here it has been made vegan-friendly by replacing the dairy ingredients with cubes of firm vegan cheese or tofu feta, and a mixture of coconut and almond milk.

30ml/2 tbsp sunflower oil or light olive oil
2 bay leaves
10ml/2 tsp ginger purée
10ml/2 tsp garlic purée
1 fresh green chilli, finely chopped
2.5ml/½ tsp ground turmeric
5ml/1 tsp ground coriander
2.5ml/½ tsp ground cumin
2.5–5ml/½–1 tsp chilli powder
150g/5oz frozen or fresh peas
2.5cm/1in piece of cinnamon stick
250g/9oz potatoes, peeled and cut into 2.5cm/1in chunks
2.5ml/½ tsp salt, or to taste
300ml/½ pint/1¼ cups coconut milk (canned or see page 40)
300ml/½ pint/1¼ cups almond milk (see page 28)
200g/7oz firm smoked coconut 'cheese' (see page 94) or tofu 'feta' (see page 100), cut into 2.5cm/1in chunks
2.5ml/½ tsp garam masala
a mixture of wild and basmati rice, to serve

SERVES 4

Cook's tip
Wild rice is particularly beneficial in a vegan diet because it is high in protein, unlike true rice. It provides useful amounts of the essential amino acid lysine, which is a building block of protein, aids calcium absorption, and is involved in the production of various hormones, enzymes and antibodies in the body.

1 Heat half of the oil in a large, non-stick pan over a low heat and add the bay leaves, ginger, garlic and chilli. Fry gently for 3–4 minutes, until the garlic softens but does not brown.

2 Add the ground turmeric, coriander, cumin and chilli powder. Stir and cook for 2 minutes.

3 Meanwhile, put the peas in a bowl, cover with boiling water and leave until tender. Drain and keep to one side.

4 Reduce the heat to medium and pour the remaining 15ml/1 tbsp oil into the pan of spices. Add the cinnamon and sizzle for 20 seconds.

5 Next add the potatoes and salt, then slowly add the coconut and almond milks, and stir to combine. Bring to the boil, reduce the heat to low and simmer, uncovered, for 20 minutes, stirring often.

6 Add the 'cheese' and peas, and simmer for 6–7 minutes. Stir in the garam masala and remove from the heat. Serve with a mixture of wild and basmati rice.

Desserts & sweet treats

For those who avoid dairy, rich ice creams, cheesecakes and treats like crème caramel may all seem off limits, but they don't have to be. Super-thick nut milks, coconut cream, cocoa 'butter' and tofu are all ingredients that can be used to make these delicious desserts. And there's no need to forgo creamy chocolate truffles or sweet and rich fudge either, as these can be dairy free, too.

Instant banana ice cream

This incredibly easy ice cream is created by blitzing frozen ripe bananas with a few spoonfuls of nut milk. It quickly blends to a smooth, sophisticated dessert that belies its simplicity. Use coconut milk if you prefer, or drizzle with some butterscotch sauce (see page 67).

4 large ripe bananas, peeled
45–75ml/3–5 tbsp light almond milk (see page 29), chilled
30ml/2 tbsp toasted flaked almonds, to serve

SERVES 4

Variation
For banana and peanut butter ice cream, add a large spoonful or two of smooth peanut butter when blending the frozen bananas.

1 Roughly cut the bananas into chunks and put them in a large airtight container, in a single layer if possible. Freeze for at least 2 hours, or until the slices are completely frozen but not rock-hard.

2 Meanwhile, chill your food processor bowl or food blender, and the serving dishes or glasses, in the fridge.

3 Put the banana into the food processor or blender and pour over 45ml/3 tbsp of the almond milk. Pulse briefly to chop up the bananas, then blend to form a smooth ice cream, adding more milk if needed.

4 Spoon the ice cream into the chilled glasses or bowls and serve immediately, scattered with a few toasted flaked almonds.

Chocolate avocado ice cream

This is a not-too-sweet ice cream in which avocados add a wonderful smooth texture, although their flavour is barely detectable. If time allows, chill the coconut cream and coconut milk overnight in the fridge. Use coconut evaporated milk in place of coconut milk for a richer result.

1 Pour and scrape the coconut cream and coconut milk into a blender or food processor. Add the avocados and maple syrup and blend briefly until the avocados are very finely chopped,

2 Sift in the cacao or cocoa powder, add the vanilla, then blend again until the mixture is completely smooth. Taste and add more maple syrup if liked (bear in mind that it will taste slightly less sweet when frozen).

3 Churn the mixture in an ice-cream maker until it is firm enough to scoop. Alternatively, pour the mixture into a suitable freezer container and freeze it for 1 hour, or until the sides and base are just frozen and the middle is soft. Whisk with a fork for 30 seconds, to break up and combine the frozen and less-frozen parts, then return to the freezer and repeat an hour later. Freeze for at least 2 hours or until solid enough to scoop.

4 Serve the ice cream in bowls or glasses, decorated with shards or curls of dark chocolate.

150ml/$\frac{1}{4}$ pint/$\frac{2}{3}$ cup coconut cream (see page 40)
400ml/14fl oz can of coconut milk (or see page 40)
2 small ripe avocados, peeled and diced
about 90ml/6 tbsp maple syrup
40g/1$\frac{1}{2}$oz/$\frac{1}{3}$ cup raw cacao powder or unsweetened cocoa powder, sifted
5ml/1 tsp vanilla extract
vegan dark chocolate shards or curls, to decorate

SERVES 4–6

Coconut milk ice cream

This creamy vegan coconut and lime ice cream is bliss on sultry days and particularly welcome as a cooling dessert to follow a hot and spicy main meal. Make sure you use full-fat and not reduced-fat coconut milk for this ice cream. Top with toasted coconut shavings.

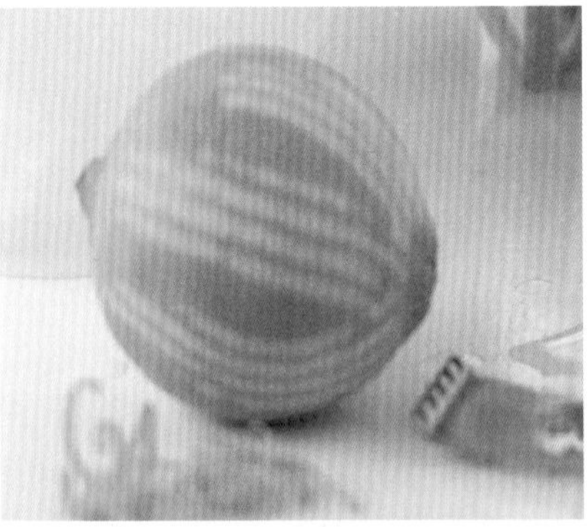

150ml/¼ pint/⅔ cup water
115g/4oz/½ cup caster/superfine sugar
2 limes
400ml/14fl oz can of full-fat coconut milk (or see page 40)
toasted coconut shavings, to garnish (see Cook's tip)

SERVES 4–6

Cook's tip
Spread flaked coconut on a baking sheet lined with baking parchment. Bake at 150°C/300°F/Gas 2 for 12–15 minutes, turning often, until golden. Cool.

1 Put the water in a small pan. Tip in the sugar and bring to the boil, stirring constantly, until it has all dissolved. Remove the pan from the heat and leave the syrup to cool, then chill well.

2 Grate the limes finely, taking care to avoid the bitter pith. Squeeze the limes and pour the juice and rind into the pan of syrup. Add the coconut milk and stir briefly.

3 Churn the mixture in an ice-cream maker until it is firm enough to scoop. If you don't have an ice-cream maker, pour the mixture into a suitable freezer container and freeze it for 1½ hours, or until the sides and base are just frozen and the middle is a soft slush. Beat using an electric whisk for 30 seconds. Quickly return it to the freezer and repeat twice more at hourly intervals, then freeze for at least 2 hours.

4 Remove the ice cream from the freezer 20 minutes before serving to soften. Serve, garnished with a few toasted coconut shavings.

Strawberry soya milk and tofu ice cream

Smooth, silken tofu gives this pretty pink dairy-free ice cream a remarkably creamy taste. Here, it is combined with soya milk, but you can use almond or cashew milk for a slightly richer and nuttier flavour. You can also use other berries – raspberries or blueberries work well.

1 Reserve 60ml/4 tbsp of the milk, then pour the remainder into a large pan and bring to the boil over a medium heat. Blend the sugar and cornflour with the reserved milk. Add to the hot milk with the vanilla and simmer, stirring, for 2 minutes, until thick enough to coat the back of a spoon. Pour into a bowl, cover the surface with a piece of wet greaseproof or waxed paper to prevent a skin forming, then leave to cool.

2 Place the strawberries in a food processor or blender with the tofu, oil and maple syrup and process until smooth. Mix into the vanilla custard.

3 Churn the mixture in an ice-cream maker until it is firm enough to scoop. Alternatively, pour into a freezerproof container and freeze for 2 hours. Whisk the half-frozen mixture until smooth, then return to the freezer for 1 hour. Whisk again and freeze until solid.

4 Remove the ice cream from the freezer 20 minutes before serving, to soften. Serve garnished with strawberry slices and a wafer, if you like.

450ml/¾ pint/scant 2 cups soya milk (see page 43)
50g/2oz/¼ cup caster/superfine sugar
20ml/4 tsp cornflour/cornstarch
5ml/1 tsp vanilla extract
250g/9oz/2 cups strawberries, washed and hulled
500g/1¼lb silken tofu
15ml/1 tbsp sunflower oil
30ml/2 tbsp maple syrup
vegan wafers (shop-bought or see page 180; cut into wedges rather than rolling into cones), to serve (optional)

SERVES 8

Pistachio ice cream

Full-bodied pistachio milk makes a rich ice cream with a subtle nut flavour and delicate pale green colour. Make it with unstrained nut milk so that you get flecks of nut in the mixture.

45ml/3 tbsp cornflour/cornstarch
45ml/3 tbsp caster/superfine sugar
small pinch of salt
475ml/17fl oz/2 cups unstrained pistachio milk (see page 33)
1.5ml/¼ tsp vanilla extract
250ml/9fl oz/1 cup oat cream or soya cream, chilled
1–2 drops green food colouring (optional)
vegan wafer cones (shop-bought or see below), dipped in melted vegan chocolate and chopped nuts if liked, to serve (optional)

SERVES 4

Cook's tip
Let the ice cream soften in the fridge for 20 minutes before scooping and serving.

1 Blend the cornflour, sugar and salt with 75ml/5 tbsp of the pistachio milk in a bowl. Pour the rest of the milk into a heavy pan and heat until steaming hot, but do not boil.

2 Gradually whisk the hot milk into the cornflour mixture, then pour back into the pan. Simmer over a low heat for 5 minutes, until the custard thickens, stirring all the time. Remove the pan from the heat and stir in the vanilla. Cover the custard with a sheet of wet greaseproof paper or baking parchment to prevent a skin forming, and leave to cool.

3 When the custard is cold, stir the oat or soya cream into the custard. If you want your ice cream to be a slightly more intense shade of green, stir in 1–2 drops of green food colouring.

4 Churn the mixture in an ice-cream maker until it is firm enough to scoop. If you don't have an ice-cream maker, pour the mixture into a suitable freezer container and freeze it for 1 hour, or until the sides and base are just frozen and the middle is soft. Whisk with a fork for 30 seconds, to break it up and combine the frozen and less-frozen parts, then return it to the freezer and repeat an hour later. Freeze the ice cream for at least 2 hours or until it's solid enough to scoop.

Wafer ice cream cones

10ml/2 tsp baking powder
30ml/2 tbsp water
15ml/1 tbsp caster/superfine sugar
25g/1oz/2 tbsp vegan margarine or 'buttery' spread (see page 72), melted and cooled
15–20ml/3–4 tsp almond milk or soya milk (see pages 28 or 43)
1.5ml/¼ tsp vanilla extract
20g/¾oz/scant ¼ cup plain/all-purpose flour
pinch of salt
sunflower oil, for brushing

MAKES 6

1 Put the baking powder and water into a mixing bowl and blend together. Stir in the sugar, followed by the margarine or spread, 15ml/1 tbsp of the milk and the vanilla extract. Sift over the flour and salt, and stir everything together; add a further 5ml/1 tsp milk if the batter seems a little bit too thick.

2 Heat a non-stick frying pan or skillet (a crêpe pan is ideal) over a medium heat. Once it is hot, turn down the heat to low and add a little sunflower oil. Ladle in 45ml–60ml/3–4 tbsp of the batter and tilt and spread out to a 15cm/6in circle. Cook for about 3 minutes or until set and the underside is golden brown. Turn over and cook the other side for 2–3 minutes, until golden. Alternatively, use a waffle maker if you have one, following the manufacturer's instructions.

3 Tip the wafer out on to a board and quickly roll it into a cone shape while still hot. Squeeze the tip of the cone to seal it. Leave to cool on a wire rack. Repeat with remaining mixture to make more cones.

Raspberry ripple creamsicles

Raspberries and almonds are perfect partners. For these sweet lollies, very thick and creamy almond milk is churned into ice cream and rippled with a thick raspberry coulis. The initial nut soaking and blending process takes a while but the result is well worth the effort.

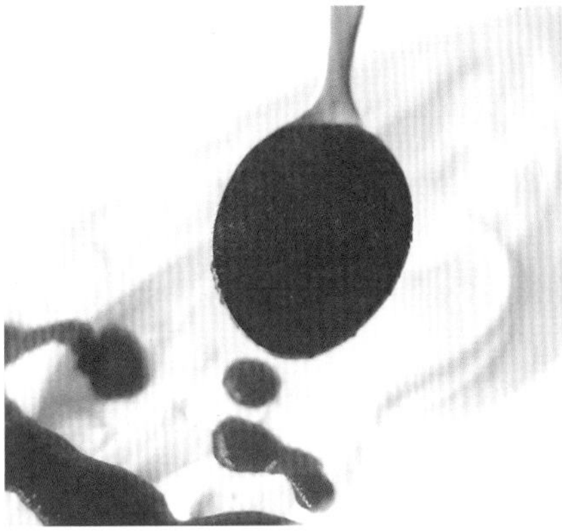

75g/3oz/½ cup raw unsalted unblanched almonds
150ml/¼ pint/⅔ cup filtered water, plus water for soaking
2 medjool dates, pitted
150ml/¼ pint/⅔ cup oat cream or soya cream
25g/1oz/¼ cup caster/superfine sugar
2.5ml/½ tsp vanilla extract
75g/3oz/½ cup fresh raspberries
6 ice lolly (popsicle) sticks

MAKES 6

1 Put the almonds in a heatproof bowl and pour over enough boiling water to cover the nuts by about 2.5cm/1in. Leave to soak until the water is tepid and the almonds cool enough to handle. Drain the almonds, then squeeze the nuts out of the skins. Discard the skins.

2 Return the nuts to the bowl and pour over enough cold water to cover by about 2.5cm/1in. Leave to soak at room temperature for at least 8 hours or place in the fridge and soak for up to 24 hours.

3 Drain and rinse the almonds, then tip them into a blender. Add the filtered water and dates. Pulse a few times to break up the nuts, then blend for 3–4 minutes or until the mixture is smooth. Add the cream, vanilla and half the sugar, then blend again until silky smooth.

4 Pour into a suitable freezer container and freeze for 1 hour, or until the sides and base are just frozen and the middle is soft. Whisk for 30 seconds, to break up and combine the frozen and less-frozen parts.

5 Meanwhile, make the coulis. Blend the raspberries and remaining sugar in a blender or small food processor until smooth. Press through a fine strainer into a jug or bowl, discarding the pips. Chill until needed.

6 Drizzle the coulis over the semi-frozen ice cream and gently stir for just a few seconds to make a marbled effect. Pour into ice lolly/ice pop moulds, add the sticks and freeze for 3–4 hours or until solid. Just before serving, to remove the creamsicles, dip the moulds briefly into hot (but not boiling) water.

Cook's tips

- You will need a powerful blender to make the very smooth almond milk this recipe requires. If the milk is still grainy after blending, strain it through a nut bag or a sieve or strainer lined with muslin or cheesecloth before adding the sugar, oat cream and vanilla.
- You could make these creamsicles using blackberries instead of raspberries. You can also use cashew nuts instead of almonds.

Choc ices

Luxurious vanilla ice cream is set in ice lolly moulds then thickly coated in dark chocolate to make this decadent treat. Coconut milk is excellent for making vegan ice creams; when combined with cashews, the coconut is barely perceptible and the vanilla flavour dominates.

For the vanilla ice cream
115g/4oz/¾ cup raw unsalted cashew nuts
75ml/5 tbsp mild non-dairy milk, such as rice, light almond or soya (see pages 44, 29 or 43)
400ml/14oz can of full-fat coconut milk (or see page 40)
60ml/4 tbsp agave syrup or maple syrup
7.5ml/1½ tsp vanilla extract

For the chocolate coating
100g/3½oz/½ cup cocoa butter
50g/2oz/½ cup raw cacao powder or unsweetened cocoa powder
15ml/1 tbsp agave syrup
pinch of salt (optional)

MAKES 8

Cook's tip
If you don't have time to make chocolate coating, melt 150g/5oz vegan dark chocolate in a bowl over a pan of very hot (not boiling) water. Leave until just cool before dipping the ices.

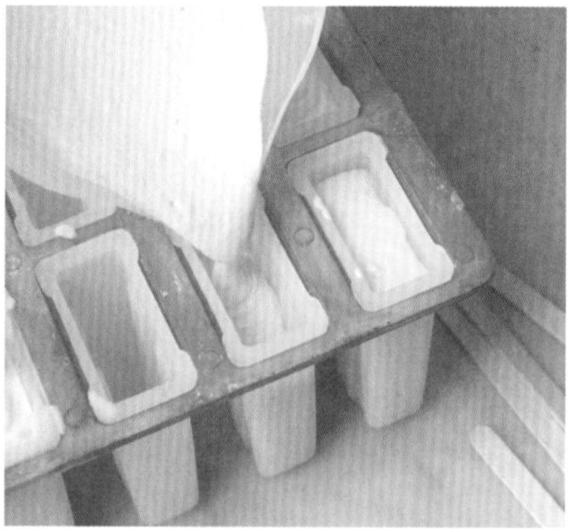

1 Put the cashew nuts in a bowl and pour in enough cold water to cover them by 2.5cm/1in. Leave to soak at room temperature for 5–6 hours or for up to 24 hours in the fridge. Drain and rinse.

2 Put the soaked cashews in a blender with the milk, three-quarters of the coconut milk, and the agave or maple syrup and vanilla. Pulse a few times to break up the nuts, then blend until very smooth and creamy. Add the remaining coconut milk and blend again.

3 Pour the mixture into lolly/ice pop moulds, add sticks and freeze for 4–6 hours or until completely firm.

4 About half an hour before you are ready to unmould the ice creams, make the chocolate coating. Put the cocoa butter in a bowl over a pan of near-boiling water. Allow to melt, stirring occasionally.

5 Remove the bowl from the hot water. Sift over the cacao or cocoa powder and stir in. Add the agave syrup and salt if using and stir again. Leave until just cool.

6 Meanwhile, line a baking sheet with baking parchment. Remove the ice creams from the freezer and loosen the moulds by briefly dipping each into hot (not boiling) water. Put on the prepared baking sheet and return to the freezer for a few minutes to firm up. When the chocolate coating is just cool, dip each ice cream in the chocolate to coat. Place the ice creams on the prepared baking sheet and return to the freezer to set the coating before serving.

Mango and lime whip

This creamy whip combines fruit purée with non-dairy yogurt and whipped coconut cream for a really quick and easy dessert that can be made ahead. It can be varied by using other fruit purées. For this mango version, choose a variety like Alphonso, which is wonderfully fragrant.

2 large mangoes
grated rind of 1 lime
juice of ½ lime
60ml/4 tbsp coconut milk yogurt, cashew yogurt or soya yogurt (see pages 54, 55 or 52)
150ml/¼ pint/⅔ cup whipped coconut cream (see page 64 but omitting the vanilla extract)

SERVES 4

1 Using a sharp knife, cut down the cheeks of the mango on either side of the stone/pit. Using the knife or a vegetable peeler, remove the skin. Cut and reserve neat slices to use for decoration, then roughly chop the rest of the flesh into small chunks.

2 Put the chopped mango in a food processor. Add the lime rind and juice and process until completely smooth. Pour and scrape the mango and lime purée into a bowl.

3 Stir in the yogurt, then gently fold in the whipped coconut cream. Pour into four glasses or cups and chill for 1–2 hours, or for up to 24 hours. Just before serving, decorate each glass with the reserved fresh mango slices.

Chocolate and hazelnut mousse

This is a simple chocolate mousse enriched with cocoa butter and with an oat cream base. Instead of being sweetened with sugar, it contains medjool dates, which also act as a thickener. Allow 2–3 hours for the mousse to chill in the fridge and set.

25g/1oz/¼ cup raw cacao powder or unsweetened cocoa powder
15ml/1 tbsp carob powder
150ml/¼ pint/⅔ cup hazelnut milk (see page 30)
75g/3oz/6 tbsp cocoa butter
pinch of salt
2.5ml/½ tsp vanilla extract
150ml/¼ pint/⅔ cup oat cream
6 medjool dates, pitted

SERVES 4

1 Sift the cacao or cocoa and carob powders into a small pan. Gradually blend in the hazelnut milk, using a whisk. Add the cocoa butter and salt.

2 Put the pan over a low heat and whisk until the cocoa butter has melted and the mixture is smooth. Remove from the heat and stir in the vanilla extract and oat cream.

3 Pour the mixture into a blender, add the dates and blend until the mixture is creamy and very smooth.

4 Divide between four glasses and chill for several hours, until the chocolate mousse has thickened and is lightly set.

White chocolate and strawberry parfaits

Although you can buy dairy-free white chocolate, it is often packed with additives. Rich and smooth cacao butter is vegan and has a delicious depth of flavour and smoothness that really lifts this sumptuous dessert. High in protein, and with low-sugar alternatives for sweetening, it is a healthy and satisfying end to a meal. Allow enough time ahead to soak the nuts.

115g/4oz/1 cup raw unsalted unblanched almonds
50g/2oz/½ cup raw unsalted cashew nuts
115g/4oz/½ cup cacao butter
2 ripe avocados, flesh scooped out and roughly chopped
350g/12oz/3 cups strawberries, hulled, plus 6 whole strawberries, to decorate
120ml/4fl oz/½ cup maple syrup
juice of ½ lemon
5ml/1 tsp vanilla bean paste
90g/3½oz/1 cup rolled oats
50g/2oz/½ cup lucuma powder
50g/2oz/½ cup mesquite powder

SERVES 6

Cook's tip
Many people consider lucuma and mesquite to be 'superfoods' as they are high in antioxidants and micro-nutrients. Lucuma is a sub-tropical fruit that can be dried and ground into a powder. It has a subtle caramel flavour and colour, and makes an excellent alternative to sugar as it is naturally very sweet. Mesquite comes from the dried pods of the mesquite tree. Mild and sweet, it has subtle hints of molasses.

1 Put the almonds and cashew nuts into separate bowls, and pour in enough cold water to cover them by 2.5cm/1in. Leave them to soak at room temperature for 5–6 hours or for up to 24 hours in the fridge. Drain and rinse.

2 Put the cacao butter in a large heatproof bowl set over a pan of barely simmering water. When melted, remove the bowl from the heat.

3 Discard the soaking water from the cashews and put them in a blender. Add the melted cacao butter, avocados, strawberries, maple syrup, lemon juice and vanilla. Blend on high for about 30 seconds, until combined. Add a little water, if needed. Pour the creamy mixture into six dessert glasses.

4 Drain the almonds, then process them in a food processor with the oats to make the crumbly topping.

5 Transfer the almond mixture to a mixing bowl, add the lucuma and mesquite powders, then stir in 30ml/2 tbsp cold water with a fork to form some crumbly clumps.

6 Spoon the crumbly topping evenly over the parfaits, top each dessert with a decorative strawberry, and chill until ready to serve.

Crème caramel

Most traditional recipes for crème caramel are made with an oven-baked egg custard. This vegan version, delicately flavoured with vanilla, is thickened with cornflour and lightly set with agar agar. Served with fresh seasonal fruit, it makes a delicious dairy-free dessert.

1 Put the sugar into a heavy pan and gently dissolve over a medium heat until the sugar melts to a syrup and turns a golden colour. Do not stir it during the process or you may cause the sugar to crystallize. Once the syrup is golden, immediately remove the pan from the heat and very carefully stir in 15ml/1 tbsp water – it will spit and sputter so take great care. Return to a low heat and stir until the caramel is smooth.

2 Warm an ungreased 900-ml/1½-pint baking dish or six 150-ml/¼-pint ramekins with near-boiling water, then tip out the water. Pour the caramel over the base of the dish or divide between the ramekins. Using oven gloves or a cloth, tilt the dish or ramekins to coat the base evenly with the hot caramel. Set aside.

3 To make the custard, blend the cornflour, maple syrup and agar agar with some of the almond milk in the pan. Stir in the rest of the milk. If using a vanilla pod, make a slit along its length, open it out and scrape out the seeds using the tip of the knife. Add both these and the pod to the milk mixture.

4 Put the pan over a medium heat and whisk until the mixture thickens and boils. Gently simmer for 5 minutes, stirring occasionally.

5 Remove from the heat and leave to cool for a few minutes. Remove the vanilla pod, if used, or stir in the vanilla extract.

6 Pour the mixture into the prepared dish or ramekins. Leave to cool and then chill for at least an hour, and up to 2 days.

7 To serve, loosen around the edge with a knife and tip the dish to ease the custard away from the sides. Select a serving dish that is flat in the middle but with a deep enough rim to contain the caramel syrup. Invert the serving dish over the baking dish and turn upside down. If using ramekins, turn them out on to small plates. Serve immediately.

75g/3oz/scant ½ cup caster/superfine sugar
30ml/2 tbsp cornflour/cornstarch
30ml/2 tbsp maple syrup
5ml/1 tsp agar agar
550ml/18fl oz/2¼ cups light almond milk (see page 29)
1 vanilla pod/bean or 7.5ml/1½ tsp vanilla extract

SERVES 6

Cook's tip
Unlike gelatine, agar agar has a fairly high melting point. These caramels are therefore perfect when you are serving puddings on a hot day (or in a hot climate) as the custards will hold their shape better when taken out of the fridge.

Chocolate cashew 'cheesecake'

This is a lovely vegan dessert for those who love both cheesecake and chocolate. It's easy to make once you have a batch of mild-tasting cashew nut cheese (see page 104) and it doesn't need baking or a setting agent, but remember to allow a few hours for it to firm up in the freezer.

250g/9oz/3 cups desiccated/ shredded unsweetened coconut
225g/8oz/1½ cups raw unsalted mixed nuts of your choice, chopped roughly
200g/7oz fresh dates
batch of soft fermented cashew nut 'cheese' (see page 104)
100ml/3½fl oz/scant ½ cup agave syrup
100ml/3½fl oz/scant ½ cup coconut oil, melted
15ml/1 tbsp lemon juice (optional)
2.5ml/½ tsp tamari (optional)
75g/3oz/⅔ cup raw cacao powder or unsweetened cocoa powder
fresh raspberries, to decorate

SERVES 6

1 Make the crust by putting the coconut and nuts in a food processor and blending together a little. Stone/pit and chop the dates, then add them to the mixture, and process again to form a dough-like texture.

2 Line a round loose-bottomed cake tin or pan with cling film or plastic wrap – or use a springform tin or silicone dish. Press the crust mixture into the tin to make the base, levelling it smooth with the back of a spoon. Chill in the fridge while you make the filling.

3 Put the remaining ingredients except the cacao or cocoa into a food processor and mix until smooth. Blend in the cacao or cocoa powder.

4 Pour the filling into the crust and smooth level with a spatula. Place the cake in the freezer for 2–4 hours.

5 Remove the cheesecake from the freezer and unmould it on to a serving plate. Cut into slices to serve, decorated with a few fresh raspberries if you like. If it's not eaten straight away, store it in the fridge, where it will keep for at least a week.

Tofu berry 'cheesecake'

Dairy cheesecakes often contain high levels of fat, but this vegan recipe has a simple bran flake crust and uses low-fat tofu and soya yogurt to make a wonderfully creamy topping without the addition of lots of sugar. It makes the perfect foil to delicious summer berries.

1 To make the base, place the spread or soya margarine and 30ml/2 tbsp of the apple juice in a pan and heat them gently until melted. Crush the bran flakes and stir into the apple juice mixture. Transfer the mixture into a 23cm/9in loose-based round flan tin or pan, and press down firmly with your fingers. Leave the base to cool. Chill until set.

2 To make the filling, place the tofu and yogurt in a food processor and process together until smooth. Heat the remaining 90ml/6 tbsp apple juice, then add the jelly crystals and stir until dissolved. Add to the tofu mixture and blend until smooth.

3 Spread the tofu mixture over the base, smoothing it evenly. Chill for 1–2 hours, until the filling has set. Carefully remove the tin and place the cheesecake on a serving plate. Arrange the fruits on top of the cake.

4 If you would like a glaze, heat the lemon juice and combine it with the redcurrant jelly. Stir until the jelly has completely melted. Leave to cool slightly, then spoon or brush it over the fruit. Chill until required and then serve.

50g/2oz/¼ cup vegan margarine or 'buttery' spread (see page 72)
120ml/4fl oz/½ cup apple juice
115g/4oz/6 cups bran flakes
425g/15oz firm tofu
300g/11oz/scant 2 cups soya yogurt (see page 52)
1 sachet of vegan jelly crystals (choose a flavour to suit your fruit topping)
175g/6oz soft fruits, such as raspberries, strawberries, blackberries and blueberries
30ml/2 tbsp lemon juice (optional)
30ml/2 tbsp redcurrant jelly (optional)

SERVES 6

Creamy pumpkin pie

This classic American dessert is delicious during the autumn months when pumpkins are readily available. The dairy-free wholemeal pastry is flavoured with pumpkin seeds and filled with a delicately spiced puréed pumpkin and tofu custard. It is creamy and satisfying.

For the base

250g/9oz/2½ cups wholemeal/wholewheat flour
pinch of salt
7.5ml/1½ tsp ground cinnamon
75ml/2½fl oz/⅓ cup pumpkin seed oil or rapeseed/canola oil
15ml/1 tbsp pumpkin seed butter (see page 86)
75ml/2½fl oz/⅓ cup sweetened soya milk (see page 43)

For the filling

450g/1lb pumpkin, deseeded and cut into 2.5cm/1 in cubes
350g/12oz silken tofu
260g/9½oz/generous 1 cup soft light brown sugar
75ml/2½fl oz/⅓ cup rapeseed/canola oil
15ml/1 tbsp carob molasses or agave syrup
7.5ml/1½ tsp ground cinnamon
5ml/1 tsp vanilla extract
2.5ml/½ tsp ground ginger
2.5ml/½ tsp ground nutmeg
2.5ml/½ tsp sea salt
icing/confectioners' sugar, for dusting

SERVES 6–8

Cook's tip

If you prefer, decorate the pie with a sprinkle of cinnamon or flakes of cinnamon sticks, or toasted sugared pumpkin seeds, or a mixture of all three.

1 Make the base. Rub together the flour, salt, cinnamon, oil and pumpkin seed butter until it resembles breadcrumbs. Add the soya milk to form a soft dough.

2 Preheat the oven to 180°C/350°F/Gas 4 and put a baking sheet in to heat. Roll out dough and use it to line an oiled 20cm/8in loose-based round flan tin or pan.

3 Meanwhile, for the filling, place the pumpkin cubes in a large pan with enough water to cover. Boil until the pumpkin is tender, about 15–30 minutes, depending on the size of the cubes. Drain and mash the pumpkin using a potato masher.

4 Add the tofu and all the other filling ingredients to the pumpkin, put in a food processor and blend until smooth and creamy. Alternatively, blend the ingredients together in the pan using a stick blender.

5 Pour the filling into the unbaked pastry case, and bake on the hot baking sheet in the oven for 50 minutes–1 hour, until golden brown.

6 Leave the pie to cool in the tin, then carefully transfer it on to a plate. Chill in the fridge before serving, dusted with a little icing sugar.

Creamy peach tart

Gluten-free and sugar-free as well as dairy-free, this easy-to-make fresh peach tart is summery and incredibly luscious. The base can be made up to three days in advance, but it's best to assemble it with the topping on the day of serving to avoid the base becoming too moist.

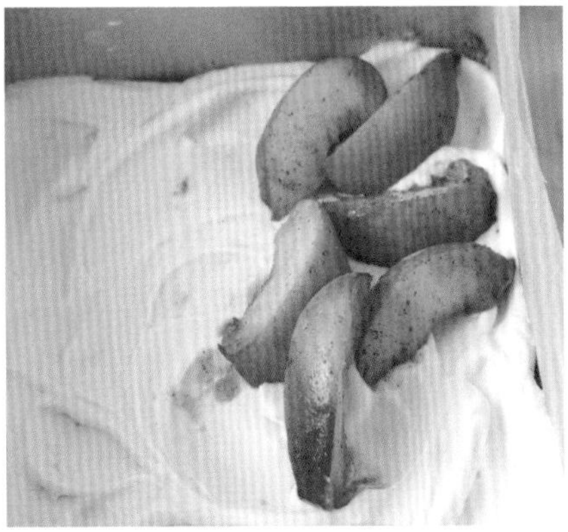

For the filling
30ml/2 tbsp maple syrup
2.5ml/½ tsp ground cinnamon, plus extra for sprinkling
15ml/1 tbsp warm water
4 ripe peaches, stones/pits removed and sliced into 10–12 segments each
160ml/5½fl oz canned coconut cream, poured into a mixing bowl and chilled

For the base
115g/4oz/¾ cup walnuts, almonds or pecans, chilled in the freezer
150g/5oz/2 cups desiccated/ shredded unsweetened coconut
10 dried pitted dates, soaked for 1 hour in 50ml/2fl oz/¼ cup boiling water

SERVES 9

1 Grease a 20cm/8in square cake tin or pan and line with baking parchment.

2 To make the filling, mix the maple syrup and cinnamon with 15ml/ 1 tbsp warm water. Put the sliced peaches in a shallow dish, drizzle with the sweet marinade, and set aside in the fridge for 1 hour.

3 To make the base, put the chilled nuts in a food processor and pulse for 1–2 minutes. Add the shredded coconut and pulse for about 10 seconds until broken down and combined. Add the dates in their soaking liquid and pulse for about 2 minutes to form a paste. Remove the blade and mix with your hands if it's too sticky to process.

4 Press the date mixture into the bottom of the prepared baking tin or pan with the back of a spoon. Set aside in the fridge for at least 1 hour.

5 When the tart is ready to assemble, put the chilled coconut cream in a mixing bowl and, using an electric whisk on low and slowly increasing the speed, whip for about 2 minutes. The colder the cream, the fluffier it will become when whipped. Spread the cream evenly over the base. Cover the whipped cream with an even layer of peach slices.

6 Chill the tart for at least 1 hour to set, but remove from the fridge before serving to bring to room temperature. Lift the whole tart out of the tin or pan using the baking parchment and slide it off the paper and on to a serving platter. Sprinkle with cinnamon and serve. The tart will keep in the fridge for up to 3 days.

Cook's tip

If you like, you could use a large ripe avocado for the topping instead of the canned coconut cream. Put the avocado in a bowl and mash with a fork. Add the syrup and cinnamon macerating juices, mix until combined and then spread evenly over the pastry before topping with the peach slices.

Coconut milk rice pudding with oranges

Rice pudding is always a comforting dessert and here it's given a new twist with the addition of tangy citrus fruit and a mixture of creamy coconut milk and nourishing cashew or soya milk. It doesn't really need sweetening, so do taste it first before sprinkling with more sugar.

400ml/14fl oz/1⅔ cups water
150g/5oz/¾ cup short grain rice
500ml/17fl oz/generous 2 cups full-fat coconut milk (canned or see page 40)
500ml/17fl oz/generous 2 cups cashew milk or soya milk (see pages 26 or 43)
sugar, to taste
5ml/1 tsp vanilla extract
5ml/1 tsp ground cinnamon, plus extra for dusting
2–3 fresh oranges, peeled

SERVES 4–6

1 Bring the water to the boil in a pan, then slowly add the rice so that the water continues to boil. Reduce the heat and simmer for 10–15 minutes until the water is absorbed.

2 Add the coconut and nut milks to the rice, return to the boil, then simmer for 30–40 minutes or until the rice is cooked. Sweeten to taste with sugar. Add the vanilla extract and cinnamon and stir to combine. Turn into a bowl and leave to cool.

3 Segment the oranges, cutting down between each piece and its membrane to release and lift out. Cut each segment into three.

4 Fold most of the orange pieces into the rice pudding. Serve at room temperature in little dishes, topped with a dusting of cinnamon and the remaining orange pieces.

Rhubarb and almond crumble

Crumbles are a family favourite and rhubarb is a great choice for a filling as it contrasts well with a sweet, crisp topping. Here, the crumble is made with almond butter blended with vegan butter, combined with dried almond flour left over from making almond milk, or with ground almonds.

450g/1lb rhubarb
50g/2oz/¼ cup sugar
30ml/2 tbsp redcurrant jelly
30ml/2 tbsp water
30ml/2 tbsp almond butter (see page 78)
150g/5oz/¾ cup vegan margarine or 'buttery' spread (see page 72)
175g/6oz/1½ cups plain/all-purpose flour
50g/2oz/½ cup almond flour (see page 11) or ground almonds
75g/3oz/⅓ cup brown sugar
40g/1½oz/½ cup rolled oats
vegan vanilla ice cream (see page 184), to serve

SERVES 4

1 In a pan, cook the rhubarb with the sugar, redcurrant jelly and water until soft but still holding its shape.Transfer to a deep pie dish.

2 For the topping, put the almond butter and dairy-free spread in a bowl and blend together. Chill for about 30 minutes, until hardened. Preheat the oven to 200°C/400°F/Gas 6.

3 Sift the flour into a bowl, stir in the almond flour or ground almonds, then add the chilled almond butter mixture and rub into the flour until it resembles rough breadcrumbs. Stir in the sugar and oats.

4 Sprinkle the crumble topping evenly over the fruit. Bake the crumble at the top of the preheated oven for 20 minutes, or until the top is crunchy and slightly brown. Serve warm with some ice cream if you like.

Variation
So many fruits can be used in a crumble: try apple, or course, strawberry and gooseberry, blueberry, raspberry or a mixture of summer fruits.

Vegan vanilla fudge

While classic fudge is usually made with butter and milk or cream, you can use coconut condensed milk and margarine to make an equally delicious vegan version. A sugar thermometer is useful, but not essential, for making the fudge. Flavour it as well if you like, see the box for ideas.

450g/1lb/2¼ cups golden caster/superfine sugar
320g/11¼oz can of sweetened condensed coconut milk
100g/3½oz/scant ½ cup vegan hard margarine
10ml/2 tsp vanilla extract

MAKES ABOUT 49 PIECES

1 Line the base and sides of an 18cm/7in square tin or pan with baking parchment. Put the sugar, sweetened condensed coconut milk and margarine in a deep heavy pan. Gently heat, stirring occasionally, until the margarine has melted and the sugar has completely dissolved.

2 Turn up the heat a little and boil the mixture for 6–8 minutes, stirring occasionally to make sure it doesn't stick on the bottom of the pan, until a sugar thermometer placed in the mixture reads 115°C/238°F. This is the soft ball stage, when a teaspoonful of the mixture dropped into cold water can then be rolled between the fingers to a soft ball.

3 Remove the pan from the heat and, when the bubbles subside a little, add the vanilla extract. Beat the mixture with a wooden spoon until it turns from being thin and shiny to having a thicker matt appearance and a slightly grainy texture.

4 Pour the fudge into the prepared tin, quickly spreading it into the corners. Leave for about 2 hours or until cold and completely set.

5 Remove the fudge from the tin and peel away the lining paper. Cut it with a long, sharp knife lengthwise into seven 2.5cm/1in-wide strips, then do the same crosswise to make 49 squares. You can also cut it into eight strips each way to make 64 smaller squares. Store in an airtight container.

Cook's tip

Don't overbeat the mixture; as soon as it thickens and a few grains form, pour it into the tin or else the fudge will be crumbly rather than smooth.

Flavouring ideas

Add one of the following flavourings to the fudge mixture after removing the pan from the heat and before beating the mixture:

Chocolate – Stir in 100g/3½oz dark vegan chocolate, chopped roughly.

Alcohol – Stir in about 15ml/1 tbsp rum or other alcohol, such as chocolate, hazelnut or almond liqueur.

Fruit – Stir in 25g/1oz/¼ cup cranberries or other small dried fruits.

Nut – Stir in 25g/1oz/¼ cup chopped skinned nuts, such as hazelnuts, pecans or almonds.

Ginger – Stir in 1.5ml/¼ tsp ground ginger and 25g/1oz/scant ¼ cup finely chopped crystallized ginger.

Chocolate coconut truffles

These moist, tender and very sweet truffles are made with shredded coconut and condensed coconut milk, and coated with vegan dark chocolate and a dusting of cocoa powder. Store in the fridge and serve them as an after-dinner treat with coffee or mint tea.

250g/9oz/3 cups desiccated/shredded unsweetened coconut
320g/11¼oz can of sweetened condensed coconut milk

For the chocolate coating
150g/5oz vegan dark chocolate, chopped, or chocolate coating (see page 184)
raw cacao powder or unsweetened cocoa powder, or desiccated/shredded coconut, to decorate (optional)

MAKES ABOUT 20

Flavouring ideas
Add one of the following flavourings to the coconut truffle mixture before rolling into balls:

Ginger – Stir in 1.5ml/¼ tsp ground ginger and 25g/1oz/scant ¼ cup finely chopped crystallized ginger.

Pistachio – Stir in 25g/1oz/¼ cup chopped raw unsalted skinned pistachio nuts.

Lime – Stir in the finely grated zest of 1 lime.

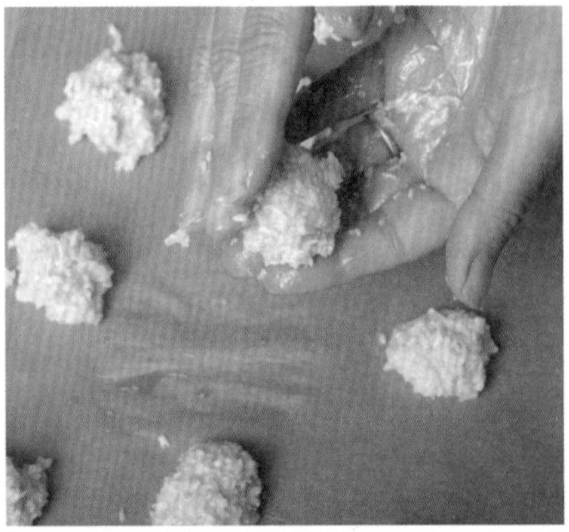

1 Put the coconut and sweetened condensed coconut milk in a bowl and stir together. Cover and chill in the fridge for 15 minutes to allow the coconut to start soaking up the moisture and for the mixture to thicken.

2 Roll the mixture into small balls, making them slightly smaller than your desired truffle size as they will become larger when they are coated in chocolate. Place the balls on a plate and return to the fridge for a few more minutes to firm a little more; the mixture will still be slightly soft and sticky to handle, but that's fine.

3 If using chocolate, chop or break it into small pieces and put in a heatproof bowl. Place the bowl over a pan of steaming hot (not boiling) water and leave for a few minutes, stirring occasionally, until the chocolate has completely melted and is smooth. Remove the bowl from the hot water and leave until just cool and slightly thickened, but not starting to set.

4 Using two forks, carefully dip the truffles, one at a time, into the melted chocolate or the chocolate coating, turning to coat on all sides. Allow any excess to drip off, then place the truffles on a board covered with waxed paper or baking parchment. If liked, roll them gently in a little sifted cacao or cocoa powder, sprinkle over a little desiccated coconut, or for a flamboyant gift, decorate with edible gold leaf.

5 Leave to set at room temperature before removing from the paper. Keep the truffles chilled in the fridge until ready to serve either in a small bowl or individual paper cases.

Berry and mint yogurt treats

Frozen summer berries make a great standby ingredient for these summery-tasting treats. They are sweet, fruity and creamy, but good for you as well – there is vitamin C in the fruits and protein levels are boosted with the quinoa flakes and sunflower seeds. Great for kids too.

115g/4oz/1 cup rolled oats
75g/3oz/¾ cup quinoa flakes
150g/5oz/scant 1 cup cashew nuts
3 tbsp/45ml sunflower seeds
150g/5oz/1 cup frozen mixed berries, no need to defrost
4 tbsp/60ml soya or other dairy-free yogurt (see page 52)
a handful of mint leaves
a little desiccated/shredded coconut, for rolling (optional)

MAKES 20

1 Add the oats, quinoa flakes, nuts and sunflower seeds to a food processor and blitz together to make a powder.

2 Spoon in the frozen berries, non-dairy yogurt and mint leaves,and blitz again until well mixed and smooth.

3 Scoop the mixture out of the food processor, and roll little pieces in the palm of your hand to make about 20 balls.

4 Roll the berry balls in a little desiccated coconut if you like, and serve. To store, pack them into a plastic container, interleaving the layers with pieces of baking parchment. They will keep happily in the refrigerator for up to 2 days.

Espresso power balls

Medjool dates, coconut, chia and toasted hazelnuts combined with strong espresso coffee and almond milk make this a winning combo, perfect for a pick-me-up. Mixing the naturally sweet dates with protein-rich nuts and high-fibre oats will give the body a sustained energy boost.

1 Line the base of a grill pan with a piece of foil, fold up the edges then grill the hazelnuts for 2–3 minutes. Rub in a kitchen towel to remove the brown skins.

2 Add the dates to a food processor with the oats and chia seeds, and blitz briefly until roughly chopped. Add the hazelnuts, coconut, cacao and maple syrup, and then the coffee and almond milk. Process together until finely chopped and beginning to clump together.

3 Take the mixture out, and cut into 20 pieces. Roll each piece in the palm of your hands to make a smooth ball. These can be stored in the refrigerator for up to 3 days.

50g/2oz/⅓ cup hazelnuts
150g/5oz/8 Medjool dates, stoned
150g/5oz/1½ cup rolled oats
2 tbsp/30ml chia seeds
40g/1½oz/½ cup desiccated/ shredded unsweetened coconut
1 tbsp/15ml cacao powder
1 tbsp/15ml maple syrup
2 tbsp/30ml strong black coffee
2 tbsp/30ml almond milk (page 28)

MAKES 20

Baking

While you can sometimes convert your favourite baking recipe by simply swapping ingredients such as butter with vegan margarine, this won't always work. Dairy-free vegan baking often needs a lot more tweaking, requiring adjustments in quantities and slightly different techniques. However, as revealed in this chapter, crunchy cookies, light-as-air sponge cakes, squidgy chocolate brownies and even eggless meringues with creamy fillings can all still be enjoyed, once you know how.

Brown scones with oat milk

Oat milk is inexpensive and easy to make and here it's used to make lovely light brown flour scones. Because they are virtually fat-free, you should eat them while they are very fresh – warm from the oven if possible, but definitely on the day of baking.

- vegetable oil, for greasing
- 115g/4oz/1 cup self-raising/self-rising flour, plus extra for dusting
- 115g/4oz/1 cup wholemeal/whole-wheat self-raising/self-rising flour
- 5ml/1 tsp baking powder
- 1.5ml/½ tsp salt
- about 350ml/12fl oz/1½ cups oat milk (see page 45), plus extra for glazing

MAKES 8

1 Preheat the oven to 220°C/425°F/Gas 7. Grease a baking sheet with oil and dust with flour.

2 Sift the flours, baking powder and salt into a bowl, adding the bran left in the sieve or strainer. Make a well in the centre, pour in almost all the milk and stir, adding milk as needed to make a soft, moist dough. Do not overmix.

3 Lightly dust a surface with flour, turn out the dough and dust it with flour. Press out the dough to a thickness of 4cm/1½in. Cut out eight scones with a 5cm/2in fluted pastry cutter. Place on the baking sheet and brush the tops with oat milk or leave unglazed and dust with flour.

4 Bake the scones for about 12 minutes, until well risen and golden brown. Remove to a cooling rack and enjoy warm.

'Buttermilk' soda bread

If you need a loaf of bread quickly, this non-yeasted version can be prepared and baked in under an hour. It relies on the acidity of buttermilk to boost the rise and give it an airy texture; the vegan buttermilk used here is just as effective as the traditional dairy one.

1 Preheat the oven to 200°C/400°F/Gas 6, and grease a baking sheet.

2 Combine the dry ingredients in a mixing bowl and stir in enough of the vegan 'buttermilk' to make a fairly soft dough. Turn the dough out on to a work surface dusted with a little wholemeal flour and knead lightly until smooth.

3 Form the dough into a circle, about 4cm/1½in thick. Lay on the baking sheet and mark a deep cross in the top with a floured knife.

4 Bake for about 45 minutes, or until the bread is browned and sounds hollow when tapped on the base. Cool on a wire rack. If a soft crust is preferred, wrap the loaf in a clean dish towel while it is cooling.

vegetable oil, for greasing
450g/1lb/4 cups wholemeal/wholewheat flour
175g/6oz/1½ cups plain/all-purpose flour
7.5ml/1½ tsp bicarbonate of soda/baking soda
5ml/1 tsp salt
about 450ml/¾ pint/scant 2 cups vegan 'buttermilk' (see page 213)

MAKES 1 LOAF

Sunflower milk seeded spelt bread

A mixture of quinoa and spelt flour is used to make this rustic loaf. Spelt is an ancient grain (dating back more than 5,000 years), and has a lower gluten content than wheat flour. Quinoa flour offers protein content. The seeds and sunflower milk provide slow-release carbohydrates.

225g/8oz/2 cups quinoa flour
225g/8oz/2 cups spelt flour
10ml/2 tsp easy-blend/rapid-rise dried yeast
25g/1oz/¼ cup chopped raw unsalted nuts, such as walnuts or hazelnuts
25g/1oz/¼ cup mixed seeds (sunflower, pumpkin, flax and poppy seeds), plus 15ml/1 tbsp extra for sprinkling
60ml/4 tbsp sugar
10ml/2 tsp salt
250ml/9fl oz/1 cup sunflower seed milk (see page 38), plus extra to glaze
50ml/2fl oz/¼ cup boiling water
vegetable oil, for greasing

MAKES 1 LOAF

Cook's tip

You can use a breadmaker to make this loaf, using a basic wholegrain programme. Add the nuts and seeds to the dough halfway through the cycle, or follow the manufacturer's instructions.

1 Sift the flours into a large bowl, add the dried yeast, chopped nuts, seeds, sugar and salt, and stir to combine. Make a well in the centre.

2 Mix the milk and water together in a bowl and pour into the well. Stir, mixing in the flour gradually, to form a pliable dough. Transfer the dough to a floured board, and knead by hand for 6–8 minutes, or in an electric mixer with a dough hook for 4–5 minutes, until soft and elastic.

3 Place the dough in a clean bowl, cover it with a damp cloth and leave it in a warm place for 1–1½ hours, until nearly doubled in size.

4 Knock back/punch down the dough and knead it for a couple of minutes. Cover it with the damp cloth again and set it aside to prove for another 30 minutes, until doubled in size. Preheat the oven to 220°C/425°F/Gas 7.

5 Oil a 450g/1lb loaf tin/pan, or a baking sheet. Shape the dough to neatly fill the tin or, if using the baking sheet, split it into three strands and braid it for a more decorative loaf.

6 With a sharp knife, score the top of the loaf lengthways and across, to help the dough rise. Brush the top with milk and sprinkle with seeds.

7 Bake for 35–40 minutes, until the loaf is risen and golden, and sounds hollow on the base when tapped (you will have to remove it from the tin to test this). Remove from the tin or baking sheet, and cool on a wire rack for at least 20 minutes.

Squash and 'buttermilk' cornbread

A combination of grated orange butternut squash and fine yellow cornmeal gives this cornbread a wonderful texture and vibrant golden colour. It's made with vegan buttermilk, which contrasts with the sweetness of the squash. It's a delicious accompaniment to soups and casseroles.

- 200g/7oz butternut squash, peeled and coarsely grated
- vegan 'buttermilk' (see below) made with 10ml/2 tsp lemon juice or vinegar and 250ml/9fl oz/1 cup rice milk or soya milk (see pages 44 or 43)
- 40g/1½oz/3 tbsp coconut oil or vegan 'buttery' spread (see page 72)
- 30ml/2 tbsp maple syrup
- 115g/4oz/⅔ cup fine yellow cornmeal
- 115g/4oz/1 cup plain/all-purpose flour, preferably unbleached
- 7.5ml/1½ tsp baking powder
- 2.5ml/½ tsp bicarbonate of soda/baking soda
- 2.5ml/½ tsp salt
- 5ml/1 tsp vegan powdered egg replacer
- 20ml/4 tsp warm water

SERVES 6–8

1 Preheat the oven to 200°C/400°F/Gas 6. Line a 20cm/8in round cake tin or pan with baking parchment and lightly grease.

2 Put the grated butternut squash in a pan and pour over the vegan buttermilk. Add the coconut oil or non-dairy spread, and maple syrup. Gently heat, stirring occasionally, until the fat has just melted. Turn off the heat.

3 Put the cornmeal, flour, baking powder, bicarbonate of soda and salt into a large bowl and mix together. Make a hollow in the middle. Blend the powdered egg replacer with the warm water and pour into the hollow with the warm milk and butternut squash mixture. Stir together to make a smooth, thick batter.

4 Pour and scrape the mixture into the prepared tin and spread evenly. Bake for 15–20 minutes or until golden and a skewer inserted into the middle comes out clean. Leave in the tin for 5 minutes, then turn out and cut into wedges. Serve warm.

Cook's tips

- Cornbread is best eaten on the day it is made. If that isn't possible, it can be frozen for up to a month, then allowed to defrost and gently warmed before serving.
- Instead of the vegan 'buttermilk', you can use a mixture of half non-dairy yogurt and half non-dairy milk.

Vegan 'buttermilk'

To make vegan buttermilk, put 20ml/4 tsp lemon juice, apple cider vinegar or white wine vinegar in a measuring jug. Add enough non-dairy milk (of your choosing) to reach the 450ml/¾ pint mark. Stir well, then leave to stand at room temperature for 4–5 minutes before using. Adjust the proportions to suit your recipe.

Nut pulp crackers

These simple crackers are made with the leftover pulp from making almond or other nut milks. Their light, delicate texture makes them ideal for serving with rich and creamy non-dairy cheeses. Make them plain, sprinkle with a little salt, or try the smoked paprika or dill versions for a change.

175g/6oz/1 cup damp almond pulp (left over from making almond milk, see page 28) or pulp from other nut milks
2.5ml/½ tsp baking powder
45ml/3 tbsp nutritional yeast flakes
30ml/2 tbsp ground flax seeds
pinch of ground black pepper
30ml/2 tbsp olive oil
sea salt crystals, for sprinkling

MAKES ABOUT 25

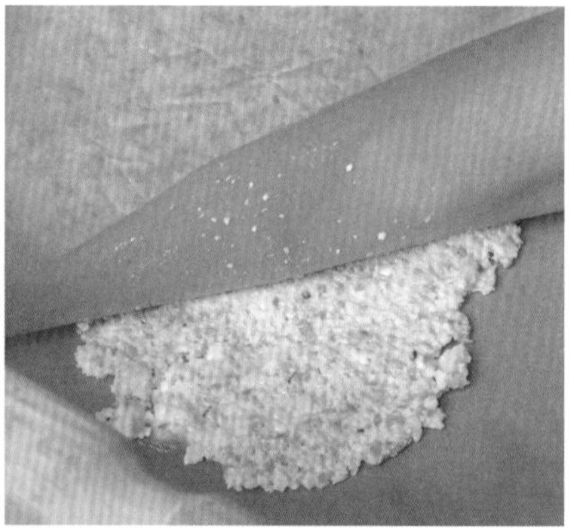

Cook's tips
• 175g/6oz/1 cup of almonds, blanched, soaked and made into almond milk should produce the same quantity of slightly damp nut pulp, which you can use immediately to make these crackers; there's no need to dry out the pulp first.
• Make sure the crackers are dry and crisp; they should just be starting to brown at the edges. Store them in an airtight container as soon as they are cool because they soften quickly.

1 Preheat the oven to 180°C/350°F/Gas 4. Line a baking sheet with baking parchment.

2 Put the almond pulp in a bowl and stir with a fork to break up any clumps. Sprinkle over the baking powder, nutritional yeast, flax seeds and black pepper. Stir with the fork to mix thoroughly (the nutritional yeast flakes will dissolve in the damp nut pulp).

3 Drizzle over the olive oil and stir again with the fork, then use your hands to bring the mixture together into a soft dough.

4 Roll out the dough between two sheets of baking parchment to about 3mm/⅛in thick. Gently prick the dough all over with a fork, then use a sharp knife to cut into 6cm/2½in squares.

5 Using a palette knife, carefully transfer the crackers to the prepared baking sheet. Sprinkle over a little sea salt, then bake the crackers for 5 minutes. Turn down the oven to 150°C/300°F/Gas 2 and bake for a further 15–20 minutes.

6 Leave on the baking sheet for 5 minutes, then transfer to a wire rack and leave to cool completely.

Variation
For smoked paprika crackers, sprinkle 5ml/1 tsp smoked paprika over the nut pulp before mixing. For dill crackers, add 5ml/1 tsp dried dill.

Cashew nut butter cookies

These dairy-free cookies are quick and easy to make and contain just a few ingredients. If you enjoy sneaking a spoonful of nut butter from the jar, you will love these! Half are plain, half are chocolatey. You can use any smooth nut butter you like here, so feel free to experiment.

225g/8oz/1 cup smooth cashew butter (see page 79)
30ml/2 tbsp maple syrup
10ml/2 tsp raw cacao powder or unsweetened cocoa powder
2.5ml/½ tsp icing/confectioners' sugar

MAKES 12

Variation
If liked, sandwich the cookies together in pairs with some chocolate hazelnut spread (see page 81). Beat the spread first to soften it.

1 Preheat the oven to 180°C/350°F/Gas 4. Line a baking sheet with baking parchment.

2 Put the cashew butter and maple syrup into a bowl and combine well with a spoon. Transfer half the nut mixture to a separate bowl and sift over 7.5ml/1½ tsp of the cacao or cocoa powder. Stir until blended.

3 Shape each batch of mixture into six walnut-sized balls. Flatten these slightly, then arrange on the baking sheet, spacing them slightly apart to allow room for the cookies to spread.

4 Bake for 5–7 minutes, until beginning to brown around the edges. Remove from the oven and allow to cool a little on the baking sheet.

5 Dust the plain ones with icing sugar and the chocolate ones with the remaining cacao or cocoa powder. These cookies can be stored in an airtight container for up to 4 days.

Peanut butter cookies

There are many versions of the well-known peanut butter cookie. These are dairy-free, and rolled in peanuts for a crunchier texture. They are very quick to bake, and will be eaten up in a trice but otherwise can be stored in an airtight container for up to 5 days.

250g/9oz/1 cup smooth peanut butter (see page 74)
115g/4oz/½ cup light muscovado (brown) sugar
5ml/1 tsp vegan powdered egg replacer
30ml/2 tbsp warm water
150g/5oz/1¼ cups self-raising/self-rising flour
2.5ml/½ tsp baking powder
175g/6oz/1½ cups raw unsalted skinned peanuts, chopped

MAKES 12

1 Preheat the oven to 180°C/350°F/Gas 4, and line a large baking sheet.

2 Put the peanut butter and sugar in a bowl and beat together until creamy. Mix the egg replacer with the warm water in a small bowl and blend well into the peanut butter mixture.

3 Sift over the flour and baking powder and stir everything together.

4 Put the chopped peanuts on a plate. Scoop up heaped teaspoons of the mixture and roll into balls (the mixture will be quite sticky, so chill for a few minutes first if necessary). Roll the balls in the chopped nuts and place them on the baking sheet, spacing well apart, and flatten slightly.

5 Bake for 8–10 minutes, or until lightly brown. Leave on the baking sheet for 5 minutes to firm up then transfer to a wire rack to cool.

Lemon and almond milk magdalenas

These simple oil-based cupcakes are often served at breakfast time with coffee in Spain, where they originate. They are always made with a mild-tasting olive oil rather than butter and contain an unusual combination of both lemon zest and vanilla.

200ml/7fl oz/scant 1 cup light almond milk (see page 29)
100ml/3½fl oz/scant ½ cup light olive oil
150g/5oz/¾ cup caster/superfine sugar
finely grated rind of 1 lemon
5ml/1 tsp vanilla extract
200g/7oz/generous 1⅔ cups self-raising/self-rising flour
5ml/1 tsp baking powder

MAKES 12

1 Preheat the oven to 180°C/350°F/Gas 4. Line a 12-cup tin or pan with paper cases.

2 Put the almond milk, olive oil, sugar, lemon rind and vanilla in a mixing bowl and beat together with an electric whisk or wooden spoon until well combined.

3 Sift the flour and baking powder together into a separate bowl. Slowly add the dry ingredients to the wet ingredients, beating continuously on a low speed or with the wooden spoon, until just combined.

4 Divide the mixture equally between the cupcake cases so that they are about three-quarters full. Bake for 18–20 minutes in the preheated oven, until a skewer inserted into the middle comes out clean. Leave the cakes to cool in the tin before serving.

Chocolate banana cupcakes

As well as being gluten and dairy free, these cupcakes are made without eggs, using ground flax seeds instead. They are sweetened primarily with bananas, so make sure you choose very ripe ones, with skins starting to turn black and very soft inside.

1 Preheat the oven to 180°C/350°F/Gas 4. Line a 12-cup tin or pan with paper cases.

2 Mash the bananas in a medium mixing bowl. Add the oil, maple syrup and coconut milk, then combine using a fork.

3 Mix all of the other ingredients together in a large mixing bowl. Add the wet ingredients to the dry ingredients and mix to combine, using a spoon, working quickly.

4 Spoon the batter into the cupcake cases so that they are about three-quarters full.

5 Bake for about 20 minutes in the middle of the oven, until they spring back when lightly pressed, and a skewer inserted into the middle comes out clean.

6 Remove the tin from the oven and place on a wire rack to cool before turning out and serving.

4 large, ripe bananas
150ml/¼ pint/⅔ cup sunflower oil
90ml/6 tbsp maple syrup
90ml/6 tbsp coconut milk (canned or see page 40)
115g/4oz/1 cup brown rice flour
75g/3oz/½ cup buckwheat flour
45ml/3 tbsp ground flax seeds/linseeds
35g/1½oz/¼ cup unsweetened cocoa powder
35g/1½oz/¼ cup carob powder
30ml/2 tbsp ground almonds
5ml/1 tsp bicarbonate of soda/baking soda
2.5ml/½ tsp ground cinnamon
2.5ml/½ tsp xanthan gum

MAKES 12

Sweet potato brownies

Brownies are traditionally made with lots of melted butter and sugar, whereas this healthier vegan version is made with steamed sweet potato and mashed banana, with just a few tablespoons of maple syrup. It also contains no flour so it's gluten free, too.

350g/12oz/2 small sweet potatoes, peeled and cut into small chunks
50g/2oz vegan dark chocolate, broken into pieces, plus extra, chopped, for topping (optional)
45ml/3 tbsp smooth peanut butter (see page 74)
45ml/3 tbsp coconut oil
45ml/3 tbsp maple syrup
1 large banana, peeled and broken into pieces
5ml/1 tsp vanilla extract
2.5ml/½ tsp ground cinnamon
15ml/1 tbsp vegan powdered egg replacer
90ml/6 tbsp warm water
50g/2oz/½ cup unsweetened cocoa powder
7.5ml/1½ tsp baking powder
50g/2oz/scant ⅓ cup Brazil nuts, roughly chopped

MAKES 12

Cook's tip

Starchy sweet potatoes are used here instead of flour. You can use steamed butternut squash instead but if you do so, you'll need to add 15ml/1 tbsp cornflour/cornstarch to the mixture with the cocoa and baking powder in step 5.

1 Preheat the oven to 180°C/350°F/Gas 4. Line a shallow 20cm/8in square cake tin or pan with a piece of baking parchment.

2 Cook the sweet potato in a steamer for 10–15 minutes, until just soft when pressed with a knife.

3 Meanwhile, put the chocolate and the peanut butter, oil and maple syrup in a small pan and heat gently, stirring, until the chocolate has melted and the mixture is smooth. Take off the heat.

4 Transfer the sweet potato to a food processor, add the banana, vanilla and cinnamon and blend until smooth. Mix the powdered egg replacer with the warm water, then gradually mix in a little at a time. Add the melted chocolate mixture and beat until smooth.

5 Mix the cocoa and baking powder together. Add to the food processor and blend again until smooth.

6 Spoon into the lined tin. Sprinkle over three-quarters of the nuts and spread level, then sprinkle with the rest of the nuts. Bake for 20–25 minutes, until well risen and cracked around the edges with a slightly soft middle. Put the tin on to a wire rack and sprinkle with the extra diced chocolate, if using. Leave to cool in the tin.

7 Lift the paper and brownies out of the tin, peel off the paper and cut into 12 bars. Store in the fridge for up to 3 days.

Chocolate cake

Everyone needs a go-to vegan chocolate cake. This is a light and airy cake with a rich non-dairy cream cheese and jam filling, and succulent dark chocolate sauce topping. The vinegar helps the cake to rise while the yogurt helps to moisten and bind. If you prefer a plainer cake, leave out the walnuts and citrus zests. It is a very versatile cake, good for dessert and for teatime.

For the cake
250g/9oz/2¼ cups wholemeal/wholewheat self-raising/self-rising flour
225g/8oz/1 cup soft light brown sugar
150ml/¼ pint/⅔ cup soya milk (see page 43)
120ml/4fl oz/½ cup rapeseed/canola oil, plus extra for greasing
115g/4oz/1 cup broken walnuts (optional)
grated rind of 2 oranges (optional)
30ml/2 tbsp of unsweetened cocoa powder
15ml/1 tbsp soya or almond yogurt (see page 52) or silken tofu
15ml/1 tbsp balsamic vinegar
pinch of salt
10ml/2 tsp carob powder
25g/1oz vegan dark chocolate

For the filling
60ml/4 tbsp vegan cream cheese
5ml/1 tsp finely grated lime rind (optional)
60ml/4 tbsp orange or apricot jam

For the chocolate sauce
75g/3oz vegan dark chocolate
15ml/1 tbsp agave syrup
250ml/9fl oz/1 cup soya cream

SERVES 8

1 Place all the ingredients for the cake mixture, apart from the chocolate, in a large bowl. Mix with a wooden spoon until they are thoroughly combined.

2 Coarsely grate or chop the chocolate, then stir it into the cake mixture until evenly distributed.

3 Preheat the oven to 180°C/350°F/Gas 4. Lightly oil two 20cm/8in deep cake tins or pans and line the bases with baking parchment. Spoon in the cake mixture, evenly between the two tins.

4 Bake the cakes in the oven for about 20–30 minutes or until a metal skewer inserted in the middle comes out clean.

5 Meanwhile, put the cream cheese for the filling into a bowl and mix in the grated lime rind if using. Set aside until ready to use.

6 When the cakes are baked turn them out on to a wire rack. Leave them to cool completely.

7 When the cakes are cool, spread the cream cheese evenly over one of the cakes. Spread the other with jam. Sandwich them together, with the two fillings facing each other, then place carefully on a serving plate.

8 Make the chocolate sauce. Break the chocolate into chunks and melt it in a bowl set over a pan of very hot (not boiling) water. Mix in the agave syrup, and then the soya cream, adding a little at a time while continuously stirring.

9 Pour the sauce over the cake and spread to cover. Leave to cool slightly, then serve with extra sauce alongside if you like.

Variations

• For a decadent dessert cake, add a tablespoon of orange liqueur to the sauce, or, for a Black Forest-style gâteau, use cherry jam and decorate with pitted fresh cherries.
• Instead of the sauce topping, you could decorate the cake with chocolate-flavoured frosting (see page 69).

Pear and cashew yogurt sponge

Thin slices of pear make an attractive fruity topping for this light sponge, which is flavoured with ginger and lime. You can either leave this to cool and serve it as a cake, or serve it while still warm as a dessert with creamy vanilla custard (see page 65) or a dollop of cashew yogurt.

175g/6oz/¾ cup light muscovado/brown sugar
120ml/4fl oz/½ cup sunflower oil, plus extra for greasing
finely grated rind of 1 lime
10ml/2 tsp vegan powdered egg replacer
60ml/4 tbsp warm water
120ml/4fl oz/½ cup cashew yogurt (see page 55)
175g/6oz/1½ cups plain/all-purpose flour
7.5ml/1½ tsp baking powder
7.5ml/1½ tsp ground ginger
3 firm ripe pears

MAKES 9

1 Grease a loose-bottomed 18cm/7in square tin or pan and line the base with baking parchment. Preheat the oven to 180°C/350°F/Gas 4.

2 Beat together the sugar, oil and lime rind in a bowl. Blend the egg replacer with the warm water, then add to the sugar and oil mixture, a third at a time, beating well after each addition. Stir in the yogurt. Sift the flour, baking powder and ginger over the mixture and fold in.

3 Halve the pears, then scoop out the cores with a teaspoon. Cut the pear halves into very thin slices. Working quickly (before they start to brown), arrange the slices on the bottom of the tin. Spoon the cake mixture over the sliced pears and level the top.

4 Bake for 40–45 minutes, or until golden brown and firm to the touch. Cover with foil towards the end of cooking if the top starts to brown too much. Leave to cool in the tin for 10 minutes before turning out and carefully removing the lining paper. Cut into 9 squares and serve warm.

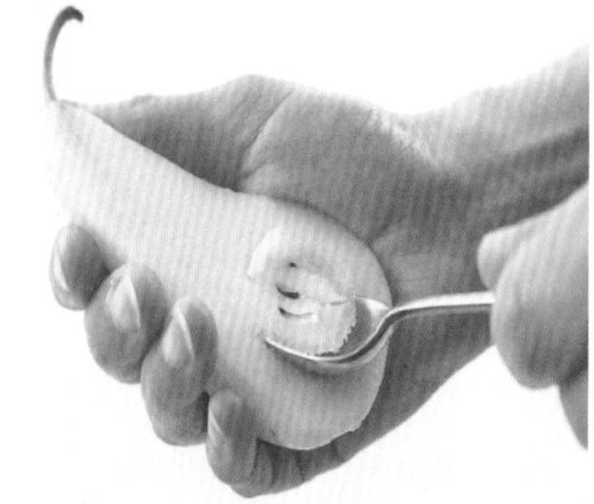

Mini Victoria sponges

These light and airy little vegan sponge cakes are perfect with mid-morning coffee or as a dainty treat for afternoon tea. Despite being low in fat and dairy free, they have a lovely moist texture and taste every bit as good as a traditional Victoria sponge.

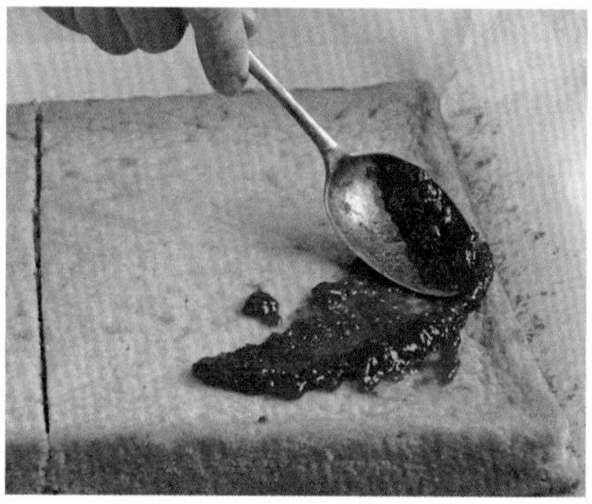

1 Preheat the oven to 180°C/350°F/Gas 4. Grease and line a 35 x 25cm/ 14 x 10in deep baking tin/pan with baking parchment.

2 Put the spread or margarine and sugar in a mixing bowl and whisk for about 5 minutes, until very light and creamy. It is important to whisk in as much air as possible as this will give lightness to the cake.

3 Sift together the flour, bicarbonate of soda and baking powder, then whisk into the creamed mixture. Add the milk, yogurt and vanilla, and stir to ensure everything is combined.

4 Spoon the mixture into the tin and bake for 25–30 minutes until the cake is firm and springs back to your touch and a knife comes out clean when inserted into the middle. Leave to cool.

5 Cut the cake in half so that you have two rectangles and spread jam over one. Place the second rectangle on top and cut into 24 squares. Dust with icing sugar to serve. Store for up to 2 days in an airtight container.

225g/8oz/1 cup 'buttery' spread (see page 72) or vegan margarine
225g/8oz/1 cup caster/superfine sugar
300g/10oz/2 cups self-raising/ self-rising flour
2.5ml/½ tsp bicarbonate of soda/ baking soda
1 tsp/5ml baking powder
120ml/4fl oz/½ cup rice milk or soya milk (see pages 44 or 43)
250ml/9fl oz/1 cup soya yogurt (see page 52)
1 tsp/5ml vanilla extract
4 tbsp/60ml fruity jam
icing/confectioners' sugar, for dusting

MAKES 24

Tropical fruit meringue cake

Once discarded as a waste product, the cooking liquid from a can of chickpeas has found recognition as a wonder ingredient dubbed aquafaba (or 'bean water'). It's the gloopy, creamy fibres of the beans, and in many recipes it acts similarly to egg whites.

1 Preheat the oven to 110°C/225°F/Gas ¼. Line three baking sheets with non-stick baking parchment and draw a 20cm/8in circle on each.

2 For the meringue, pour the chickpea liquid (aquafaba) into a large bowl and whisk for 7–8 minutes or until the mixture has doubled in volume and is white with soft peaks. Sprinkle over the cream of tartar, then slowly add the sugar, spoonful by spoonful, whisking continuously until the mixture is very thick with stiff peaks.

3 Spoon the mixture on to the trays, spreading out into circles according to the guide lines. Bake for 2½ hours, switching the baking sheets round after 1½ hours so the meringues cook evenly. Turn off the oven and leave the meringues to cool in the oven for 1 hour, then remove and leave to cool completely before carefully peeling away the baking parchment.

4 For the filling, add the water drained from one can of chickpeas into a large bowl and whisk for approximately 5 minutes until it's more than doubled in size, white and foamy. Add the cream of tartar and powdered vanilla and whisk again for another minute. Slowly start adding in the icing sugar, whisking until the mixture forms stiff, glossy peaks.

5 Carefully melt the cacao butter or white chocolate and coconut oil together, then slowly, a little at a time, whisk into the aquafaba mixture.

6 Put one meringue on to a serving plate, layer with half the filling and fruit, top with a second meringue, then spoon over the remaining filling and fruit. Top with the final meringue and dust with sugar before serving.

For the meringue
2 x 400g/14oz cans of chickpeas, liquid drained and saved
5ml/1 tsp cream of tartar
225g/8oz/1 cup plus 30ml/2 tbsp caster/superfine sugar
15ml/1 tbsp icing/confectioners' sugar, for dusting

For the filling
400g/14oz can of chickpeas, water drained and saved
2.5ml/½ tsp cream of tartar
2.5ml/½ tsp vanilla powder
115g/4oz/1 cup icing/confectioners' sugar
200g/7½oz cacao butter or vegan white chocolate
50g/2oz/¼ cup coconut oil
selection of tropical fruits, such as mango, papaya, passion fruit and kiwi, peeled and sliced

SERVES 8

Variation

For a raspberry meringue cake, use 450g/1lb/2½ cups fresh raspberries instead of the tropical fruits and omit the lime rind.

Cook's tip

Meringue made with aquafaba is not as stable as that made with regular meringue, so assemble it only when you are ready to serve.

Nutritional information

The nutritional analysis for each recipe is calculated per quantity or item, or per smaller serving. It does not include optional ingredient suggestions.

Cashew milk (800ml) Energy 507kcal/2121kJ; Protein 11.7g; Carbohydrate 44g, of which sugars 23g; Fat 35.3g, of which saturates 7g; Cholesterol 0mg; Calcium 0mg; Fibre 3.1g; Sodium 660mg.

Almond milk (800ml) Energy 100kcal/419kJ; Protein 3.3g; Carbohydrate 3.6g, of which sugars 0g; Fat 8.3g, of which saturates 0g; Cholesterol 0mg; Calcium 0mg; Fibre 4.4g; Sodium 533mg.

Light almond milk (800ml) Energy 133kcal/558kJ; Protein 3.3g; Carbohydrate 16.7g, of which sugars 16.7g; Fat 6.7g, of which saturates 0g; Cholesterol 0mg; Calcium 0mg; Fibre 0g; Sodium 533mg.

Hazelnut milk (800ml) Energy 440kcal/1842kJ; Protein 4.8g; Carbohydrate 52g, of which sugars 25.6g; Fat 22.4g, of which saturates 0g; Cholesterol 0mg; Calcium 0mg; Fibre 0g; Sodium 0mg.

Pecan milk (750ml) Energy 100kcal/419kJ; Protein 3.3g; Carbohydrate 3.6g, of which sugars 0g; Fat 8.3g, of which saturates 0g; Cholesterol 0mg; Calcium 0mg; Fibre 4.4g; Sodium 533mg.

Walnut milk (750ml) Energy 546kcal/2285kJ; Protein 12g; Carbohydrate 24g, of which sugars 0g; Fat 48g, of which saturates 6g; Cholesterol 30mg; Calcium 0mg; Fibre 8g; Sodium 363mg.

Macadamia milk (400ml) Energy 192kcal/804kJ; Protein 2.1g; Carbohydrate 3.7g, of which sugars 1.3g; Fat 20.3g, of which saturates 3.2g; Cholesterol 0mg; Calcium 0mg; Fibre 3g; Sodium 13mg.

Pistachio milk (400ml) Energy 349kcal/1451kJ; Protein 11.9g; Carbohydrate 16.1g, of which sugars 4.5g; Fat 26.8g, of which saturates 3.2g; Cholesterol 0mg; Calcium 0mg; Fibre 8.1g; Sodium 11mg.

Brazil nut milk (600ml) Energy 122kcal/512kJ; Protein 2.4g; Carbohydrate 16.8g, of which sugars 15.1g; Fat 7.2g, of which saturates 2.4g; Cholesterol 0mg; Calcium 0mg; Fibre 0g; Sodium 0mg.

Peanut milk (800ml) Energy 500kcal/2093kJ; Protein 20g; Carbohydrate 20g, of which sugars 0g; Fat 36.7g, of which saturates 0g; Cholesterol 0mg; Calcium 0mg; Fibre 0g; Sodium 0mg.

Chestnut milk (800ml) Energy 208kcal/864kJ; Protein 19.2g; Carbohydrate 4g, of which sugars 1.6g; Fat 12.8g, of which saturates 1.9g; Cholesterol 0mg; Calcium 104mg; Fibre 4g; Sodium 256mg.

Tiger nut milk (1.2 litres) Energy 188kcal/785kJ; Protein 3.1g; Carb 25g, of which sugars 0g; Fat 6.2g, of which saturates 0g; Cholesterol 0mg; Calcium 0mg; Fibre 0g; Sodium 0mg.

Pumpkin seed milk (400ml) Energy 71kcal/299kJ; Protein 14.4g; Carb 0g, of which sugars 0g; Fat 25.6g, of which saturates 0g; Cholesterol 0mg; Calcium 0mg; Fibre 1.6g; Sodium 0mg.

Sunflower seed milk (400ml) Energy 300kcal/1256kJ; Protein 10.4g; Carbohydrate 10.3g, of which sugars 1.5g; Fat 26.1g, of which saturates 2.2g; Cholesterol 0mg; Calcium 0mg; Fibre 5.8g; Sodium 15mg.

Hemp seed milk (500ml) Energy 501kcal/2090kJ; Protein 23.8g; Carbohydrate 28.5g, of which sugars 24.9g; Fat 33.2g, of which saturates 4.8g; Cholesterol 0mg; Calcium 95mg; Fibre 6.3g; Sodium 0mg.

Coconut milk and cream (250ml) Energy 301kcal/1251kJ; Protein 3.5g; Carbohydrate 13g, of which sugars 13g; Fat 26.5g, of which saturates 22.8g; Cholesterol 0mg; Calcium 59mg; Fibre 0g; Sodium 196mg.

Coconut flour (100g) Energy 443kcal/1854kJ; Protein 0g; Carbohydrate 63.3g, of which sugars 7.1g; Fat 15g, of which saturates 13.9g; Cholesterol 0mg; Calcium 0mg; Fibre 48.6g; Sodium 0mg.

Pea milk (800ml) Energy 313kcal/1308kJ; Protein 25g; Carbohydrate 18.8g, of which sugars 0g; Fat 15.6g, of which saturates 0g; Cholesterol 0mg; Calcium 0mg; Fibre 0g; Sodium 0mg.

Soya milk (1.2 litres) Energy 260kcal/1080kJ; Protein 24g; Carbohydrate 5g, of which sugars 2g; Fat 16g, of which saturates 2.4g; Cholesterol 0mg; Calcium 130mg; Fibre 5g; Sodium 320mg.

Rice milk (1.2 litres) 600kcal/2511kJ; Protein 1.2g; Carbohydrate 120g, of which sugars 0g; Fat 12g, of which saturates 0g; Cholesterol 0mg; Calcium 0mg; Fibre 0g; Sodium 0mg.

Oat milk (800ml) Energy 412kcal/1727kJ; Protein 1.5g; Carbohydrate 7.5g, of which sugars 36.2g; Fat 9g, of which saturates 0g; Cholesterol 0mg; Calcium 0mg; Fibre 0g; Sodium 0mg.

Cocoa flavoured milk (250ml) Energy 112kcal/465kJ; Protein 8.8g; Carbohydrate 3g, of which sugars 0.5g; Fat 7.3g, of which saturates 2.5g; Cholesterol 0mg; Calcium 52mg; Fibre 3.7g; Sodium 222mg.

Carob flavoured milk (250ml) Energy 88kcal/368kJ; Protein 7.4g; Carbohydrate 2.1g, of which sugars 0.5g; Fat 5.6g, of which saturates 1.6g; Cholesterol 0mg; Calcium 42mg; Fibre 2.5g; Sodium 151mg.

Goji berry flavoured milk (250ml) Energy 482kcal/390kJ; Protein 10.3g; Carbohydrate 23.8g, of which sugars 14.4g; Fat 4.3g, of which saturates 0.6g; Cholesterol 0mg; Calcium 32mg; Fibre 2g; Sodium 80mg.

Açai berry flavoured milk (250ml) Energy 134kcal/290kJ; Protein 6.7g; Carbohydrate 5g, of which sugars 2.8g; Fat 4g, of which saturates 0.6g; Cholesterol 0mg; Calcium 32mg; Fibre 1.4g; Sodium 80mg.

Chia seed flavoured milk (250ml) Energy 87kcal/364kJ; Protein 7g; Carbohydrate 1.5g, of which sugars 0.6g; Fat 5.8g, of which saturates 0.8g; Cholesterol 0mg; Calcium 58mg; Fibre 3.8g; Sodium 130mg.

Coconut water kefir (1 litre) Energy 373kcal/1561kJ; Protein 0g; Carbohydrate 67.8g, of which sugars 0g; Fat 0g, of which saturates 0g; Cholesterol 0mg; Calcium 0mg; Fibre 0g; Sodium 0mg.

Water kefir (900ml) Energy 144kcal/603kJ; Protein 0g; Carbohydrate 20.7g, of which sugars 0g; Fat 0g, of which saturates 0g; Cholesterol 0mg; Calcium 0mg; Fibre 0g; Sodium 0mg.

Soya milk yogurt (475ml) Energy 347kcal/1468kJ; Protein 10g; Carbohydrate 61.3g, of which sugars 57.5g; Fat 8.6g, of which saturates 1.4g; Cholesterol 0mg; Calcium 66mg; Fibre 3.3g; Sodium 114mg.

Coconut milk yogurt (400ml) Energy 107kcal/460kJ; Protein 1.3g; Carbohydrate 24.6g, of which sugars 24.2g; Fat 1.2g, of which saturates 0.8g; Cholesterol 0mg; Calcium 116mg; Fibre 0g; Sodium 446mg.

Cashew yogurt (300ml) Energy 228kcal/956kJ; Protein 4.6g; Carbohydrate 26.4g, of which sugars 17.8g; Fat 13.3g, of which saturates 2.6g; Cholesterol 0mg; Calcium 0mg; Fibre 1.2g; Sodium 260mg.

Simple nut cream (300ml) Energy 647kcal/2707kJ; Protein 21.6g; Carbohydrate 0g, of which sugars 0g; Fat 57.5g, of which saturates 7.2g; Cholesterol 0mg; Calcium 0mg; Fibre 0g; Sodium 0mg.

Cashew cream (500ml) Energy 967kcal/4046kJ; Protein 26.7g; Carbohydrate 57.3g, of which sugars 0g; Fat 76.7g, of which saturates 0g; Cholesterol 0mg; Calcium 0mg; Fibre 0g; Sodium 433mg.

Sour cream (200ml) Energy 731kcal/3055kJ; Protein 78.8g; Carbohydrate 40.8g, of which sugars 0.1g; Fat 34.4g, of which saturates 0.9g; Cholesterol 0mg; Calcium 577mg; Fibre 0g; Sodium 44mg.

Hollandaise sauce (200ml) Energy 433kcal/1795kJ; Protein 13.5g; Carbohydrate 13.8g, of which sugars 3.6g; Fat 36.4g, of which saturates 7.1g; Cholesterol 0mg; Calcium 26mg; Fibre 3.2g; Sodium 85mg.

Avocado mayo (250ml) Energy 416kcal/1720kJ; Protein 5.5g; Carbohydrate 9.2g, of which sugars 1.7g; Fat 39.9g, of which saturates 9.5g; Cholesterol 0mg; Calcium 29mg; Fibre 9.1g; Sodium 10mg.

Aioli (250ml) Energy 607kcal/2497kJ; Protein 0.7g; Carbohydrate 1g, of which sugars 0.8g; Fat 66.8g, of which saturates 9.5g; Cholesterol 0mg; Calcium 7mg; Fibre 0g; Sodium 1278mg.

Ranch dressing (250ml) Energy 846kcal/3498kJ; Protein 16.5g; Carb 28.2g, of which sugars 14.1g; Fat 75.1g, of which saturates 12.1g; Cholesterol 0mg; Calcium 131mg; Fibre 7g; Sodium 128mg.

Whipped coconut cream (150ml) Energy 88kcal/380kJ; Protein 1.2g; Carbohydrate 19.6g, of which sugars 19.6g; Fat 1.2g, of which saturates 0.8g; Cholesterol 0mg; Calcium 116mg; Fibre 0g; Sodium 440mg.

Vanilla custard (475ml) Energy 394kcal/1669kJ; Protein 11.2g; Carbohydrate 75g, of which sugars 32.2g; Fat 7.5g, of which saturates 1.1g; Cholesterol 0mg; Calcium 74mg; Fibre 2.3g; Sodium 169mg.

Warm chocolate sauce (250ml) Energy 1058kcal/4424kJ; Protein 17.2g; Carbohydrate 109g, of which sugars 103.7g; Fat 64.5g, of which saturates 41.4g; Cholesterol 5mg; Calcium 202mg; Fibre 10.6g; Sodium 393mg.

Butterscotch sauce (300ml) Energy 1713kcal/7176kJ; Protein 19.5g; Carbohydrate 156.9g, of which sugars 156.9g; Fat 112.1g, of which saturates 19g; Cholesterol 2mg; Calcium 46mg; Fibre 0g; Sodium 518mg.

Coconut dulce de leche (150ml) Energy 540kcal/2312kJ; Protein 1.3g; Carbohydrate 146.2g, of which sugars 146.2g; Fat 1.2g, of which saturates 0.8g; Cholesterol 0mg; Calcium 186mg; Fibre 0g; Sodium 479mg.

Coconut frosting Energy 655kcal/2747kJ; Protein 0.5g; Carbohydrate 94.8g, of which sugars 94.8g; Fat 33g, of which saturates 28.6g; Cholesterol 0mg; Calcium 30mg; Fibre 0g; Sodium 21mg.

'Buttery' spread (225g) Energy 1566kcal/6438kJ; Protein 1.8g; Carbohydrate 0.4g, of which sugars 0.1g; Fat 173g, of which saturates 132.6g; Cholesterol 0mg; Calcium 10mg; Fibre 0.4g; Sodium 1006mg.

Smooth peanut butter (450g) Energy 2732kcal/11313kJ; Protein 102.6g; Carbohydrate 59g, of which sugars 30.1g; Fat 233.1g, of which saturates 57.5g; Cholesterol 0mg; Calcium 166mg; Fibre 0g; Sodium 1575mg.

Crunchy peanut butter (450g) Energy 2727kcal/11300kJ; Protein 112g; Carbohydrate 34.6g, of which sugars 19.8g; Fat 238.9g, of which saturates 42.8g; Cholesterol 0mg; Calcium 212mg; Fibre 36g; Sodium 1665mg.

Almond butter (400g) Energy 2857kcal/11959kJ; Protein 100g; Carbohydrate 92.1g, of which sugars 0g; Fat 257.1g, of which saturates 28.6g; Cholesterol 0mg; Calcium 0mg; Fibre 76.2g; Sodium 0mg.

Cashew butter (400g) Energy 2350kcal/9836kJ; Protein 75g; Carbohydrate 107.5g, of which sugars 0g; Fat 200g, of which saturates 50g; Cholesterol 0mg; Calcium 0mg; Fibre 0g; Sodium 0mg.

Hazelnut butter (400g) Energy 2798kcal/11553kJ; Protein 56.4g; Carbohydrate 24g, of which sugars 16g; Fat 276g, of which saturates 20.8g; Cholesterol 0mg; Calcium 560mg; Fibre 34.7g; Sodium 24mg.

Chocolate hazelnut spread (500g) Energy 3344kcal/13943kJ; Protein 45.2g; Carbohydrate 281.5g, of which sugars 273.1g; Fat 234.4g, of which saturates 71.3g; Cholesterol 21mg; Calcium 393mg; Fibre 29.3g; Sodium 176mg.

Chestnut butter (400g) Energy 511kcal/2166kJ; Protein 5.1g; Carbohydrate 114.4g, of which sugars 40.4g; Fat 6.8g, of which saturates 1.2g; Cholesterol 0mg; Calcium 116mg; Fibre 13.7g; Sodium 31mg.

Coconut butter (250g) Energy 1510kcal/6230kJ; Protein 14g; Carbohydrate 16g, of which sugars 16g; Fat 155g, of which saturates 133.5g; Cholesterol 0mg; Calcium 58mg; Fibre 45.7g; Sodium 70mg.

Classic tahini (200g) Energy 1194kcal/4925kJ; Protein 27.3g; Carbohydrate 1.4g, of which sugars 0.6g; Fat 120g, of which saturates 20.4g; Cholesterol 0mg; Calcium 1005mg; Fibre 15.8g; Sodium 30mg.

Toasted tahini (175g) Energy 1095kcal/4517kJ; Protein 27.3g; Carbohydrate 1.4g, of which sugars 0.6g; Fat 108.9g, of which saturates 18.9g; Cholesterol 0mg; Calcium 1007mg; Fibre 15.8g; Sodium 30mg.

Sunflower seed butter (300g) Energy 1688kcal/7063kJ; Protein 56.2g; Carbohydrate 0g, of which sugars 0g; Fat 150g, of which saturates 18.8g; Cholesterol 0mg; Calcium 0mg; Fibre 0g; Sodium 0mg.

Pumpkin seed butter (300g) Energy 1905kcal/7893kJ; Protein 73.2g; Carbohydrate 45.6g, of which sugars 3.3g; Fat 158.8g, of which saturates 23.6g; Cholesterol 0mg; Calcium 117mg; Fibre 21.2g; Sodium 54mg.

Pine nut pesto (225ml) Energy 1083kcal/4461kJ; Protein 8.6g; Carbohydrate 4.5g, of which sugars 1.9g; Fat 114.6g, of which saturates 13.7g; Cholesterol 0mg; Calcium 130mg; Fibre 1.3g; Sodium 5mg.

Simple almond milk 'cheese' (350g) Energy 1371kcal/5668kJ; Protein 37.1g; Carbohydrate 12.8g, of which sugars 8.1g; Fat 130.6g, of which saturates 12.5g; Cholesterol 0mg; Calcium 423mg; Fibre 0.1g; Sodium 25mg.

Firm sesame seed 'cheese' (350g) Energy 1032kcal/4280kJ; Protein 50.5g; Carbohydrate 24.1g, of which sugars 1.4g; Fat 84.9g, of which saturates 13.4g; Cholesterol 0mg; Calcium 846mg; Fibre 39.8g; Sodium 43mg.

Firm smoked coconut 'cheese' (350g) Energy 1093kcal/4575kJ; Protein 32.2g; Carbohydrate 45.4g, of which sugars 0g; Fat 97.8g, of which saturates 0g; Cholesterol 0mg; Calcium 1mg; Fibre 25g; Sodium 1043mg.

Courgette 'cheese' loaf (550g) Energy 1019kcal/4244kJ; Protein 75.5g; Carbohydrate 65.4g, of which sugars 9.5g; Fat 54.5g, of which saturates 7.1g; Cholesterol 0mg; Calcium 142mg; Fibre 52.7g; Sodium 168mg.

Mozzarella-style 'cheese' for melting (350g) Energy 1172kcal/4861kJ; Protein 37.3g; Carbohydrate 58.7g, of which sugars 3.5g; Fat 90.9g, of which saturates 50.8g; Cholesterol 0mg; Calcium 61mg; Fibre 17.1g; Sodium 996mg.

Mozzarella-style 'cheese' for grating (250g) Energy 714kcal/2972kJ; Protein 39.9g; Carbohydrate 50g, of which sugars 0g; Fat 43.2g, of which saturates 28.5g; Cholesterol 0mg; Calcium 178mg; Fibre 8.9g; Sodium 548mg.

Tofu 'feta' (275g) Energy 1221kcal/5106kJ; Protein 139.3g; Carbohydrate 75.1g, of which sugars 0g; Fat 51.7g, of which saturates 0.9g; Cholesterol 0mg; Calcium 908mg; Fibre 8.8g; Sodium 0mg.

'Labneh' cheese balls (makes 12) Energy 563kcal/2358kJ; Protein 10.5g; Carbohydrate 64.5g, of which sugars 60.5g; Fat 31g, of which saturates 4.6g; Cholesterol 0mg; Calcium 70mg; Fibre 3.5g; Sodium 1102mg.

White bean 'cheese' sauce (400ml) Energy 561kcal/2355kJ; Protein 61.1g; Carbohydrate 58.8g, of which sugars 1.7g; Fat 13.5g, of which saturates 5.8g; Cholesterol 0mg; Calcium 146mg; Fibre 39.3g; Sodium 775mg.

Carrot and potato 'cheese' sauce (350ml) Energy 782kcal/3254kJ; Protein 34.7g; Carbohydrate 63.4g, of which sugars 11.1g; Fat 47.3g, of which saturates 6.6g; Cholesterol 66mg; Calcium 41mg; Fibre 23.9g; Sodium 1033mg.

Soft fermented cashew nut 'cheese' (350g) 1432kcal/5935kJ; Protein 44.2g; Carbohydrate 45.2g, of which sugars 11.5g; Fat 120.5g, of which saturates 23.8g; Cholesterol 0mg; Calcium 80mg; Fibre 10.7g; Sodium 1020mg.

Matured fermented cashew nut 'cheese' (450g) Energy 1481kcal/ 6139kJ; Protein 51.8g; Carbohydrate 50.7g, of which sugars 11.5g; Fat 120.9g, of which saturates 23.7g; Cholesterol 0mg; Calcium 81mg; Fibre 15g; Sodium 2983mg.

Soft fermented macadamia 'cheese' (350g) Energy 2098kcal/ 8782kJ; Protein 17.9g; Carbohydrate 35.7g, of which sugars 0g; Fat 223.2g, of which saturates 0g; Cholesterol 0mg; Calcium 0mg; Fibre 0g; Sodium 982mg.

Soft fermented almond 'cheese' (350g) Energy 1530kcal/6335kJ; Protein 52.8g; Carbohydrate 17.2g, of which sugars 10.5g; Fat 139.5g, of which saturates 11.1g; Cholesterol 0mg; Calcium 600mg; Fibre 0g; Sodium 1018mg.

Matured fermented almond 'cheese' (350g) Energy 1545kcal/6400kJ; Protein 54g; Carbohydrate 20.7g, of which sugars 12.9g; Fat 139.3g, of which saturates 11.1g; Cholesterol 0mg; Calcium 600mg; Fibre 0.7g; Sodium 2984mg.

Garlic and herb fermented 'cheese' roll (350g) Energy 1560kcal/6470kJ; Protein 60.6g; Carbohydrate 60.4g, of which sugars 11.7g; Fat 122.2g, of which saturates 23.7g; Cholesterol 0mg; Calcium 139mg; Fibre 20.1g; Sodium 1021mg.

Paprika and tomato fermented 'cheese' balls (makes 12) Energy 205kcal/ 859kJ; Protein 2.6g; Carbohydrate 4.4g, of which sugars 0.1g; Fat 21g, of which saturates 0.3g; Cholesterol 0mg; Calcium 5mg; Fibre 0.4g; Sodium 124mg.

Savoury 'cheesy' sprinkles (seedy) (175g) Energy 939kcal/3902kJ; Protein 50.2g; Carb 44.3g, of which sugars 2.2g; Fat 64.8g, of which saturates 8.7g; Cholesterol 0mg; Calcium 161mg; Fibre 23.6g; Sodium 990mg.

Savoury 'cheesy' sprinkles (nutty) (175g) Energy 1209kcal/5018kJ; Protein 61.6g; Carb 53.8g, of which sugars 8g; Fat 86.8g, of which saturates 16.6g; Cholesterol 0mg; Calcium 56mg; Fibre 25.1g; Sodium 1009mg.

Coconut milk and quinoa porridge (serves 6) Energy 129kcal/543kJ; Protein 4.5g; Carb 25.3g, of which sugars 6.1g; Fat 1.7g, of which saturates 0.2g; Cholesterol 0mg; Calcium 37mg; Fibre 1g; Sodium 114mg.

Multigrain banana berry porridge (serves 6) Energy 52kcal/218kJ; Protein 2.1g; Carbohydrate 8.8g, of which sugars 3.6g; Fat 1.1g, of which saturates 0.1g; Cholesterol 0mg; Calcium 8mg; Fibre 0.8g; Sodium 15mg.

Multi-grain mix (5 portions) Energy 156kcal/658kJ; Protein 5.3g; Carbohydrate 28.7g, of which sugars 0g; Fat 2.9g, of which saturates 0g; Cholesterol 0mg; Calcium 16mg; Fibre 2.7g; Sodium 10mg.

Overnight oats with yogurt (berry) (serves 2) Energy 576kcal/ 2420kJ; Protein 16g; Carb 73.2g, of which sugars 26.2g; Fat 26.2g, of which saturates 1.8g; Chol 0mg; Calcium 93mg; Fibre 13.8g; Sodium 86.5mg.

Overnight oats with non-dairy yogurt (mango and chia) (serves 2) Energy 583.5kcal/2453kJ; Protein 16g; Carbohydrate 75.2g, of which sugars 28.3g; Fat 26.3g, of which saturates 1.8; Cholesterol 0mg; Calcium 92mg; Fibre 14.4g; Sodium 85.5mg.

Overnight oats with non-dairy yogurt (banana, cacao and coconut) (serves 2) Energy 599.5kcal/2518kJ; Protein 16.8g; Carbohydrate 76g, of which sugars 28.7; Fat 27.4g, of which saturates 2.3g; Cholesterol 0mg; Calcium 96.5mg; Fibre 14.2g; Sodium 131mg.

Overnight oats with non-dairy yogurt (kiwi and grape) (serves 2) Energy 579.5kcal/2436kJ; Protein 16g; Carbohydrate 74g, of which sugars 27.2g; Fat 26.4g, of which saturates 1.8g; Cholesterol 0mg; Calcium 93.5mg; Fibre 13.8g; Sodium 85.5mg.

Overnight oats with non-dairy yogurt (strawberry and raspberry) (serves 2) Energy 576.5kcal/2423kJ; Protein 16g; Carbohydrate 73.3g, of which sugars 26.5g; Fat 26.4g, of which saturates 1.8g; Cholesterol 0mg; Calcium 94mg; Fibre 14g; Sodium 86.5mg.

Fruity rice milk and buckwheat bowl (serves 3) Energy 333kcal/1402kJ; Protein 5.4g; Carbohydrate 56.6g, of which sugars 31.2g; Fat 3g, of which saturates 0g; Cholesterol 0mg; Calcium 32mg; Fibre 4.9g; Sodium 6mg.

Drop scones (makes 16) Energy 68kcal/288kJ; Protein 1.2g; Carbohydrate 14.1g, of which sugars 3.2g; Fat 1.1g, of which saturates 0.1g; Cholesterol 0mg; Calcium 45mg; Fibre 0.6g; Sodium 46mg.

Date double-deckers (makes 12) Energy 229kcal/960kJ; Protein 4.7g; Carbohydrate 31.6g, of which sugars 15.8g; Fat 10.1g, of which saturates 5g; Cholesterol 0mg; Calcium 20mg; Fibre 2.3g; Sodium 48mg.

Cranberry and apple muesli bars (makes 12) Energy 97kcal/410kJ; Protein 2.5g; Carbohydrate 15.9g, of which sugars 8.6g; Fat 3g, of which saturates 0.3g; Cholesterol 0mg; Calcium 20mg; Fibre 2.6g; Sodium 26mg.

Sugar-free muesli (350g) Energy 1755kcal/7374kJ; Protein 60.9g; Carbohydrate 233.3g, of which sugars 1.4g; Fat 70g, of which saturates 6.8g; Cholesterol 0mg; Calcium 212mg; Fibre 30.2g; Sodium 93mg.

Mushroom muffins (makes 6) Energy 400kcal/1666kJ; Protein 6.7g; Carbohydrate 34.1g, of which sugars 1.2g; Fat 27.2g, of which saturates 3.7g; Cholesterol 0mg; Calcium 93mg; Fibre 2.5g; Sodium 389mg.

Apricot bran muffins (makes 12) Energy 126kcal/534kJ; Protein 3g; Carbohydrate 23.4g, of which sugars 8.4g; Fat 2.9g, of which saturates 0.5g; Cholesterol 0mg; Calcium 80mg; Fibre 3.7g; Sodium 101mg.

Pecan milk and pear milkshake (serves 2) Energy 140kcal/594kJ; Protein 1.6g; Carbohydrate 30.1g, of which sugars 29.1g; Fat 2.4g, of which saturates 0g; Cholesterol 0mg; Calcium 15mg; Fibre 5.1g; Sodium 197mg.

Creamy coconut and hazelnut smoothie (serves 2) Energy 549kcal/2275kJ; Protein 9.3g; Carbohydrate 17.3g, of which sugars 16.1g; Fat 49.8g, of which saturates 20.3g; Cholesterol 0mg; Calcium 106mg; Fibre 3.9g; Sodium 149mg.

Brown rice and almond drink (serves 4) Energy 87kcal/368kJ; Protein 0.8g; Carbohydrate 19.5g, of which sugars 0g; Fat 1.1g, of which saturates 0g; Cholesterol 0mg; Calcium 0mg; Fibre 0g; Sodium 0mg.

Hot chocolate (serves 4) Energy 381kcal/1596kJ; Protein 3g; Carbohydrate 55.4g, of which sugars 31.3g; Fat 17.4g, of which saturates 8.4g; Cholesterol 3mg; Calcium 17mg; Fibre 1.7g; Sodium 3mg.

Turmeric almond milk latte chai (serves 4) Energy 48kcal/204kJ; Protein 0.4g; Carbohydrate 10.7g, of which sugars 10.7g; Fat 0.7g, of which saturates 0g; Cholesterol 0mg; Calcium 2mg; Fibre 0g; Sodium 89mg.

Coconut milk golden soup (serves 4) Energy 205kcal/858kJ; Protein 4.9g; Carbohydrate 19.3g, of which sugars 13.1g; Fat 12.4g, of which saturates 1.7g; Cholesterol 0mg; Calcium 76mg; Fibre 5.7g; Sodium 200mg.

Mushroom and hemp milk soup (serves 4) Energy 124kcal/515kJ; Protein 6.2g; Carbohydrate 5.8g, of which sugars 5g; Fat 8.6g, of which saturates 1.2g; Cholesterol 0mg; Calcium 28mg; Fibre 3.1g; Sodium 8mg.

Curried cauliflower and cashew milk soup (serves 4) Energy 197kcal/823kJ; Protein 10.1g; Carbohydrate 17.6g, of which sugars 10.1g; Fat 10.5g, of which saturates 2g; Cholesterol 0mg; Calcium 68mg; Fibre 5.2g; Sodium 175mg.

Aubergine dip with tahini-almond yogurt (serves 4) Energy 71kcal/298kJ; Protein 3g; Carbohydrate 4.8g, of which sugars 4.4g; Fat 4.6g, of which saturates 0.7g; Cholesterol 0mg; Calcium 17mg; Fibre 4.1g; Sodium 6mg.

Mini baked potatoes with 'blue cheese' (20) Energy 78kcal/328kJ; Protein 5.8g; Carb 10.8g, of which sugars 0.7g; Fat 1.8g, of which saturates 0.1g; Cholesterol 17mg; Calcium 37mg; Fibre 0.9g; Sodium 33mg.

Courgette and 'feta' fritters (serves 4) Energy 318kcal/1328kJ; Protein 24.2g; Carbohydrate 25.3g, of which sugars 3.4g; Fat 15.1g, of which saturates 1.1g; Cholesterol 0mg; Calcium 171mg; Fibre 3.7g; Sodium 10mg.

Fried 'mozzarella' sticks (makes 20) Energy 106kcal/442kJ; Protein 4.3g; Carbohydrate 10.9g, of which sugars 0.2g; Fat 5.5g, of which saturates 2.5g; Cholesterol 0mg; Calcium 27mg; Fibre 1.2g; Sodium 80mg.

'Cheesy' nachos bake with guacamole (serves 6) Energy 418kcal/1747kJ; Protein 12g; Carbohydrate 37.5g, of which sugars 4.6g; Fat 25.9g, of which saturates 7.7g; Cholesterol 0mg; Calcium 114mg; Fibre 10.5g; Sodium 525mg.

'Cheese' and tomato quesadillas (serves 4) Energy 599kcal/2514kJ; Protein 18.1g; Carbohydrate 79.1g, of which sugars 5.6g; Fat 26g, of which saturates 14g; Cholesterol 0mg; Calcium 132mg; Fibre 9.3g; Sodium 566mg.

Chicory avocado salad with tofu cream (serves 4) Energy 443kcal/ 1826kJ; Protein 12g; Carbohydrate 3.5g, of which sugars 2g; Fat 42.3g, of which saturates 6.9g; Cholesterol 0mg; Calcium 484mg; Fibre 5.1g; Sodium 97mg.

Creamy slaw salad with vegan mayo (serves 4) Energy 127kcal/531kJ; Protein 2.1g; Carbohydrate 14.8g, of which sugars 6.5g; Fat 7g, of which saturates 1g; Cholesterol 0mg; Calcium 69mg; Fibre 7.3g; Sodium 228mg.

Margherita pizza (serves 4) Energy 589kcal/2477kJ; Protein 18.7g; Carbohydrate 83.4g, of which sugars 4.4g; Fat 23g, of which saturates 8.9g; Cholesterol 0mg; Calcium 173mg; Fibre 7.2g; Sodium 146mg.

Grilled 'cheese' polenta with mushrooms (serves 4) Energy 729kcal/3037kJ; Protein 24.1g; Carbohydrate 77.1g, of which sugars 7.5g; Fat 30.3g, of which saturates 12.9g; Cholesterol 0mg; Calcium 100mg; Fibre 6.7g; Sodium 228mg.

Leek and 'feta' tart (serves 4) Energy 844kcal/3522kJ; Protein 54.1g; Carbohydrate 62.8g, of which sugars 3.1g; Fat 46.5g, of which saturates 5.5g; Cholesterol 1mg; Calcium 434mg; Fibre 6.4g; Sodium 264mg.

Macaroni 'cheese' (serves 4) Energy 797kcal/3349kJ; Protein 26.5g; Carbohydrate 106.7g, of which sugars 10.7g; Fat 33.7g, of which saturates 6g; Cholesterol 0mg; Calcium 98mg; Fibre 8g; Sodium 413mg.

Vegetable moussaka with tofu topping (serves 8) Energy 348kcal/1451kJ; Protein 26.8g; Carbohydrate 22.2g, of which sugars 10.3g; Fat 18.8g, of which saturates 1.4g; Cholesterol 0mg; Calcium 222mg; Fibre 5.3g; Sodium 350mg.

Vegetable and almond milk lasagne (serves 6) Energy 374kcal/1563kJ; Protein 8g; Carbohydrate 46g, of which sugars 10.1g; Fat 18.5g, of which saturates 2.7g; Cholesterol 0mg; Calcium 76mg; Fibre 6.2g; Sodium 112mg.

Courgetti with dairy-free pesto (serves 4) Energy 348kcal/1436kJ; Protein 6.7g; Carbohydrate 13.9g, of which sugars 5.6g; Fat 29.7g, of which saturates 3.7g; Cholesterol 17mg; Calcium 92mg; Fibre 4g; Sodium 16mg.

Pasta with a creamy nut-mushroom sauce (serves 4) Energy 516kcal/2157kJ; Protein 15.8g; Carbohydrate 45.2g, of which sugars 7g; Fat 28.7g, of which saturates 4.3g; Cholesterol 0mg; Calcium 62mg; Fibre 4.8g; Sodium 19mg.

Creamy carbonara with smoked carrot 'bacon' (serves 4) Energy 701kcal/2952kJ; Protein 50.6g; Carbohydrate 91.3g, of which sugars 7.4g; Fat 19.9g, of which saturates 1.2g; Cholesterol 0mg; Calcium 269mg; Fibre 10.6g; Sodium 112mg.

Courgettes stuffed with tofu 'feta' (serves 4) Energy 605kcal/ 2512kJ; Protein 25.8g; Carbohydrate 56.9g, of which sugars 11.8g; Fat 31.5g, of which saturates 2.4g; Cholesterol 0mg; Calcium 196mg; Fibre 7.7g; Sodium 9mg.

Creamy 'paneer' curry (serves 4) Energy 553kcal/2313kJ; Protein 28.9g; Carbohydrate 40.9g, of which sugars 1.7g; Fat 34.5g, of which saturates 1.2g; Cholesterol 21mg; Calcium 169mg; Fibre 6.8g; Sodium 266mg.00g; Sodium 00mg.

Instant banana ice cream (serves 4) Energy 101kcal/429kJ; Protein 1.2g; Carbohydrate 24.4g, of which sugars 20.9g; Fat 0.5g, of which saturates 0.1g; Cholesterol 0mg; Calcium 6mg; Fibre 1.5g; Sodium 1mg.

Chocolate avocado ice cream (serves 6) Energy 364kcal/1516kJ; Protein 4.4g; Carbohydrate 17g, of which sugars 10.8g; Fat 32.7g, of which saturates 9.7g; Cholesterol 0mg; Calcium 25mg; Fibre 4.6g; Sodium 78mg.

Coconut milk ice cream (serves 6) Energy 229kcal/964kJ; Protein 1.6g; Carbohydrate 24g, of which sugars 20g; Fat 16g, of which saturates 0g; Cholesterol 0mg; Calcium 6mg; Fibre 2g; Sodium 11mg.

Strawberry soya milk and tofu ice cream (serves 8) Energy 321kcal/1343kJ; Protein 29.8g; Carbohydrate 28.1g, of which sugars 10.8g; Fat 12.5g, of which saturates 0.3g; Cholesterol 0mg; Calcium 223mg; Fibre 0.7g; Sodium 22mg.

Pistachio ice cream (serves 4) Energy 266kcal/1103kJ; Protein 5.1g; Carbohydrate 15g, of which sugars 4.6g; Fat 21g, of which saturates 12.2g; Cholesterol 0mg; Calcium 6mg; Fibre 2.4g; Sodium 9mg.

Wafer ice cream cones (makes 6) Energy 49kcal/206kJ; Protein 0.4g; Carbohydrate 5.8g, of which sugars 2.7g; Fat 2.9g, of which saturates 1.8g; Cholesterol 0mg; Calcium 24mg; Fibre 0.2g; Sodium 210mg.

Raspberry ripple creamsicles (makes 6) Energy 205kcal/855kJ; Protein 4.1g; Carbohydrate 16.1g, of which sugars 15.8g; Fat 14.3g, of which saturates 6.8g; Cholesterol 0mg; Calcium 43mg; Fibre 1.1g; Sodium 5mg.

Choc ices (makes 8) Energy 357kcal/1481kJ; Protein 5.1g; Carbohydrate 12.9g, of which sugars 5.4g; Fat 32.9g, of which saturates 9.6g; Cholesterol 0mg; Calcium 19mg; Fibre 3.1g; Sodium 73mg.

Mango and lime whip (serves 4) Energy 81kcal/346kJ; Protein 1.2g; Carbohydrate 14.4g, of which sugars 14.1g; Fat 2.6g, of which saturates 2g; Cholesterol 0mg; Calcium 21mg; Fibre 2.7g; Sodium 40mg.

Chocolate and hazelnut mousse (serves 4) Energy 370kcal/1531kJ; Protein 3.8g; Carbohydrate 15.6g, of which sugars 13.3g; Fat 32.8g, of which saturates 21.7g; Cholesterol 1mg; Calcium 23mg; Fibre 2.4g; Sodium 98mg.

White chocolate and strawberry parfaits (serves 6) Energy 604kcal/2504kJ; Protein 11g; Carbohydrate 50.1g, of which sugars 22.3g; Fat 41.7g, of which saturates 14.3g; Cholesterol 1mg; Calcium 83mg; Fibre 17.4g; Sodium 26mg.

Crème caramels (serves 6) Energy 95kcal/404kJ; Protein 0.5g; Carbohydrate 22.9g, of which sugars 18g; Fat 0.8g, of which saturates 0g; Cholesterol 0mg; Calcium 8mg; Fibre 0g; Sodium 65mg.

Chocolate cashew 'cheesecake' (serves 6) Energy 955kcal/3956kJ; Protein 20.4g; Carbohydrate 38.3g, of which sugars 17.8g; Fat 81.1g, of which saturates 39.4g; Cholesterol 0mg; Calcium 137mg; Fibre 12.3g; Sodium 308mg.

Tofu berry 'cheesecake' (serves 6) Energy 454kcal/1903kJ; Protein 35.3g; Carbohydrate 43.5g, of which sugars 17.4g; Fat 18.7g, of which saturates 4.6g; Cholesterol 0mg; Calcium 255mg; Fibre 3.7g; Sodium 202mg.

Creamy pumpkin pie (serves 8) Energy 533kcal/2237kJ; Protein 24.9g; Carbohydrate 67g, of which sugars 36.7g; Fat 21.5g, of which saturates 1.1g; Cholesterol 0mg; Calcium 188mg; Fibre 4.7g; Sodium 7mg.

Creamy peach tart (serves 9) Energy 312kcal/1294kJ; Protein 4.5g; Carbohydrate 17.6g, of which sugars 17.3g; Fat 25.3g, of which saturates 15.2g; Cholesterol 0mg; Calcium 29mg; Fibre 5.3g; Sodium 8mg.

Coconut milk rice pudding with oranges (serves 6) Energy 318kcal/1331kJ; Protein 6.2g; Carbohydrate 28.8g, of which sugars 3.6g; Fat 21.5g, of which saturates 0.2g; Cholesterol 0mg; Calcium 34mg; Fibre 3.8g; Sodium 41mg.

Rhubarb and almond crumble (serves 4) Energy 704kcal/2951kJ; Protein 11.3g; Carbohydrate 82.3g, of which sugars 39.6g; Fat 39.4g, of which saturates 21.1g; Cholesterol 0mg; Calcium 212mg; Fibre 6.3g; Sodium 163mg.

Vegan vanilla fudge (makes 49) Energy 73kcal/309kJ; Protein 0.6g; Carbohydrate 13.2g, of which sugars 13.2g; Fat 2.3g, of which saturates 0.8g; Cholesterol 2mg; Calcium 22mg; Fibre 0g; Sodium 23mg.

Vegan chocolate fudge (makes 49) Energy 84kcal/352kJ; Protein 0.7g; Carbohydrate 14.5g, of which sugars 14.5g; Fat 2.9g, of which saturates 1.1g; Cholesterol 3mg; Calcium 22mg; Fibre 0.1g; Sodium 24mg.

Vegan liqueur chocolate fudge (makes 49) Energy 74kcal/312kJ; Protein 0.6g; Carbohydrate 13.2g, of which sugars 13.2g; Fat 2.3g, of which saturates 0.8g; Cholesterol 2mg; Calcium 22mg; Fibre 0g; Sodium 23mg.

Vegan fruit fudge (49) Energy 75kcal /315kJ; Protein 0.6g; Carb 13.6g, of which sugars 13.6g; Fat 2.4g, of which saturates 0.8g; Cholesterol 2mg; Calcium 22mg; Fibre 0g; Sodium 24mg.

Vegan ginger fudge (makes 49) Energy 74kcal/314kJ; Protein 0.6g; Carbohydrate 13.5g, of which sugars 13.5g; Fat 2.4g, of which saturates 0.8g; Cholesterol 2mg; Calcium 22mg; Fibre 0g; Sodium 24mg.

Chocolate coconut truffles (makes 20) Energy 167kcal/697kJ; Protein 2.4g; Carbs 14.4g, of which sugars 14.4g; Fat 11.5g, of which saturates 8.9g; Cholesterol 6mg; Calcium 52mg; Fibre 2.5g; Sodium 26mg.

Coconut ginger truffles (makes 20) Energy 169kcal/706kJ; Protein 2.4g; Carbohydrate 15g, of which sugars 15g; Fat 11.5g, of which saturates 8.9g; Cholesterol 6mg; Calcium 52mg; Fibre 2.5g; Sodium 28mg.

Coconut pistachio truffles (makes 20) Energy 175kcal/728kJ; Protein 2.7g; Carbohydrate 14.5g, of which sugars 14.4g; Fat 12.2g, of which saturates 9g; Cholesterol 6mg; Calcium 53mg; Fibre 2.6g; Sodium 33mg.

Coconut lime truffles (makes 20) Energy 167kcal/697kJ; Protein 2.4g; Carbohydrate 14.5g, of which sugars 14.4g; Fat 11.5g, of which saturates 8.9g; Cholesterol 6mg; Calcium 52mg; Fibre 2.5g; Sodium 26mg.

Berry and mint yogurt treats (makes 20) Energy 94kcal/393kJ; Protein 3.1g; Carbohydrate 9.1g, of which sugars 1.8g; Fat 5.3g, of which saturates 0.9g; Cholesterol 0mg; Calcium 17mg; Fibre 1.9g; Sodium 35mg.

Espresso power balls (makes 20) Energy 90kcal/377kJ; Protein 2.1g; Carbohydrate 11.5g, of which sugars 5.8g; Fat 4.2g, of which saturates 1.3g; Cholesterol 0mg; Calcium 20mg; Fibre 2.5g; Sodium 26mg.

Brown scones with oat milk (makes 8) Energy 116kcal/492kJ; Protein 3.2g; Carbohydrate 20.5g, of which sugars 2.6g; Fat 1g, of which saturates 0.1g; Cholesterol 0mg; Calcium 56mg; Fibre 2.3g; Sodium 126mg.

'Buttermilk' soda bread (1 loaf) Energy 2239kcal/9504kJ; Protein 74.5g; Carb 428g, of which sugars 33.8g; Fat 17.6g, of which saturates 1.7g; Cholesterol 0mg; Calcium 416mg; Fibre 61.2g; Sodium 19mg.

Sunflower milk seeded spelt bread (makes 1 loaf) Energy 293kcal/1225kJ; Protein 10.7g; Carbohydrate 48.1g, of which sugars 8.1g; Fat 7.5g, of which saturates 0.6g; Cholesterol 0mg; Calcium 9mg; Fibre 0.9g; Sodium 493mg.

Squash and 'buttermilk' cornbread (serves 8) Energy 197kcal/824kJ; Protein 3.1g; Carb 26.8g, of which sugars 6.3g; Fat 6.4g, of which saturates 4.4g; Cholesterol 0mg; Calcium 35mg; Fibre 1.6g; Sodium 125mg.

Nut pulp crackers (makes 25) Energy 63kcal/261kJ; Protein 2.7g; Carbohydrate 1.6g, of which sugars 0.3g; Fat 5.2g, of which saturates 0.5g; Cholesterol 0mg; Calcium 17mg; Fibre 1g; Sodium 5mg.

Cashew nut butter cookies (makes 12) Energy 119kcal/499kJ; Protein 3.7g; Carbohydrate 6.8g, of which sugars 1.5g; Fat 9.6g, of which saturates 2.5g; Cholesterol 0mg; Calcium 3mg; Fibre 0.1g; Sodium 8mg.

Peanut butter cookies (makes 12) Energy 299kcal/1246kJ; Protein 7.7g; Carbohydrate 22.6g, of which sugars 11.7g; Fat 20.3g, of which saturates 4.3g; Cholesterol 19mg; Calcium 64mg; Fibre 0.5g; Sodium 176mg.

Lemon and almond milk magdalenas (makes 12) Energy 157kcal/660kJ; Protein 1.6g; Carbohydrate 26g, of which sugars 13.6g; Fat 5.8g, of which saturates 0.8g; Cholesterol 0mg; Calcium 62mg; Fibre 0.7g; Sodium 72mg.

Chocolate banana cupcakes (makes 12) Energy 238kcal/993kJ; Protein 3.9g; Carbohydrate 28g, of which sugars 12.1g; Fat 12.4g, of which saturates 2g; Cholesterol 0mg; Calcium 27mg; Fibre 3.4g; Sodium 77mg.

Sweet potato brownies (makes 12) Energy 176kcal/734kJ; Protein 4.8g; Carbohydrate 14.4g, of which sugars 8.6g; Fat 11.4g, of which saturates 5.3g; Cholesterol 58mg; Calcium 34mg; Fibre 2.1g; Sodium 86mg.

Chocolate cake (serves 8) Energy 441kcal/1848kJ; Protein 6.6g; Carbohydrate 56.4g, of which sugars 32.4g; Fat 22.5g, of which saturates 3.5g; Cholesterol 0mg; Calcium 141mg; Fibre 3g; Sodium 169mg.

Pear and cashew yogurt sponges (makes 9) Energy 248kcal/1043kJ; Protein 2.4g; Carbohydrate 42.1g, of which sugars 27.2g; Fat 8.9g, of which saturates 1.1g; Cholesterol 0mg; Calcium 40mg; Fibre 2.4g; Sodium 6mg.

Mini Victoria sponges (makes 24) Energy 164kcal/687kJ; Protein 1.5g; Carbohydrate 22.4g, of which sugars 13g; Fat 8.2g, of which saturates 1.7g; Cholesterol 0mg; Calcium 49mg; Fibre 0.6g; Sodium 114mg.

Tropical fruit meringue cake (serves 8) Energy 369kcal/1554kJ; Protein 2.2g; Carbohydrate 63.8g, of which sugars 62.1g; Fat 13.4g, of which saturates 9.6g; Cholesterol 2mg; Calcium 23mg; Fibre 0.8g; Sodium 5mg.

Index

Published by Lorenz Books
an imprint of Anness Publishing Ltd
www.lorenzbooks.com; info@anness.com

Publisher: Joanna Lorenz
Editorial and layout: Lucy Doncaster
Concept design: Adelle Mahoney
Special photography: William Shaw
Additional food styling: Heather Whinney
Nutritional consultant: Clare Emery
Index: Marie Lorimer

With thanks to the contributors, in particular Asa Simonsson for the fermented cheeses, and Ysanne Spevack and Sara Lewis for some of the desserts and sweet treats.

The advice and information in this book are believed to be accurate and true at the time of going to press, but neither the author nor the publisher can accept legal responsibility or liability for any errors or omissions nor for any loss, harm or injury that comes about from following this book. The reader should not regard the recommendations, ideas and techniques described as substitutes for the advice of a medical practitioner or other qualified professional before embarking on major dietary changes.

A CIP catalogue record for this book is available from the British Library.

COOK'S NOTES

For all recipes, quantities are given in both metric and imperial measures and, where appropriate, in standard US cups and spoons. Follow one set of measures, but not a mixture, because they are not interchangeable.
Standard spoon and cup measures are level. 1 tsp = 5ml, 1 tbsp = 15ml, 1 cup = 250ml/9fl oz.
Australian standard tablespoons are 20ml. Australian readers should use 3 tsp in place of 1 tbsp for measuring small quantities. American pints are 16fl oz/2 cups. American readers should use 20fl oz/2½ cups in place of 1 pint when measuring liquids. Bracketed terms are intended for American readers.
Since ovens vary, you should check with your manufacturer's instruction book for guidance.
The nutritional analysis given for each recipe is calculated per portion (i.e. serving or item), unless otherwise stated. If the recipe gives a range, such as Serves 4–6, then the nutritional analysis will be for the smaller portion size, i.e. 6 servings.
The analysis does not include optional ingredients, such as salt added to taste.